Gender in Contemporary Iran

This book examines gender and the dynamics of social change in contemporary Iran, documenting the changes in women's lives and showing how women now have now become agents of social change rather than victims.

Bringing together the detailed primary research of a number of eminent scholars working in Iran, this collection provides unique perspectives on the past decade in Iranian society. Chapters document and examine how different Iranian groups and classes are negotiating, resisting, and pressing for political and social change, and explore the complexity of a society that often is portrayed in monolithic stereotypes in the international media. Thematically arranged sections explore discourses around gender and the impact of these discourses upon women; the gendered impact of educational, employment, communications, and cultural changes; changing gender attitudes among the post-revolutionary generation of youth; and the ways economic changes have been affecting women.

Providing an important basis for understanding social and political developments in a country that has been a focus of international attention for much of the past decade, this collection will be an important reference for scholars of Iranian studies, gender studies, political science and sociology.

Roksana Bahramitash is Research Director at the Canada Research Chair of Islam, Pluralism and Globalization at the University of Montreal, Canada

Eric Hooglund is Senior Research Scholar in Contemporary Interpretations of Islam and Muslim Cultures in the Centre for Middle Eastern Studies at Lund University, Sweden.

Iranian studies

Edited by Homa Katouzian
University of Oxford
and
Mohamad Tavakoli
University of Toronto

Since 1967 the International Society for Iranian Studies (ISIS) has been a leading learned society for the advancement of new approaches in the study of Iranian society, history, culture and literature. The new ISIS Iranian Studies series published by Routledge will provide a venue for the publication of original and innovative scholarly works in all areas of Iranian and Persianate Studies.

Gender in Contemporary Iran

Pushing the boundaries

**Edited by Roksana Bahramitash and
Eric Hooglund**

 Routledge
Taylor & Francis Group

LONDON AND NEW YORK

First published 2011
by Routledge
2 Park Square, Milton Park, Abingdon, Oxon OX14 4RN

Simultaneously published in the USA and Canada
by Routledge
711 Third Avenue, New York, NY 10017

Routledge is an imprint of the Taylor & Francis Group, an informa business

British Library Cataloguing in Publication Data
A catalogue record for this book is available from the British Library

Library of Congress Cataloging in Publication Data
Gender in contemporary Iran : pushing the boundaries / edited by Roksana
Bahramitash and Eric Hooglund.
p. cm. – (Iranian studies ; 10)
Includes bibliographical references and index.
1. Women–Iran–Social conditions. 2. Iran–Social conditions–1997– I.
Bahramitash, Roksana, 1956- II. Hooglund, Eric J. (Eric James), 1944–
HQ1735.2.G46 2011
305.48'89155–dc22
2010041908

ISBN: 978-0-415-78101-5 (hbk)
ISBN: 978-0-203-83071-0 (ebk)

Typeset in Times New Roman
by Wearset Ltd, Boldon, Tyne and Wear
Printed and bound by TJI Digital, Padstow, Cornwall

Acknowledgements

We are sincerely grateful to literally hundreds of wonderful people who helped the editors and the individual contributors in multiple ways with the research for and compiling of this volume. A few people provided valuable assistance at key points, and we would like to mention their names, trusting that the many other colleagues and friends who are not cited will understand that space constraints make it impractical to list the names of each and every one of you. This project began as a series of conferences, sponsored by the journal *Middle East Critique*, to present research by scholars doing field research in Iran on various dimensions of gender. Four members of *Critique*'s Editorial Board, Hossein Akhavi-Pour, Nasrin Jewel, Mahnaz Kousha, and Navid Mohseni, encouraged the project from the outset and at critical points raised funds to support the convening of the conferences. Long-time friends of *Critique*, Iraj Beheshti, Perry Ketchum, Helen Metz, Nahid Navab, and Abdul-Hossein Ostad-Hosseini understood our goals and offered insights from their own personal experiences with gender issues. Sadly, Perry Ketchum, like contributor Louise Halper, succumbed to a fatal form of cancer before this book was published. Perry and Louise both had a deep respect for Iranian culture and a nuanced understanding of Iranian society, and we believe their spirits inspired the book's completion. That latter phase has been successful thanks to Joe Whiting and Suzanne Richardson at Routledge. In addition, we are grateful to the co-editors of Iranian studies series, Homa Katouzian and Mohammad Tavakoli, who recognized the originality of the research and decided to include the book in this highly regarded Routledge series.

Separately, Roksana Bahramitash would like to thank her children for their patience during her work on this project: Mahsana, Arash, Eiman, and Atena Sadegh. She also would like to thank her mother; her cousin, Zohreh Bahramast, and her wonderful children, Marzieh, Reza, and Hanieh Diba; many friends in Iran; and her colleague in Montreal, Anthony Synott.

Eric Hooglund would like to thank friends and colleagues in Iran who have been especially helpful during his research there: Turaj Azkia, Jabbar Bagheri, Ayatollah Mohammad Jafar Mahallati, and Gholam-Hosain Vatandoust.

Finally, we both would like to dedicate this book:

To the academic community in Iran, especially women whose diverse activities on behalf of gender equity in legal matters, education, and the workplace are changing Iranian society, and to their fathers, brothers, husbands, and sons, whose support sustains and encourages these women to push onward.

Contents

Contributors

Niki Akhavan received a PhD from the University of California at Santa Cruz. Her doctoral dissertation, "The Iranian Internet: Interventions in New Media and Old Politics," interrogates the cultural politics and political significance of Net-directed modes of transnational expression and activism among Iranians, both in Iran and in the diaspora. She is currently based in Washington DC, where she continues her research into the cultural politics of the Iranian diaspora and works as an NGO consultant on Iran and Persian Gulf regional affairs.

Roksana Bahramitash is a graduate of McGill University's Sociology Department and has received two post-doctorate awards from the Social Sciences and Humanities Council of Canada (SSHRC). She is the winner of the Eileen D. Ross award (2003–2004) for her work on female poverty, globalization, Islamization and women's employment. In 2006 she won a three-year research grant from the SSHRC and in 2008 she was given a grant by the Council for the Arts to write her memoir. Bahramitash has taught many courses at McGill University and Concordia University, and has worked with international development agencies, including the Canadian Development Agency (CIDA), the International Development Research Centre (IDRC), the United Nations Development Program (UNDP) and a World Bank-funded project through the Center for Teaching and Research on Arab Women (CAWTAR). Bahramitash is the author of more than twenty refereed journal articles and book chapters. Her first book, *Liberation from Liberalization: Gender and Globalization in Southeast Asia* (Zed Press, 2005, reprint edn, 2008), has been translated into Persian and published by SAMT in Tehran. Her most recent book (Syracuse University Press, forthcoming), is co-edited with Hadi S. Esfahani.

Zohreh Fanni is Associate Professor of Geography at Shahid Beheshti University in Tehran, Iran. She obtained a BA degree from Tarbiat Modaress University in Tehran, and masters and doctoral degrees from the University of Tehran. She has published four books in Persian pertaining to the geography of development, including a translation of J. Momsen's *Gender and Development* (University of Tehran Press, 2004), and six articles in scholarly journals.

Her research has focused on the role of small cities in the Tehran metropolitan region and assessing gender inequality indices for women in urban society. More broadly, her research interests include urban planning issues, human and sustainable development, and gender geography.

Elhum Haghighat-Sordellini is Associate Professor of Sociology at Lehman College, City University of New York. She received her higher education degrees from Rutgers University (BA), University of Texas (MA) and University of Maryland (PhD). Her areas of expertise are the demography of the Middle East and North Africa (MENA), women's social status in MENA, including employment, education and migration issues as they pertain to gender and social inequality. She has received numerous grants and published several reports and articles on education, immigration and development issues and policies, including in academic journals such as *International Review of Sociology/Revue Internationale de Sociologie, Identities: Journal of Politics, Gender and Culture, Industrial Relations*, and *International Journal of Sociology and Social Policy*. Her recent book is *Women in the Middle East and North Africa, Continuity and Change* (Palgrave Macmillan, 2010). She has worked as a consultant and policy and quantitative analyst for the US Department of Labor, the World Bank and the Educational Testing Service.

Louise Halper (1944–2008) was Professor of Law at Washington & Lee University and Director of the Frances Lewis Law Center there. She received her JD degree from Rutgers University and her LLM from New York University. Before entering academia, she practiced public interest law for 15 years and appeared at every level of state and federal court, including the Supreme Court of the United States. Her scholarship on law and gender in the Middle East concentrated on Iran and Turkey. She travelled widely in the area, visiting at Koc University in Istanbul and American University in Cairo, as well as teaching at Marmara University in Istanbul as a Fulbright Fellow. In 2002, she spent part of her sabbatical in Iran. She published articles in the *Harvard Journal of Law & Gender*, the *Yale Journal of Law & Humanities* and the *Cornell Journal of Law & Public Policy*, as well as in numerous other publications. At the time of her unexpected death (see further in Introduction), she was editing for publication a collection of papers presented at a March 2007 symposium on Gender-Relevant Legislative Change in Muslim and non-Muslim Countries that was jointly sponsored by the Frances Lewis Law Center and the Islamic Legal Studies Program at Harvard Law School.

Eric Hooglund has been Editor of *Middle East Critique* since 1995. He is also Senior Research Scholar in Contemporary Interpretations of Islam in the Centre for Middle Eastern Studies, Lund University, Sweden. His main research focus is Iran, where he has been undertaking field research since the early 1970s. He is the author or editor of several books about Iran and also has written more than 100 articles and book chapters examining diverse aspects of Iranian culture, history and politics. His most recent publications include "Thirty Years of Islamic Revolution in Iran," *Middle East Report*, no. 250 (spring 2009); *Iran, A Country Study*, co-edited with Glenn Curtis (Library of Congress, 2008); *Encyclopedia of the Modern Middle East*, associate editor for Iran and Turkey (Gale-Thomsen, 2007); "Iran, Wary Neutral," in *The Iraq War: Causes and Consequences*, edited by R. Fawn and R. Hinnebusch (Lynne Rienner, 2006); *Encyclopedia of the Modern Middle East, 2nd edn*, co-edited with Philip Mattar *et al.* (Gale-Thomson, 2004); and *Twenty Years of Islamic Revolution: Political and Social Transition in Iran Since 1979* (Syracuse University Press, 2002).

Shala Kazemipour is Associate Professor of Sociology at Tehran University and Deputy Director of the Population Studies and Research Centre in Asia and the Pacific. She has done extensive research on development and population studies and has worked with a number of professional associations, including the Demographic Research Section at the Institute of Social Studies and Research and Head of the Advisory Board for Student Affairs at the Faculty of Social Sciences at Tehran University. She is the author of many books and articles in both English and Persian, including *Primary Methods in Population Analysis* (Tehran: Payam-e Nur University, 1991); *A Sociological Study of the City of Tehran* (Tehran: Population Studies and Research Centre in Asia and the Pacific, 2001); "Myth and Realities of the Impact of Islam on Women: Women's Changing Marital Status in Iran" (with Roksana Bahramitash) in *Middle East Critique*, 15, 2 (summer 2006); and (with Roksana Bahramitash) "Economy, Informal Economy," in *Today: An Encyclopedia of Life in the Islamic Republic*, ed. Mahran Kamrava and Manochehr Dorraj (Greenwood Press, 2008).

Farhad Khosrokhavar is Professor of Sociology at the École des Hautes Études en Sciences Sociales, Paris. He has been a Rockefeller Fellow and a Visiting Scholar to Yale in 2008 and to Harvard in 2009. His main topics of interest are Islamic radicalism in Europe and the Middle East and post-revolutionary Iran. He is currently working on "Jihadism Worldwide" for Paradigm Publishers, and which focuses on the convergences between Shi'i and Sunnite radicalism. His publications include 17 books, three of which have been translated into English: *Suicide Bombers, The New Martyrs of Allah* (Pluto Press 2005), *Muslims in Prison* (with James Beckford and Daniele Joly, 2006), and *Inside Jihadism: Understanding Jihadist Movements Worldwide* (Yale Cultural Sociology Series, Paradigm Publishers, 2009).

Azadeh Kian is Professor of Sociology and Director of the Centre for Gender and Feminist Studies, University of Paris 7-Diderot, co-director of National Federation of Research on Gender in France (Fédération RING), and a Researcher at Mondes iranien et indien, CNRS. Her research projects include state, gender, ethnicity and identity in Iran, gender, and post-colonial theories. Her books include *La République islamique d'Iran: de la maison du Guide à la raison d'Etat* (Editions Michalon, 2005; Greek trans., 2006), *Famille et* *mutations socio-politiques* (Editions de la Maison des Sciences de l'Homme, 2005), *Les femmes iraniennes entre islam l'état et famille* (Maisonneuve & Larose, 2002), and *Secularization of Iran, a Doomed Failure? The New Middle Class and the Making of Modern Iran* (Peeters, 1998). Her recent articles include "Féminisme islamique en Iran: nouvelle forme d'assujettissement ou l'émergence de sujets agissants?," *Critique Internationale*, January–March 2010; "Crafting Iranian Nationalism: Intersectionality of Aryanism, Westernism and Islamism" (with Gilles Riaux), in Susana Carvalhi and François Gemenne (eds) *History, Nationalism and the (Re)construction of Nations* (Palgrave, 2009), "From Motherhood to Equal Rights Advocates: The Weakening of Patriarchal Order," in Homa Katouzian and Hossein Shahidi (eds) *Iran in the 21st Century. Politics, Economics and Conflict* (Routledge, 2008); "Erving Goffman: de la production sociale du genre à l'objectivation sociale des différences biologiques," in D. Chabaud-Rychter, V. Descoutures, A.M. Devreux and E.Varikas (eds) *Sous les sciences sociales, le genre* (Editions la Découverte, 2010), "Mondialisation, 'guerre antiterroriste,' néo-orientalisme, renouveau des nationalismes et redéploiement de violence de genre," in Dan Ferrand-Bechmann and Abou Ndiaye (eds) (éditions Desclée de Brouwer, 2010) *Violences et Société* pp. 215–232.

Fatemeh Etemad Moghadam is Professor of Economics at Hofstra University. She received a DPhil in Economics from Oxford University and MA and BA degrees from Barnard College of Columbia University. She has published extensively on agrarian economy, economic history, and women and development in Iran. She is the author of *From Land Reform to the Revolution: The Political Economy of Agricultural Development in Iran (1960–1979)* (I.B. Tauris Academic Studies). Her publications on gender and development in Iran include: "Iran's New Islamic Home Economics: An Exploratory Attempt to Conceptualize Women's Work in the Islamic Republic," in *Research in the Middle East Economics*, 4 (2001); "Women and Labor in the Islamic Republic of Iran," in Lois Beck and Guity Nashat (eds) *Women in Iran from 1800 to the Islamic Republic* (University of Illinois Press, 2004), and "Undercounting Women's Work in Iran," *Iranian Studies*, Special Issue on Women and Gender, Janet Afary guest editor, 42, 1 (2008). She has served as Executive Secretary and President of the Middle East Economic Association and as a board member of several scholarly organizations and academic journals. She also has worked as a consultant for UNDP and the World Bank.

Goli M. Rezai-Rashti is Associate Professor of Sociology of Education and Women Studies at the University of Western Ontario, in London, Canada. Her research and teaching is focused on anti-racism, feminism, globalization and education. She is currently involved in two SSHRC research projects: (1) dealing with the participation of women in higher education in Iran; and (2) dealing with a critique of male elementary schools and the notion of role modelling. She has numerous publications.

Jaleh Taheri has a MSc in Development Studies from Lund University in Sweden. She received a BA in Politics from Bates College in Lewiston, Maine, where she completed an Honours thesis, based on original field research in Iran, about the differences between how Iranian women are depicted in the West and how they perform in Iran. She has travelled widely in Europe, India, Pakistan and the Middle East and spent one year as a Research Fellow at the Centre for Middle East Studies at the University of Durham in the United Kingdom. She writes on the topics of religion, gender and politics in Iran, Syria and Pakistan. She is currently the project manager of Women for Sustainable Growth Initiative, a programme at the Centre for Middle Eastern Studies, Lund University, which aims to encourage and connect female business leaders in Scandinavia and the Middle East.

Introduction

The case for a gendered analysis of contemporary Iran

Roksana Bahramitash and Eric Hooglund

The objective of this book is to present a gendered analysis of the dynamics of social change in contemporary Iran. A gendered analysis deliberately focuses on the impact of societal changes upon women without ignoring the reality that women do not represent a monolithic category but themselves may be agents of and/or resistors against changes that affect them and their families. The importance of a gendered understanding of Iranian society was demonstrated in June 2009, when millions of Iranian women of all ages and backgrounds joined Iranian men in a week of nationwide mass rallies in support of a leading candidate (Mir-Hosain Musavi) and two others who were challenging incumbent President Mahmud Ahmadinejad in a presidential election. After the Ministry of Interior collected ballot boxes – without following the normal procedure of having local precinct committees tabulate the votes – and subsequently announced that Ahmadinejad had won a majority of votes, these same women and men, as well as the candidates whom they had supported, became convinced that the "official tally" was fraudulent. They again took to the streets of cities, towns, and even villages, this time in a week of mass demonstrations to demand a transparent recount or a strictly monitored re-vote. The international media had paid scant attention to the pre-election rallies, which had included candidate Musavi campaigning alongside his wife, but they became fascinated with the post-election mass protests and the presence of women in them. Thousands of photographs, taken by cell phone cameras and sent all over the world via the internet, documented the protests and the active role of women.

One reason why these protests attracted international attention was because they were so counter to the stereotypes about Iranian society, especially with respect to the role of women, which have prevailed since the Islamic Revolution of 1978 to 1979. That earlier mass, nationwide movement was also one in which the presence of women had been important. However, because religion, in this case Islam rather than a secular ideology, was a main inspiration motivating the revolution against a monarch whom Iranians rejected en masse for being unjust but whom the self-identified "developed world" (Australia, Canada, Europe, Japan, and the United States) perceived as being modern and progressive, there has been a general tendency in the West to view the post-revolutionary creation of the Islamic Republic of Iran as being not a "modern" society but one in which "traditional" religious values repress everyone, especially women. Because this view has been prevalent among both those whose political views are on the Left and those whose political views are on the Right, it ought not to be surprising that negative stereotypes about Iranian women have been pronounced in academic disciplines as well as in the popular media. Indeed, a characteristic of mainstream feminist writing in the West has been to portray Iranian women in particular and all Muslim women in general, as categorical victims.

Such representation of Muslim women has been criticized by post-colonial feminist theorists. For example, Chandra Mohanty, who studies gender and development in the Muslim world, argues that mainstream gender and development literature about women in the Muslim world remains in a framework set by modernization theories and Western feminist discourse. Mohanty argues that this literature, "like most other scholarship does not comprise merely 'objective' knowledge about a certain subject. It is also a directly political and discursive practice insofar as it is purposeful and ideological." This is so because "feminist scholarly practice exists within power-relations which they counter, redefine or even implicitly support."[1] Here Mohanty is referring to the unequal power relations that exist between the Western world and the developing world. Other post-colonial feminists, such as Eiman O. Zein-Elabdin and S. Charusheela, argue that, "As a discipline, it [economics] has upheld the narrative of 'development' as the centerpiece of its theoretical construction of formerly colonized regions, presuming the ontological precedence of modern European societies as a basis for its theory of history."[2] Similarly, Paul Feyerabend argues that "the discourse on development in effect renders patterns of life outside the (Western) industrial world as a 'mistake'."[3] With respect to women and development in the Middle East, feminist scholars such as Leila Abu-Lughod, Leila Ahmed, Margot Badran, Laura Deeb, Sondra Hale, Frances Hasso, Deniz Kandiyoti, Reina Lewis, Saba Mahmood, Fatima Mernissi, Jennifer Olmsted, and Meyda Yegenoglu all argue for the need to understand how women have agency.[4]

In the case of Iran, several feminist scholars have argued that analyses which view women in Iran as victims and overlook their agency are unable to provide readers with a complete picture. These scholars include, among others, Roksana Bahramitash, Golbarg Bashi, Shala Haeri, Azadeh Kian, Ziba Mir-Hosseini, Mino Moalem, Valentine Moghadam, Parvin Paidar, Elaheh Rostami-Povey, and Nayereh Tohidi, among others.[5] They all recognize that women in Iran continue to face major challenges in terms of achieving gender equality, but their research also documents how Iranian women are constantly resisting and pressing for changes. As noted above, the Iranian Revolution had been a catalyst for women's activism, initially through their political mobilization in support of the prolonged, nationwide movement to overthrow the regime of Mohammed Reza Shah Pahlavi (r. 1941–1979), the king who, by 1978, had become widely perceived as a repressive dictator responsible for virtually every kind of injustice in Iranian society.[6] After the revolutionary movement concluded with the deposition of the monarchy and the establishment of the Islamic Republic, Iranian women, as the aforementioned feminist scholars have demonstrated, did not return to their homes and forget about politics. Rather, many women remained actively engaged in the process of creating a new society, although such women have not comprised a unified bloc. Some women activists, for example, accepted traditionally conservative interpretations of Islamic texts and supported new laws that discriminated against women,[7] while other women activists used liberal interpretations of Islam to contest these same laws. A few women even joined militant opposition groups, such as secular Marxist parties or the religious Mojahedin-e khalq organization; the latter initiated an unsuccessful armed uprising in 1981.[8] A result of these diverse activities of acquiescence and resistance among women has been a dynamic society where both positive and negative changes have impacted upon the economic, legal, political, and social status of women.

It is this process of resistance and change that the contributors to this volume examine in post-revolutionary Iran, a process that has been the result of women activists pressing for social change. Their gendered examination of contemporary Iran provides insights on social change and how women have been agents of this transformation. The objective of undertaking a gendered study of social developments in Iran had its origins in a series of academic conferences that began in 1992 under the auspices of the (then new) journal *Critique*.[9] Because *Critique*'s intellectual purpose was to present analyses of the Middle East from a post-colonialist perspective that challenged the dominant American academic paradigms embedded in Eurocentric power dynamics (i.e., national security studies) and mainstream economic theories (first modernization and then neoliberalism), its conferences did not focus exclusively on Iran or women. Nonetheless, each conference featured at least one panel devoted to an exploration of issues that are of particular concern to women in the Middle East. In 2002, *Critique* organized a panel on current field research in the Middle East for the First World Conference of Middle East Studies (WOCMES), held in Mainz, Germany, and thereafter regularly organized panels for other international conferences, including for the annual meetings of the Middle East Studies Association (MESA) of North America and the Society for Iranian Studies (SIS). These *Critique*-sponsored panels provided opportunities for younger women scholars to present fascinating fieldwork data they had gathered about women's political and social activism and about significant changes that affected women in several Middle East countries, particularly Iran. This experience prompted these writers (Bahramitash and Hooglund) to organize specific panels about research on women in Iran. The chapters in this volume originated as papers presented on *Critique*-sponsored panels at conferences, especially the one at the MESA Conference in Montréal, Canada, in November 2007.

What is significant about the approach in this volume is that all the contributors are active scholars who ground their arguments on field research they have undertaken in Iran (with the exception of Niki Akhavan who examined web blogs of Iranian women, a project which she began to research outside of Iran, although she did travel to Iran to complete this research) For that reason, the empirical evidence is both unique and essential for an understanding of the changes that have been transforming Iranian society generally in the past three decades. With respect to women specifically, the empirical research documents a complex and nuanced process of social change that contradicts prevalent stereotypes outside the country about their role and status. In particular, this research contradicts the prevalent stereotype which assumes that Iranian (and Muslim) women are victims of their society. Such stereotypes reinforce a dichotomy of Western women as being agents and liberated while Iranian/Muslim women are oppressed victims of Muslim men. A fundamental underpinning of the chapters here is that although women in Iran have experienced many challenges and hardships, they have never ceased to press for change and are constantly pushing boundaries for social transformation. One political result of their activism is illustrated in the aforementioned 2009 presidential election. Rather than accept the government's contention that Ahmadinejad had won a second term, millions of women took to the streets to demonstrate their disbelief and outrage. Although these street protests were eventually suppressed, the political elite was obviously shaken by the magnitude and nationwide character of the protests, especially the obvious presence of women in them, and thus sought to balance its coercion with some concessions. Ahmadinejad, for example, nominated three women to be ministers for his second term as President. Although the *Majlis* eventually rejected two of them, it is significant that it approved Gohar Sharifeh Dastgerdi to be Minister of Health, the first post-revolutionary female cabinet minister.

While each of the chapters examines a unique aspect of activities, attitudes, or changes affecting women in Iran, the co-editors have given careful thought to arranging the chapters in a thematically coherent structure. The initial three chapters, for instance, analyze the discourses around gender and the impact of these discourses upon women in the spheres of law (Louise Halper), politics (Azadeh Kian), and religion (Fatemeh Etemad Moghadam). The next three chapters assess the gendered impact of educational, employment, communications, and cultural changes (Goli Rezaei-Rashti, Nikki Akhavan, and Jaleh Taheri). Chapters 7 and 8 present specific case studies about changing gender attitudes among the post-revolutionary generation of youth, especially women, in an urban (Farhad Khosrokhavar) and a rural (Eric Hooglund) area of Iran. The last three chapters (Roksana Bahramitash and Shala Kazemipour, Bahramitash and Zohreh Fanni, and Elhum Haghighat-Sordellini) examine some of the ways in which economic changes have been affecting women.

The first chapter, "Authority, modernity and gender-relevant legislation in Iran" by Louise Halper, provides an overarching gendered framework for the book by focusing on legal changes and religious discourses as they apply to Iranian women. Halper, a legal scholar who practiced law for 15 years before becoming an academic expert on law, carried out field research in Iran during the mid-2000s. She originally presented this chapter as a paper for a panel organized by *Middle East Critique* for the Middle East Studies Association annual meeting in Montreal, Canada, in November 2007. Halper had agreed to have her paper included in this book project and was working on a revised draft when, unfortunately, she passed away suddenly in June 2008. We remain saddened by the loss of such a rare legal scholar but are pleased that we can present her final work here, with only the preliminary edits she had approved. It is a tribute to a wonderful individual, an exceptional scholar and teacher, a committed feminist, and a person who had a sharp legal mind.[10] In this chapter, Halper examines how discourses regarding laws of marriage and divorce have been forced to change from a religious perspective as the result of pressures brought to bear by women's rights activists. Specifically, she notes that the discourse on gender-relevant law in Iran has often focused on the Islamic Republic's reinstatement of religious law to govern issues of marriage, divorce, and family; less attention, however, has been paid to legislation that continues to shape the law and its application. In this respect, Halper examines several modifications to the law of marriage and divorce, changes that have not only been enacted by the *Majlis*, but changes that the Council of Guardians has approved as being compatible with religious law. This chapter links these legal modifications to enhanced political participation by women, one consequence of which has been more flexible interpretations of religious law. Halper suggests that the mobilization of women into political life evoked by the Revolution of 1979 has changed the space within which religio-legal interpretation takes place. She concludes that, although a misogynist current underlies much traditional jurisprudence and legal practice with respect to the place of women in family and in society, the political need to mobilize women in support of the Islamic Revolution and thereafter to maintain that support prevailed. That mobilization, in practice, has given rise to a marriage and family code with modern characteristics, as well as a social space in which women are and continue to be active, as evidenced by the outcome of the 2007 municipal elections.

In Chapter 2, "Gendering Shi'ism in post-revolutionary Iran," Azadeh Kian complements Halper's chapter by examining the ways in which women activists, both Islamists and secularists, have been challenging a masculinized construct of the Islamic state that relies on essentialist discourses and gendered concepts of citizenship. In this process, argues Kian, women activists continuously contest and reinterpret Islamic doctrines and laws as well as traditional values and norms. They do so by producing contexts to become involved in public debates, to interact with political and religious leaders and institutions, and to create new meanings. Against those who use Islam to justify gender discrimination and to perpetuate patriarchal codes and male domination, many Iranian women now refer to Islamic law and sacred texts and, through their own interpretations and new readings, oppose gendered social relations. Kian argues that such women contribute tremendously to the social construction of secularism and the emergence of a democratic system whose prerequisite condition is respect for human rights and separation between the religious and political spheres.

In Chapter 3, "Women and social protest in the Islamic Republic of Iran," Fatemeh Etemad Moghadam traces the historical origins of contemporary peculiarities in the freedom of female labor and women's participation in public space in Iran. She applies an approach similar to those applied by Emma Boserup and other political economists. She argues that two important factors have left lasting impacts upon the contemporary ambiguities about freedom of female labour and on commoditization of female sexuality and reproductive labor: the production systems that historically dominated the general geographic area of contemporary Iran; and the Shi'i version of the Islamic law (*shari'a*). With a reference to historical debates over women's role in the production system, Moghadam argues that the economic and technological changes accompanied by modernization and the growing interaction with the West have created a new era of change.

In Chapter 4, "Exploring women's experience of higher education and the changing nature of gender relations in Iran," Goli M. Rezai-Rashti assesses women's participation in higher education since the 1990s. Recent statistics indicates that there is a steady reduction of the gender gap for literacy, elementary, secondary, and especially higher education. This chapter is based on empirical investigation that deals with the lives of female and male students and faculty members in several Iranian universities. Male students and faculty members were interviewed in order to show the significance of gender relations and the relational aspects of the gender regimes in Iran. The discussion presents women's and men's views of their participation in higher education, and discusses their aspirations, expectations, and desires for getting a university education. Furthermore, it investigates how women and men perceive their experience in universities as a basis for examining questions of agency, gender relations, and participation in the broader Iranian society. This involves their perception of employment opportunities, relationships, and attitudes toward marriage.

Given the significant presence of women in higher education, it is perhaps not surprising to learn that women are active users of the internet. In Chapter 5, "Exclusionary cartographies: gender liberation and the Iranian blogosphere," Niki Akhavan analyses the writings of female web blogists in Iran and documents how Iranian women have deployed the internet to interrogate various gender issues. She notes that in the decade since Iranians have made use of the internet as a site for political and cultural production, proliferating sets of discourses have glorified the *weblogistan* as a site where bloggers effectively challenge the state, and where women in particular find liberation. While Iranian women have a significant presence online and have deployed the Net in variously interrogating issues of gender, mainstream and celebratory accounts of the internet remain problematic for several reasons. According to Akhavan, the most worrisome shortcomings of such discourses concern the ways in which certain kinds of women are excluded from consideration. Depending upon and reifying several uncritical categories such as East/West, Progressive/Regressive, Liberal/ Religious, popular accounts about the Iranian blogosphere privilege the viewpoints of largely middle- to upper-class and self-identified secular women while completing ignoring, and thus erasing, the voices of women who may not fit these prescribed criteria. In considering examples of Iranian women whose participation online thus far has been largely absent from mainstream accounts, the author challenges and complicates exclusionary narratives that have dominated discourses about the liberatory potential of the Iranian internet. Akhavan argues that the discourse around female web blogists must be examined closely, since writers on this subject tend to overlook the web blogs of religious women.

Next, in Chapter 6, "Areas of Iranian women's voice and influence," Jaleh Taheri tackles the female victimhood stereotypes about Iran by discussing different activities Iranian women undertake to improve their lives. She focuses on their participation in cinema, education, the labor force, politics, and publishing. With respect to political activity, for example, Taheri notes how women have managed to increase their presence in local and municipal elections as well as in the wider political arena. She also examines how women have become involved in informal politics as volunteers in NGOs and by participating in both pro- and anti-government protests. In addition, the past decade has witnessed their increased participation in the labor force and education to the extent that today there are more women in universities than there are men. Furthermore, women have become employed in traditionally male-oriented jobs such as police officers, taxi driving, and firefighting. She discusses those women who support the regime and/or are Islamist and have become highly active in such organizations as the religious morality police, known as the *khaharan Basij-e*. In fact, being engaged as state supporters has empowered women of a certain class and religious background, and this process has worked against secular women while opening a door for pro-government women. Having recognized this, it should be noted that many women in the pro-government camp have questioned the state's exercise of power in such institutions as the *shora-ye farhangi-ye zanha* Women's Social and Cultural Council. Pro-state women conduct a vibrant discussion over how to advocate a state position through creative ways and by encouraging women voluntarily to follow government politics.

In Chapter 7, "Post-revolutionary Iranian youth: the case of Qom and the new culture of ambivalence," sociologist Farhad Khosrokhavar focuses on the attitudes of seminary students in the city of Qom, the center of theological education in Iran. His data reveal a major transformation regarding attitudes about family authority in general and the authority of the father in particular, as well as changing attitudes about gender relations and the role of the state. The significance of these attitudinal changes has been a decline in the acceptance of traditional sources of authority towards more equalitarian views. With regard to the family, for instance, young men and women no longer agree to prearranged marriages. Although they still respect their parents' views, they no longer allow their parents to choose their future partners. This is particularly significant in the case of girls who can reject their father's choice. This is a major shift and decline of the father's authority. However, with regard to sexual freedom, Qom remains conservative in comparison to Tehran where premarital sexual relations are freer. In Qom, girls in particular are extremely conscious of their reputation. With regard to the authority of the state, young people no longer seem to support the idea of a religious state as was the case during the early days of the Revolution. In fact, there are doubts about whether the politicization of religion has been beneficial for the Islamic faith and a growing belief that mixing religion and politics has hurt spirituality and religion. Even with regard to religion itself, the new generation has no problem with music as was the case a generation before.

Attitudinal changes among youth are also the subject of Chapter 8. In this case, the views are those of young rural women who live in villages near the city of Shiraz in south central Iran. In "Changing attitudes among women in rural Iran," Eric Hooglund assesses the views of young women toward family, education, employment, marriage, religion, politics, and aspects of international relations. The data are derived from informal interviews conducted in the early 2000s and show that young rural women are questioning traditional family authority in matters such as marriage and employment outside of the home. The research indicates that the attitudes of some rural women are becoming more similar to those of young urban women, especially with respect to an understanding of women's rights and the expectations of what women can do.

In Chapter 9, "Women's employment trends: advance or retreat?," Roksana Bahramitash and Shala Kazemipour first provide a discussion of women's overall employment in the formal sector and then focus on women's participation in the informal sector. They argue that the statistical decline in employment for women in post-revolutionary Iran was largely a rural phenomenon, and it was related directly to an increase in education for rural girls, rural-to-urban migration, and a decline in the global price of Iranian carpets, which led to the loss of 340,000 carpet-weaving jobs for women in the rural areas during the early 1980s. They argue that economic rather than cultural/religious reasons contributed to the initial post-revolutionary decline in female employment. Official employment figures after 1986 support this argument, since they document that overall employment for women in fact has increased, although more for urban women than for those in rural areas. Formal employment, however, is only part of the narrative about women's work. As the authors demonstrate, thousands of Iranian women are employed in the informal economic sector, which is not documented in statistics. Contrary to stereotypical assumptions that Islamization leads to a decline in female employment (as was obviously the case in Afghanistan during the five-year rule of the Taliban), the opposite has been the reality in Iran.

In Chapter 10, Bahramitash and Zohreh Fanni examine the challenges faced by low-income women who live in urban settlements established illegally on land that had previously been vacant. "Extra-legal/informal settlements: does gender matter?" provides data on two such communities: Islamabad, which is adjacent to Tehran; and Shirabad, which is adjacent to Zahedan, the center of Sistan and Baluchestan province on the border with Afghanistan and Pakistan. This chapter is significant because the authors present data about women in low-income households, a social group that tends to be absent in much of the literature about women in the Middle East and North Africa region. As the authors demonstrate, these women face multiple challenges, among which are: the psychological insecurity of knowing that at any time officials could evict their families and destroy their homes; the economic insecurity of (often) not having sufficient income for living expenses; and the social insecurity of living in neighborhoods plagued with high crime, especially drug trafficking and addiction in the case of Shirabad. Because women of low-income households tend to be the ignored subalterns in the literature about women in Muslim countries, this chapter may be read as the start of an overdue discussion.

In our final chapter, "Iran within a regional context: socio-demographic transformations and effects on women's social status," Elhum Haghighat-Sordellini compares Iran on gender issues with other countries that comprise the Middle East and North Africa (MENA) group. She argues that unlike what is often depicted by the media and a body of academic literature, Iranian society continues to experience economic development, modernization, and urbanization, and it has improved its employment and educational attainment for both men and particularly women during the past three decades. This chapter compares Iran with other MENA countries, and shows how social forces continue to transform Iranian society. Iranian women have found ways to improve their social status through factors such as achieving higher educational attainment and gainful employment. Due to Iran's economic development, Iranian women have benefited from access to better healthcare facilities and a very successful family planning program which had lowered Iran's Total Fertility Rate to one of the lowest birth rates in the world. Although Iranian woman continue to struggle to gain equal social and legal rights, higher levels of political participation, as well as a higher level of gainful employment (Iran has also been experiencing one of the highest unemployment rates in the MENA region for men and particularly for women), its women are significant and vibrant agents of social change, and active participants in improving Iranian society and their own social status.

To sum up, each chapter in this volume examines challenges and opportunities which women in Iran have faced and documents ways in which women have continued to press for change at different levels. Sometimes they have made gains, such as an overall achievement in education, employment, health, the legalization of some extra/legal settlements, in making their voices heard through the internet, and in changing attitudes of their society. Sometimes they have not been successful, such as in the last presidential election, when women were not united, with some supporting the conservative Ahmadinejad, while others – perhaps a majority of women – supported the reformist Green Movement. Even though the results of that election were disappointing for those women who opposed a second term for Ahmadinejad, the election still revealed that Iran is a country where women participate actively in politics. Indeed, in that election, Zahra Rahnavard, the wife of Green Party leader Musavi, campaigned beside her husband, a first for Iran, and other candidates promised to appoint female ministers and advisers.

Notes

1 C.T. Mohanty, *Feminist Without Borders: Decolonizing Theory, Practicing Solidarity* (Durham, NC: Duke University Press, 2003), p. 50.
2 E.O. Zein-Elabin and S. Sharusheela, *Post-Colonialism Meets Economics* (London: Routledge, 2004), p. 2.

10   *R. Bahramitash and E. Hooglund*

3 P. Feyerabend, *Farewell to Reason* (London: Verso, 1987), p. 4.
4 For representative arguments by these scholars, see Leila Abu-Lughod, "Introduction: Feminist Longings and Postcolonial Conditions," in *Remaking Women: Feminism and Modernity in the Middle East* (Princeton: Princeton University Press, 1998), pp. 3–31; Leila Ahmed, *Women and Gender in Islam* (New Haven, CT: Yale University Press, 1992); Margot Badran, *Feminists, Islam and Nation* (Princeton, NJ: Princeton University Press, 1995); L. Deeb, *An Enchanted Modern: Gender and Public Piety in Shi'i Lebanon* (Princeton, NJ: Princeton University Press, 2007); S. Hale, "Colonial Discourse and Ethnographic Residuals: The 'Female Circumcision' Debate and the Politics of Knowledge," in O. Nnaemeka (ed.) *Female Circumcision and the Politics of Knowledge: African Women in Imperialist Discourses* (Westport, CT: Praeger, 2005), pp. 209-218; F.S. Hasso, "Problems and Promise in Middle East and North Africa Gender Research," *Feminist Studies*, 31, 3 (2005), pp. 653–679; R. Lewis, *Gendering Orientalism: Race, Femininity and Representation* (London: Routledge, 1996); R. Lewis and S. Mills (eds), *Feminist Postcolonial Theory: A Reader* (Edinburgh: Edinburgh University Press, 2003); J.C. Olmsted, "'Globalization' Denied: Gender and Poverty in Iraq and Palestine," in A. Cabezas, E. Reese, and M. Waller (eds) *The Wages of Empire: Neoliberal Policies, Armed Repression, and Women's Poverty* (Boulder, CO: Paradigm, 2007); and M. Yegenoglu, *Colonial Fantasies: Towards a Feminist Reading of Orientalism* (Cambridge: Cambridge University Press, 1998).
5 Representative publications by Roksana Bahramitash, Golbarg Bashi, Shala Haeri, Azadeh Kian, Ziba Mir-Hosseini, Mino Moalem, Valentine Moghadam, Parvin Paidar, Elaheh Rostami-Povey, and Nayereh Tohidi are cited in the bibliography.
6 The development of opposition to the Shah's regime among different social forces and groups in Iran is analyzed in Ervand Abrahamian's classic history, *Iran Between Two Revolutions* (Princeton, NJ: Princeton University Press, 1982), pp. 450–524.
7 For examples of two religiously conservative and politically active women, see Janet Afary, "Portraits of Two Islamist Women: Escape from Freedom or from Tradition?," *Critique*, 19 (2001), pp. 47–77.
8 The film, *The Hidden Half*, written and directed by feminist Tahmineh Milani, is a fictional account of a young woman involved with Marxist groups during and immediately after the 1978 to 1979 Revolution. There is still a need for a comprehensive study about the aspirations and motivations of the religious women who were attracted to, and died for, the Mojahedin-e khalq; for a preliminary overview see Abrahamian, *The Iranian Mojahedin* (New Haven, CT: Yale University Press, 1989), pp. 232–235.
9 For early articles that attempted to examine the disconnect between the rhetoric about and reality of women's roles in post-revolutionary Iran, see Mahnaz Kousha, "Women, History, and Change: The Politics of Gender in Iran," *Critique*, 1 (1992), pp. 25–37; Hammed Shahidian, "National and International Aspects of Feminist Movements: The Example of Iranian Revolution of 1978–79," *Critique*, 2 (1993), pp. 33–53; and Faegheh Shiarazi-Mahajan, "The Politics of Clothing in the Middle East: The Case of *Hijab* in Post-revolutionary Iran," *Critique*, 2 (1993), pp. 54–63.
10 For an obituary of Louise Halper, see: http://feministlawprofs.law.sc.edu/?=3719 (accessed May 11, 2010).

1 Authority, modernity and gender-relevant legislation in Iran

Louise Halper

A widely accepted view, both in scholarly and more general writing, is that Muslim women benefit from a regime of secular law and suffer under religious law. Thus, we are accustomed to conflating the situation of women in countries as diverse as Iran and Afghanistan and thinking that the status of women in both is dreadful. In fact, however, indicators of women's advancement in Iran[1] are quite comparable to those of women in Turkey, which has had a secular tradition since 1924. In contrast, the situation of women in Afghanistan continues to be abysmal. At a glance, then, it appears that the presence or absence of *shari'a* as the law of the state is, at the least, non-determinative, whatever influence it may have. It is in fact my hypothesis that the situation of women is impacted less by the nature of the legal regime than by their political status; that is to say, the salience of women to the political process and their active involvement in it. Iran is my key example of this hypothesis, and modifications in the law of marriage and divorce there since the Islamic Revolution of 1978 to 1979 constitute my data.

Let me first set out some actual data. With respect to literacy, illiterates as a percentage of Iranian women aged 15 to 24 declined from over one-third in 1980 to under 10 percent in 2000.[2] Over the same period, the illiteracy rate for the entire population of adult women was cut in half, from about 60 percent to about 30 percent.[3] As for education, the number of women in secondary school as a percentage of the eligible age group more than doubled from about 30 percent to almost 80 percent.[4] As of 1999, for every 100 boys in primary school, 96 girls were enrolled, indicating that boys and girls were almost equally likely to be learning basic literacy and numeracy skills.[5] In 2000, one-half of all Iranian university students were women,[6] as were 60 percent of entering students,[7] who were selected on the basis of a difficult nationwide exam. Twenty-seven percent of working-age women were in the labor force as of 2000, up from 20 percent in 1980.[8] In terms of health, life expectancy went up by 11 years between 1980 and 2000 for both Iranian men and women.[9] With respect to family planning, "levels of childbearing have declined faster than in any other country," falling from an average of 5.6 births per woman in 1985 to only 2.0 births in 2000,[10] a drop accomplished by a voluntary, but government-sponsored, birth control program.[11]

As these figures reveal, women in Iran are, since the Islamic Revolution, more literate and have more years of education than under the monarchy. They also are longer-lived and more likely to be in the workforce after schooling. They are likely to marry later and have greater control of their reproductive lives than under the monarchy. Some of these changes (e.g., longevity and education) are certainly at least in part due to the redistributive character of the Islamic Republic which, while it has not had a great deal of success in growing the economy, has readjusted the share of national wealth going to lower income quintiles. Both men and women in this group have benefited from the expanded availability of schools and healthcare facilities for the popular classes. However, beyond the redistribution of wealth, these data bespeak a residue of attention to and focus on the situation of women that is barely predictable if we turn our attention to the Islamic Republic's initial commitment to *shari'a*, interpreted in the patriarchal terms familiar to Islamic jurisprudence in Iran under the monarchy.

How are these data compatible with the reinstantiation of *shari'a* as the law of the state under the Islamic Republic? To what extent does that law continue to govern? By what mechanism/s have the improvements reflected in these data been effectuated? What role have women themselves played in this improvement? These are important questions, since they strongly implicate the issues of religion, law, gender, and activism.

I would like to examine these questions through the lens of the law of marriage and divorce. It is probably the case that the law of marriage and divorce is the central locus of gendered contact with the law in the courts and on the books. Most women will not have to testify in a criminal or commercial case, will not be victims of criminal acts, and will not commit acts denominated sexual crimes, but most will be married, and many divorced. They will be a party to a marriage contract whose terms will shape their lives, and many will find that same contract governing the terms under which their marriage is dissolved and their futures arranged. Thus, the law of marriage and divorce is of importance to women and is, in fact, the site at which their active intervention to shape the law is most likely to be seen. This is indeed the case in Iran where the law of marriage and divorce, since the Islamic Revolution, has been a topic of interest to many women and an issue for women's organizations, as well as the women's press.[12] Women's involvement in this issue has had consequences for the law of marriage and divorce, demonstrating both the extent to which women's activism impacts upon the concerns of the state and the extent to which the state must respond to women as a constituency.

In this discussion, I will focus particularly on two legislative innovations in the law of marriage and divorce from the mid-1990s, in the period following the death of Ayatollah Khomeini in 1989 and the election of Mohammad Khatami as President of the Islamic Republic in 1997. The starting point should be the status of the law of marriage and divorce before the Islamic Republic constitutionally denominated *shari'a* as the law of the state. Prior to that, the law of marriage and divorce was supposed to be compatible with *shari'a*, as interpreted by leading clerics. Under Mohammad Reza Shah (r. 1941–1979), a new law, the Family Protection Law (FPL), was adopted in 1967 and amended in 1975. That law, which compliant clerics had held to be *shari'a*-compatible, constrained the unilateral power over divorce which was the husband's under classical Islamic law. Instead, the FPL said no divorce was final until ratified by a judge, who had to be satisfied with arrangements for custody and for the family's post-divorce maintenance. Moreover, the new law added maltreatment and addiction to the very limited circumstances (long desertion, insanity, impotence) under which the wife could initiate an action for divorce. Moreover, the husband could not register a second marriage without the first wife's consent, thus limiting his rights to polygynous marriage. These changes were procedural, but had an impact on the substantive law.

Following the overthrow of the shah in early 1979 and almost immediately after he had returned to Iran on 1 February from 13 years in exile, Ayatollah Ruhollah Khomeini declared the FPL "un-Islamic" and declared that any person who remarried after being divorced under the FPL was an adulterer. Even though Khomeini abrogated the FPL and replaced lay judges with clerics who would administer *shari'a*, no particular legislation was put in its place. Instead, judges were left to decide on their own how to apply the broad outlines of *shari'a* to particular cases. Nor were procedural rules amended, leading judges to try to fit the new legal structure into the old procedures and vice versa. This state of affairs continued, with bits of mending and amending, for more than a decade. Not until the Divorce Reform Law of 1989 were the sources of law applying to marriage and divorce in the Islamic Republic of Iran (IRI) agreed upon, and legislation passed to rationalize them with existing rules and opinions. In 1992, that law was amended further, resulting in the creation of a new family code that, while similar to the FPL, actually went further in protecting women with respect to divorce and custody rights.[13] That law was amended further in 1993 and 1996, on both occasions to the wife's advantage. By the time Mohammad Khatami was elected President of Iran (May 1997), with a stunning 80 percent of the women's vote, the law of marriage and divorce was not only the equivalent of the FPL in terms of its provisions for women, but in some cases it exceeded the former FPL protections.[14] I want to focus in particular on the amendments of 1993 and 1996, as I think they indicate a new approach to the ways in which the Islamic law of marriage and divorce can be applied in a state context through new or reclaimed interpretive strategies. To do so requires a brief examination of classical marriage law.[15]

As indicated above, in *shari'a*, marriage is considered a contract entered into by the two parties, each having different rights and responsibilities which are gendered. Thus, the husband is required to maintain the wife for both their lifetimes and for hers, if she survives him or if he divorces her by *talaq* [repudiation]. In order to provide for her support, he is required, upon marriage, to endow her with a capital sum, known as the *mehrieh*, which is for her maintenance should he die or divorce. He then has a right to her obedience and sexual/reproductive services. He also has the coterminous right to enter into up to three other similar contracts and the right to unilateral divorce. She has the right to be maintained and the duty to obey and provide sexual/reproductive services. She does not have a unilateral right to divorce and may seek it only in very limited circumstances. She cannot enter another such contract coterminously nor does she have any duty with regard to his support. Upon divorce, he has no further duty of support to her, although he must still maintain his children to whose custody he is entitled. The contract bespeaks an implicit view of society as heavily gendered, with economic activity the province of men.

With this as the outline of the *shari'a*-based law applied in the post-revolutionary religious divorce courts, many women were shocked to find themselves at risk late in their lives when their husbands unilaterally divorced them. Because of inflation or a marriage contract that had replaced the economic value of the *mehrieh* with some romantic conceit like a rose or a sigh, they could be left indigent with no resources at all, dependent on aged parents or grown children, and with little possibility of remarriage. Younger women who wished to divorce found it very difficult to leave a bad marriage without the consent of the very husbands from whom they were alienated and subject to being deprived of support if they separated.

Ziba Mir-Hosseini has richly described in her books and the film *Divorce Iranian Style* how these dilemmas made Qur'anic exegetes of women challenged by this religious law to gain their goals in the context of unwanted divorce or marriage. Among their strategies, for example, was the determination to insist on extracting the cash value of the *mehrieh* from a divorcing husband. Generally, payment of the *mehrieh* was deferred at the inception of the marriage, making the wife the first creditor on the husband's estate before its disbursal to heirs after his death; in case of his unilateral exercise of *talaq*, she is then entitled to it, although many women did not understand their rights in this respect until their education by the women's press. Another use of the *mehrieh* by a divorced wife was to waive its payment if the divorcing husband would give her custody of the children. Alternatively, she could buy her way out of the marriage by agreeing not to press her claim to the *mehrieh*. But all of these strategies relied upon the *mehrieh* retaining its value. In fact, however, inflation raged in Iran after the Revolution and during the Iran–Iraq war (1980–1988), making many *mehriehs*, in the words of a female member of the *Majles*, or Parliament, "barely enough to pay a wife's taxi fare to the divorce court."[16] Thus, a woman's only source of support following divorce, her potential means of obtaining a divorce or of keeping her children, might be completely valueless within a few years after the marriage.

The women's press took up this question and sought reform that would save women from destitution after divorce or the devastation caused by a bad marriage. One solution, suggested by Khomeini, was the creation of a right for the wife, upon the husband's exercise of *talaq*, to half the property acquired by him during the course of the marriage.[17] Such a provision would be included in the boilerplate marriage contract, although both sides must agree; such standardized provisions favorable to women would provide some assistance in redressing the imbalance of this gendered transaction, because "[T]he burden is shifted to the groom who must negotiate to remove the clauses he disagrees with, giving the bride's party leverage to request additional conditions of their own."[18] While such a provision could provide for the woman whose *mehrieh*, at the time of divorce, had declined dramatically in value due to inflation, this solution only served women married after the new provision was added to the contract. It did nothing for the older women whose marriage contracts were made earlier than 1982 when Khomeini had the provision added.[19]

In the decade of the 1980s, women had been crucial to maintaining popular support for the Islamic Republic during the terrible Iran–Iraq War of 1980 to 1988. They lent both active and passive support to the IRI, on the one hand, filling roles as ambulance drivers, ammunition packers, health workers, and workplace substitutes for men at the front, and, on the other hand, allowing their husbands and sons to go off to the devastating "human-wave" attacks that allowed Iran to use its population advantage to counter Iraq's weaponry advantage. By the end of the 1980s, issues of concern to women, including the laws applying to their marriages, divorces and families, had become a focus of both the administration and legislation. There had been a decade of attention to the "crisis of marriage" by women's organizations and in the women's press that had led to this outcome,[20] as both women and judges (in the revolutionary aftermath, all men) sought ways to ameliorate the impact on women of the harsh strictures of classical marriage law.

However, when the *Majles* took up this question, it at first did not provide a solution to this fundamental problem facing women, in part because it did not know how to do so. In finding a solution, it was aided by the demonstration in the women's press of the possibilities of new interpretive strategies when applied to religious law. The new "dynamic jurisprudence" [*fiqh-e puya*] experimented with women-friendly interpretations of Qur'anic texts and *hadith*.[21] This approach was a product of the thinking that devout and believing women and their allies had done about the situation of women in a religious state.

This position was advanced by the cleric Mohsen Sa'idzadeh, who in the 1990s authored a series of pseudonymous articles in the feminist magazine *Zanan* [Women], challenging traditional interpretations of *fiqh* concerning women. Sa'idzadeh was apparently the first modern cleric to make "an overt attempt to reconcile feminism with Islam," believing that religion and gender equality are reconcilable. His starting point was the strong equality claims of Islam, which allowed him to conclude that gender is a social construction, "a relative matter [that] ... has no place in the divine realm." Hence, he argued that those traditions which seem to mandate gender inequality were being misinterpreted or otherwise were incorrect.[22] *Zanan* published these articles as explicit challenges to retrograde interpretations of the situation of women and in order to provide women with ammunition in legal actions regarding their own marriages.

At the same time, there were a number of female *Majles* deputies who were interested in improving the legal situation of women and who were apparently attending to the discussions of *fiqh-e puya*. They and their male allies took up the problem of the lack of support for divorced women and were able to suggest a religiously-acceptable means of providing that support. The novel solution they proposed was drawn from accepted notions of religious jurisprudence reconceptualized in a post-revolutionary context. Their solution was to turn to *mu'amalat*, the religious account of the duties people owed one another. Among them is the responsibility to compensate fairly those who labor on one's behalf, so long as that labor is volunteered and not commanded. In that situation, the laborer is worthy of his or her hire, as another monotheistic tradition has it. The corresponding concept in Islam is *ujrat al-mithal*, meaning that a fair price should be paid for any commodity, including the labor of a free person.

Now, the marriage contract, while it commits the wife to compensate her husband with her obedience and sexual/reproductive services in return for his maintenance of her, does not require her to keep house or nurse children. Yet most women do so. Thus they are entitled to be compensated for this work, should they demand it, as they might do upon divorce. Such a provision was added to the 1991 divorce law at the end of 1992, as another judicially cognizable claim a divorced woman would have upon her husband.[23] This time, the *Majles* not only required that the form contract include the provision that the wife was due her wages in case of divorce, but also made it possible for a woman married under the old form of contract to receive wages for housework implied into the old contract judicially, if a court found she had not agreed to contribute her work without pay.[24] Thus, even a woman married before the right to wages was made explicit in the form contract might be entitled to receive them, although there were limitations to this right that were a product of compromise.

The most complete answer to the problem of support for divorced women was in a sense both the simplest and the most faithful to the religious tradition. I have said that the marriage gift was intended to provide women with the assurance of support, regardless of what happened to their husbands or their marriages. The *mehrieh* ceased to accomplish that function only because of inflation, which diminished the value of the marriage gift when stated in terms of currency. The obvious solution, and the one adopted by the *Majles*, encouraged by female parliamentarians within and women's organizations and the women's press externally, was to inflation-index the marriage gift.[25] Thus, whatever amount of gold the currency-denominated gift would have bought at the time of the marriage was understood to be the ongoing value of the gift at whatever time it might be demanded by the female spouse. In one simple amendment then, the issue of support for divorced women was resolved. That amount which she and her family had believed would serve as a capital sum capable of supporting her for life would be available to her whenever the marriage ended, whether it ended by death or divorce.

All of this, occurring as it did even before the reformers' take-over in the elections of 1997, is surprising, given the standard narrative of women's situation in Iran, and it begs, but does not defy, explanation. That explanation, in my view, lies in the events surrounding the Islamic Revolution, both its precursors and sequelae, and the activism of Iranian women in that context.

Here it is necessary to review a bit of history. Although Iranian women were supporters of national independence as far back as the Qajar dynasty at the end of the nineteenth century, traditionally they were not expected or encouraged to be politically active. The notion of female suffrage was first raised in the context of the Constitutional Revolution of 1905, but was rejected soundly by both clerics and laymen. The founder of the Pahlavi dynasty, Reza Shah, ordered that women had to unveil in public and established girls' schools in major cities, but did not otherwise seek their political support. After his forced abdication in 1941, a popular front government introduced suffrage legislation but once again it was defeated. With the overthrow of Prime Minister Mohammad Mossadegh in 1953, Reza Shah's son, Mohammad Reza, undertook personal governance of the state. On the advice of his American supporters, he sought to broaden his internal base of support in the early 1960s with a package of reform plans he termed the White Revolution and which included giving women the right to vote. Enfranchising women was an issue on which Khomeini, then a relatively unknown cleric, first made known his public opposition to the Shah in 1963, denouncing women's suffrage as un-Islamic. And certainly at least in part due to his opposition, relatively few women voted in the *Majles* elections, which were in any case a sham, as the Shah brooked no opposition, electorally or otherwise.

The opposition to the Shah and his government had never declined since Mossadegh's overthrow, despite savage repression, and Khomeini, though sent into exile, continued as a public face of that opposition, which contained secular, religious and liberal figures of many political stripes. Khomeini's forces had an edge – as clerics, they were less repressible than were other groups, whose organization was perforce underground, while the clergy's was visible in every mosque and *husseiniya*. It was within the power of Khomeini and his organization to rally truly mass support for the anti-Shah movement. Nor did Khomeini scruple to include women within these forces.

Mary Hooglund (now the well-known anthropologist Mary Elaine Hegland) was conducting her thesis research in a small village near Shiraz in the summer of 1978, when the protests against the Shah entered their final and most significant stage.

She describes how women became active in the protests. She notes first that the mosque was the "most important center of revolutionary activity" in the village and that women who regularly attended were "more likely to be influenced by the revolutionary ideas." Moreover, the seven young girls in the village who went to high school were taught by a mullah whose classes "became forums for learning revolutionary ideology." Both men and women experienced "horror, rage, and frustration ... when witnessing or hearing of acts of violence against their fellow citizens."[26]

Nonetheless, village women, unlike their male counterparts, did not actually participate in demonstrations until January 1979. The demonstrations of the previous month had been enormous and there was much bloodshed, as the Shah's forces attacked the demonstrators. On a day appointed for mourning those killed in December, village women, on their own, came out of their houses and walked "a little ways up the alley," chanting slogans. "When the men heard their voices," Hooglund was told, "they came out too." This must have been a transformative moment for the village women, most of whom never left their houses socially except to clean off family graves in a group every few weeks. These demonstrations continued and grew larger. "After the first evening of chanting, they began to feel that all was possible."[27]

They began to travel to Shiraz to take part in the larger demonstrations for "independence, freedom and Islamic republic." This last was a characteristic demand of the Khomeini forces, as opposed to the more secular Left, which sought simply a republic. Hooglund's informants explained their parrticipation, so unusual for Iranian women, as justified by religious authority:

> The religious scholars and the ayatollahs have said that men and women must revolt together, they must demonstrate together for religion and for freedom for all. Islamic government is for everybody and the Islamic strug-gle is for everybody. Before women didn't do this.... If we don't speak, this government will go on for hundreds of years more.[28]

Indeed, Khomeini had sanctioned and called for women's participation on the streets, calling their involvement "one of the blessings of this movement."[29] His was a call that could not be denied, even by men completely unaccustomed to seeing women in their family as political actors. As Homa Hoodfar writes, the "unconventional presence of women in political demonstrations, wearing tradi-tional black chador, became the symbol of the popular revolution."[30] This evoca-tion of women's agency by the leading cleric and most revered political figure in the country simply swept away the customary barriers to such action.

I have spent some time on the Aliabad experience because it so clearly indi-cates the radical break with the past that the Revolution created for women there, a break duplicated hundreds of thousands of times around the country. Once the Revolution succeeded, the women who had supported it so unconventionally had some claims upon it. Those claims were in fact enhanced by the need which Khomeini felt to appeal to women for their support for the creation of the Islamic Republic itself in an election and referendum to decide the shape of the new Republic. Khomeini, who had been so opposed to the Shah's 1963 offer of suf-frage for women, did not maintain this position. He urged women to come out to vote, first for the constitution of the Islamic Republic approved in December 1979, and then in March 1980 for the election of candidates who backed him. "Women in the Islamic Republic must vote. Just as men have the right to vote, women too have that right."[31] Indeed, Khomeini went further, commanding that for women, voting was a "religious, Islamic and divine duty."[32] This, as Pavin Paidar says, "was a total reversal of the history of clerical opposition to women's participation in the economy, politics and society."[33]

Nor did the creation of the Islamic Republic of Iran in 1980 call a halt to this new phase. Immediately after the Revolution, there were a variety of independ-ent women's organizations and now-visible women's caucuses within the polit-ical formations that had been underground in the Shah's time. The leading women's group, the Women's Organization of Iran, headed by the Shah's sister, had been created in the wake of the extension of suffrage to women, a formal group recognized by the monarchy. This was disbanded in favor of Women in Support of the Islamic Revolution (WSIR), a group that replaced the WOI as the conduit to and from the government in respect of issues of concern to women. At the same time, control over publications of interest to women shifted from secular supporters of the Shah to Islamist women.

What looked to the West like anti-women policies were interpreted by these Islamist women as anti-secular. They first overcame their secular counterparts, who argued for gender equality regardless of the traditions of the *shari'a*, by espousing a version of different feminism which "stressed that the Qur'an has given different rights and responsibilities to the different creations of God."[34] However, though they agreed that women's primary roles were in the family, they also supported women who wanted or needed to work outside the home. In fact, they became advocates for interpretations of *shari'a* that were more open to the concerns of modernist women than those embraced by pre-revolutionary traditionalists.[35]

In practice, Islamist women first mobilized women's support for the Islamic Republic, then became advocates for the improvement in their status and condition. This shift in emphasis required that women engage the religious establishment with "female-centered interpretations of Islam,"[36] becoming innovators in developing an "Islamic feminist theory of women's oppression and liberation."[37] They came to argue that true religious practice would not oppress women or make them lesser persons than men; thus, any practices or laws that did so were not Islamic, but accretions that should be shed.

At the same time, while the new government may not have approved of self-conscious feminism, even in its Islamic mode,[38] it maintained its support among women by measures beneficial to the popular classes. These included literacy programs for adults, more widely available public education for both sexes, and accessible primary healthcare focused in particular on healthy mothers and children.[39] These were the kinds of policies helpful to women living in traditional families, who had rejected the state feminism of the monarchy's Women's Organization of Iran.

The war with Iraq that followed also required changes in women's roles; it evoked from the government a more conciliatory approach to women than had existed in the immediate post-revolutionary period when ideological rigor was at its peak and women judges were dismissed, some faculties were closed to women and hejab was widely imposed. During the war, women were involved in assisting in battle areas, in providing food, transport, and medical support, and in distributing arms. At home, they aided the wounded, participated in meetings, demonstrations, and conferences to support the war effort, and resettled refugees from the front. As a woman interviewed by Maryam Poya said of her activities during that period, "My husband couldn't disagree; it was all for God."[40]

And when men did not come home, or came home wounded, their mothers, wives, sisters, and children needed to be provided the means of living in order to ensure continued popular support for the terrible carnage. The impact upon women's employment was substantial. More women had to work outside the home, either because their husbands were at the front, or because the galloping inflation of the war years required families to have two incomes. Women who had never been employed outside the home were encouraged by the state to enter the workforce so that they could support their families.[41] While the early position of the Islamic Republic had discouraged women from working outside the home, this changed quickly. Labor practices favorable to working mothers, such as part-time jobs with significant full-time benefits,[42] and requirements that workplaces provide daycare,[43] were adopted to make work and motherhood compatible.

Once the war ended, women not only felt empowered, but also obliged to discuss their status and establish the continuity of their participation in public life in both politics and employment. Women demanded and society agreed that the government should undertake the task of promoting women's social partici-pation as one of its overt goals, rather than simply responding piecemeal to women's issues as it had during the war. One form this process took was institu-tional, with the creation of entities within the government that focused on women's issues directly. Until then, women's issues were the purview of government-sponsored quasi-NGOs and the women's press. In 1987, under then-President Ali Khamehni (who later replaced Ayatollah Khomeini as Supreme Leader) the government created the Women's Social and Cultural Council as a formal means of providing recommendations to the executive branch on women's issues.[44] Its creation was in effect an admission by the conservatives in control of the executive branch that women's issues had an existence independ-ent of those of society at large. Moreover, those issues had to be addressed not only through the mechanism of the *Majles*, whose female representatives might or might not raise particular questions, but in a direct and coherent fashion. Sub-sequently the Bureau of Women's Affairs was created within the President's office in 1991; after President Khatami's election in 1997 it became the Center for Women's Participation, and after President Ahmadinejad's election, the Center for Women and Families.[45]

In short, women who were supportive of the Revolution became the first to undertake an institutional challenge to the Islamic government's attempt to restore unchanged a patriarchal tradition. They insisted that change for women would not come automatically with the mere existence of Islamic government, but would require specific attention and action to women as a discrete group within the polity. Their success has demonstrated that democratic change is pos-sible in the context of Islamic law. While the male-dominated reform movement did not succeed in other legislative efforts, such as winning a free "press, stop-ping torture, [ensuring] free elections, regulating state-run Radio and TV, making [political] institutions ... accountable to [the] Majles, or the fair trial of political crimes,"[46] women have experienced numerous successes regardless of the fate of reformers. Iranian women instigated change with respect to marriage and divorce laws even before the 1997 election of the reform-minded President Mohammad Khatami; they have opened up schools, employment, and political office to women; and have modified the legal regime to their benefit.

Such successes not only have substantive, but procedural impacts. Each time women have moved in a new direction – seeking to enter previously barred occupations, taking part in sports in which women have previously not participated, running for offices which women have not yet held – they have evoked a response. Because the regime claims not only divine but also electoral authority, this response cannot be simply a pro forma negative. Explanations are demanded, interpretations offered, responses written, and arguments engaged in. Because a basis in religion is also claimed, texts are produced, authorities cited, and rationalizations proffered. Each, in its turn, can be the subject of debate. Like a public trial, such a conversation creates a process of public engagement, a space of discourse hitherto unknown, and contributes to the legitimization of multiple voices.

Notes

1 See further World Bank, "Genderstats: Capabilities and Human Capital – Iran, Islamic Rep." Available at: http://genderstats.worldbank.org/genderstats/genderRpt.asp?rpt=capability&cty=IRN,Iran,%20Islamic%20Rep.&hm=home2; and United Nations Development Program (UNDP), "Human Development Report, 2001, Iran, Islamic Republic," available at www.undp.org/hdr2001/indicator/cty_f_IRN.html.
2 Ibid.
3 Ibid.
4 Ibid.; this is the only participation in education figure for which data from both 1980 and 2000 is readily available. According to ibid., the corresponding figure for young men also increased but not as dramatically; males in school as a percentage of the eligible group increased from 52 percent in 1980 to 85 percent in 2000.
5 UNDP, "Human Development Report." Gender parity in literacy is considered by UNESCO to be "a significant indicator of the empowerment of women in society"; see further the Section for Women and Gender Equality of the Bureau of Strategic Planning, UNESCO, UNESCO's Gender Mainstreaming Implementation Framework 18 (2003). Available at: http://unesdoc.unesco.org/images/0013/001318/131854e.pdf.
6 Azadeh Kian-Thiebaut, "Women and the Making of Civil Society," in Eric Hooglund (ed.) *Twenty Years of Islamic Revolution: Political and Social Transition in Iran since 1979* (Syracuse University Press, 2002), p. 63.
7 Jaleh Shadi, "Officials Concerned About Controversy Over Women's Employment and Housewifery," *Zanan*, 77 (July 2001). Available at www.netiran.com/?fn=artd(816).
8 World Bank, GenderStats.
9 Ibid., n. 2. Life expectancy for females born in 2000 was 70, for males 68, up from 59.2 and 58.5, respectively, in 1986, according to Dr. Hamid Sadeghipour of Tehran University's School of Medicine. See further Alvin Powell, "Iranian Primary Care Produces Big Results," *Harvard Gazette*, January 21, 2003. Available at www.hno.harvard.edu/gazette/2003/01.23/07-iran.html.
10 Farzaneh Roudi-Fahimi, Population Reference Bureau, "Iran's Family Planning Program: Responding to a Nation's Needs," 1 (2002). Available at www.prb.org/pdf/IransFamPlanProg_Eng.pdf.
11 Ibid., p. 3.
12 The important women's newspapers include: *Farzaneh* (editor Mahbubeh Abasgholizadeh), *Hoghugh Zanan* (editor Ashraf Geramizadegan), *Jens Dovom* (editor Nooshin Ahmady-Khorasany), *Nashriyeh-e Bonyad-e Pazhuheshha-ye Zanan-e Irani* (editor Goli Amin), *Nimey-e Digar*, 1983–2000 (editor Afsaneh Najmabadi), *Payam Hajar*

(editor Azam Taleghani), *Zan* (editor Faezeh Hashemi), *Zan Ruz* (various editors), and *Zanan* (editor Shahla Sherkat); see further Parvin Paidar, "Gender of Democracy: The Encounter between Feminism and Reformism in Contemporary Iran." Available at: www.onlinewomeninpolitics.org/beijing12/paidar.pdf.

13 Parvin Paidar, *Women and the Political Process in Twentieth-Century Iran*, p. 276.
14 Ziba Mir-Hosseini, "Women and Politics in Post-Khomeini Iran: Divorce, Veiling and Emerging Feminist Voices," in H. Afshar (ed.) (1996), *Women and Politics in the Third World*, pp. 144–147.
15 The following paragraph is drawn from Ziba Mir-Hosseini (1993) *Marriage on Trial: A Study of Islamic Family Law*, pp. 35–39.
16 Ibid.
17 In marriages occurring after 1982, the year when post-revolutionary marriage contracts were issued, the marriage contract contains a stipulation to which the parties consent by signing. This stipulation requires the husband to pay his wife, upon divorce, up to half of the wealth he has acquired during that marriage, provided that the divorce has not been initiated or caused by any fault of the wife. See ibid., p. 57, and p. 210, n. 5.
18 Homa Hoodfar, "The Women's Movement in Iran: Women at the Crossroads of Secularization and Islamization," *Women Living Under Muslim Laws*, The Women's Movement Series No. 1, 1999, p. 35.
19 Similarly, Khomeini had also approved of the adoption of an old strategy to restrain men from exercising their polygynous rights. That strategy included a provision in the marriage contract delegating to the wife the power to act as her husband's agent in the exercise of *talaq*, his unilateral right to divorce, in the event that he took a second wife. In effect, this provision gave her the power to end her marriage. Khomeini also took other steps to protect women's interests in their marriages, including means to assure them continued custody of their children upon the death of their husbands in the bloody and almost interminable Iran–Iraq war, although the traditional understanding was that their custody went to the husband's relatives after his death (ibid., p. 34).
20 Throughout the 1980s, the women's press attacked male custody rights over children, polygyny, and inequitable division of property on divorce, and argued for alternative understandings of religious prescriptions that seemed to support them. For example, the publication *Zan-e Ruz* [Today's Woman] carried articles with headlines like: "With Polygyny, No One Adheres to Islamic Law," *Zan-e Ruz*, July 14, 1984; "Women Have Grievances with the Lack of Enforcement of the Orders of Family Courts, but We Don't Have Adequate Laws in This Regard," *Zan-e Ruz*, December 2, 1989, discussing issues of custody and support; "Family Conflict is the Primary Cause of Suicide," *Zan-e Ruz*, June 4, 1989, addressing the topic of women's suicide; and "A Wife Who Has Worked Hard in My House for Years Is a Partner in My Pension/ Benefits," *Zan-e Ruz*, July 18, 1989. See also Hoodfar, op. cit., pp. 33–34.
21 Editors' note: *hadith* are the authenticated practices and sayings of the Prophet Mohammad and the Twelve Imams of Shi'i Islam.
22 Ziba Mir-Hosseini, *Islam and Gender: The Religious Debate in Contemporary Iran* (I.B. Tauris, 2000), pp. 249–250.
23 The Guardian Council did not approve that provision until 1993, when it went into effect. Hoodfar, supra note 17, p. 35.
24 "Determination of Wages for Work Done," *Zan-e Ruz*, December 18, 1993.
25 Louise Halper, "Law, Authority and Gender in Post-Revolutionary Iran," *Buffalo Law Review*, 1137 (2007), p. 54.
26 Mary Hooglund, "The Village Women of Aliabad and the Iranian Revolution," *Review Iranian Political Economy & History* (Fall 1980), pp. 27, 33.
27 Ibid., pp. 37–38.
28 Ibid., p. 40.

29 Vanessa Martin, *Creating an Islamic State: Khomeini and the Making of a New Iran* (2000), p. 156.
30 Hoodfar, supra note 17, p. 22.
31 "The Position of Women from the Viewpoint of Imam Khomeini," in Juliana Shaw and Behrooz Arezoo (ed. and trans.) (2001), p. 58. Available at: www.iranchamber. com/history/rkhomeini/books/women_position_khomeini.pdf.
32 Nesta Ramazani, "Women in Iran: The Revolutionary Ebb and Flow," *Middle East Journal*, 47 (1993), pp. 409, 411.
33 Paidar, supra note 13, p. 257.
34 Maryam Poya, *Women, Work and Islamism* (1999), p. 61.
35 Hoodfar, supra note 17, p. 20.
36 Ibid., p. 3.
37 Paidar, supra note 13, p. 240.
38 Ibid.
39 Louise Halper, "Law and Women's Agency in Post-Revolutionary Iran," *Harvard Journal of Law and Gender* (2005), pp. 85, 113.
40 Poya, supra note 31, pp. 136–137.
41 Ramazani, supra note 30, p. 411.
42 Paidar, supra note 13, p. 328.
43 Ramazani, supra note 30, p. 414.
44 Elham Gheytanchi, "Appendix: Chronology of Events Regarding Women in Iran Since the Revolution of 1979," 67 *Soc. Res.*, 67 (2000), pp. 439, 445.
45 Nahid Motee, Population Council, "Scientific and Cultural Exchange Program between Iranian and International Researchers," 4 (2000). Available at: www. iranngos.org/reports/SciCulExch/Women011ProfilesGovAgenResWo.htm.
46 Majid Mohammadi, "Iran's Way of Constitutionalism After 1996: Interpretations of Iran's Constitution by the Judiciary and the Reformers," unpublished paper presented at the 2003 Annual Meeting of the Law and Society Association, Pittsburgh, PA, June 5, 2003, on file with the author, p. 3.

2 Gendering Shi'ism in post-revolutionary Iran

Azadeh Kian

In the aftermath of the Iranian Revolution, patriarchal order was reinforced and gender inequality was institutionalized when Islamic laws founded on traditional jurisprudential interpretations (*fiqh-i-sonnati*) were applied to women's rights and family code. Gender inequality thus became the paradigmatic form upon which the Islamic state is based. The Family Protection Law of 1967 was abrogated, and a series of regressions were imposed upon women's rights in both the public and the private realms. For example, an Islamic dress code was applied, and *hijab* became compulsory first for active women and then generalized to the female population; important limitations were set for women in matters of divorce and child custody; the minimum age of marriage for girls was lowered from 18 to nine years (increased to 13 years under the sixth *Majles* in 2002); women's access to judiciary occupations was prohibited, etc.

According to the dominant ideological discourse that considered the home the best and the most suitable place for women, the ideal model for a Muslim woman was one of a mother and a housewife as portrayed in the official mass media and schoolbooks. Faced with high rates of inflation that has led to the decrease in the purchasing power of lower and middle-class households, women's revenue-earning activity became necessary to the survival of their families. The proponents of the ideal of Islamic femininity were therefore forced to change their interpretations of the *shari'a* endorsing women's work outside the household. However, only economic and financial dimensions of women's work are emphasized to the detriment of the social dimension, women continue to be considered dependent upon their husbands, and although half of women active in the formal sector of the economy are highly educated, they are seldom given decision-making posts. Ayatollah Khamenehi, the current leader, declared in a sermon on 16 December 1992: "Islam authorizes women to work outside the home. Her work might even become necessary if it does not change her main responsibility, especially her children's education and the housework."[1] Although Islamists tolerate women's revenue-earning activity, they do not accept its logical consequence, namely women's autonomization and their questioning of men's all-out authority.

In addition to gender-segregating occupational policies, men are given overwhelming privileges in matters of marriage, divorce, guardianship of children after divorce or inheritance. For example, according to article 1105 of the Civil Code, the man is the head of the household and the wife is obliged to submit to her husband (*tamkin*). If she refuses to comply with her husband's authority and demands (including sexual demands), he is legally allowed to sanction his wife, and in certain cases is even authorized to divorce her. Likewise, men retain the exclusive right to divorce (article 1133 of the Civil Code) and to parental authority (*kifalat*) after divorce.

In the name of religion some Islamists with a positivist approach to nature essentialize gender inequality, which they consider to be a natural fact originating in the divine will. They confine women to domesticity where natural hierarchy limits the equality between men and women. Javad Mustafavi, an Iranian conservative cleric and the author of a widely read book entitled *The Paradise of the Family* (*Behesht-i khanevadeh*), argues, "God has created women to do the housework, child-bearing and child-rearing. God has created men for activities outside the home, for confronting the hardships of life." The proponents of traditional jurisprudence argue that men and women are different in their essence and should not be equal. They argue that men and women are complementary (*mokamel*). They thus reject equality and emphasize the notion of equity.

During the first decade of the Revolution, men's superior legal position led some of them to abuse their rights. For example, the number of unjustified divorces initiated by men increased, while the Islamic courts almost automatically granted the guardianship of children to men. This provoked the general discontent of the female population and forced the Islamist women parliamentarians to prepare motions to defend more adequately women's needs and rights in the private sphere of the family. They held that the teachings of Islam were not respected.[2]

The segregation laws triggered the mobilization of many women and created a common ground of protest for both secular women, many of whom had been dismissed from their posts during the revolutionary period (1979–1986), and the disillusioned educated Islamics, who had gained social mobility thanks to the revolution and the thrusting aside of secular women. They rejected their confinement at home, challenged the institutionalized gender inequalities by emphasizing their activity in the economic, social and cultural realms that are not forbidden by the religious and political elite's reading of the *shari'a*, but they also asserted their authority in the religious and judicial realms where women are denied power.[3]

Training women *mujtahids*

Because authorities justify such prohibitions by referring to the Qur'an, the *shari'a*, the *hadith* (sayings and practices attributed to the Prophet and the Imams) and Islamic traditions, women's challenge necessarily entails debates that revisit and reinterpret Islamic principles. While women have proposed legal changes and presented their own readings of the Qur'anic verses and Islamic laws, the actual implementation of change in the existing laws under the Islamic

Republic requires recourse to *ijtihad*. To this end, women *mujtahids* (doctors of jurisprudence) are needed more than ever. Following the death of Mrs. Amin-Isfahani, a woman *mujtahid*, in the early 1980s, Iran is, for the time being, devoid of female religious authorities. Their shortage has led some religious women, who believe that such undertakings necessitate the training of women in relevant fields, to create women's religious seminaries. One of the implications of this undertaking is the autonomization of women in the realm of religion. Young women, including university or high-school students, increasingly seek religious training and enroll in religious seminaries. In 1996, out of 62,731 students in religious seminaries, 9,995 or 16 percent were women, of whom 20 percent were in the age group 15 to 19, 34 percent were in the age group 20 to 24, 17 percent were in the age group 25 to 29, and 11 percent were in the age group 30 to 34. Almost 90 percent of these women resided in urban areas.[4]

Fatemeh Amini[5] founded the first religious seminary for women in Qom in 1972. She declared:

> I often visited the ulama including Ayatollahs Golpayegani, Najafi, Vahidi and Shari'atmadari. They all knew me well and trusted me. I was very active in assisting the disinherited. With the support of the late Grand Ayatollah Kazem Shari'atmadari I created *Maktab Tawhid* in Qom. I then founded several seminaries including *Maktab Ali* in Qom and *Maktab Zahra* in Yazd. After the revolution Imam Khomeini ordered that all seminaries unite and appointed a council of management. The *Maktab Towhid* thus became Jame'at-ol Zahra. I then decided to move to Tehran where I founded *Fatemeh Zahra* religious seminary in 1988. Some religious authorities from Qom later visited my seminary, which they approved and even authorized me to spend religious taxes (*sahm-i imam*) here but I preferred to remain independent. My seminary is one of the most spiritual in the country. We have over 250 students, many of whom are also university or high-school students as well as medical doctors or engineers. Like at other religious seminaries, they study for four years. We are devoted to Imam Ali and his holy family and offer courses on Imamology that is peculiar to our seminary. We also teach Arabic and even offer English courses. In addition to ordinary curricula that are common to other religious seminaries, we also offer courses on public health, ecology, home management, and the like. These are taught by university professors.[6]

A divorced woman and a mother of two highly educated daughters, Fatemeh Amini, who obtained her high-school diploma only after the Revolution at the age of 47, believes that a female *mujtahid* should be capable of solving a multitude of problems. She declared:

> Our main aim here is to form women *mujtahids*. According to the Qur'an, men and women are equal.... The society needs women doctors and engineers as well as women *mujtahids*. But there is an important resistance

against women attaining the degree of *ijtihad* (interpretation). Without these obstacles, which seriously hinder their training, we could have had many women *mujtahids* since the revolution. A lot of young women study at these seminaries but nobody encourages them. Owing to the lack of financial means I have not been able to hire an adequate number of teachers. As a result, many of my students have been enrolled for five years without being able to finish all courses. Our aim here is to educate women *mujtahids* as well as women capable of finding solutions to women's problems, including their social problems. We also financially and morally assist deprived women and have established a credit system that collect money from the pious rich and grant interest-free loans to the poor. Our goal is to contribute to women's development by giving impetus to their creativity, thereby also increasing their self-esteem.[7]

In addition to independent religious seminaries, 5,000 women are enrolled in *Jamiat ul Zahra*, the Qom religious seminary (*hawza*) for women, which is the largest of its kind in Iran and teaches official Islam. It continues to be managed by an appointed council of managers. Their curricula are common to other religious seminaries. The religious seminary also has an Office of Research and Study on Women which launched a magazine called *Zanan va Tazeha-ye Andisheh.* The editorial board rejects egalitarian views held by "radical secular feminists" and "moderate feminists" and criticized traditionalist views. For the editorial board of this magazine only the mobilization and active participation of Muslim women themselves can bring a quick and fundamental solution to their problems.

Among female students in *Jamiat ul Zahra* 800 are from foreign countries, from Kenya to China, and who attempt to attain the status of *Aalima* (a senior preacher). Zahra Merali, a 21-year-old Kenyan Muslim, who lived and studied there, later said that the experience at the seminary had given her a stronger religious foundation despite the materialism of the outside world. She started giving lectures to women at mosques in Mombasa and Arusha, in Tanzania.[8]

Role of women's magazines

Religious women's mobilization against "the dispossession of women of their power in the realm of the sacred" is not limited to training women *mujtahids*. Women's magazines, including *Zanan, Farzaneh, Payam-e Hajar* and *Payam-e Zan* (published by the Qom religious seminary) played a significant role in publicizing and disseminating relevant debates. Because several articles of the Civil Code (e.g., men's unilateral right to divorce and legalization of polygyny) find their origins in the Qur'anic verses, especially that of *Al Nisa* (women), Muslim women challenge the dominant readings by the clergy which they consider to be distorted. Through presenting their own interpretations they intend to show that Islam accommodates the equality of rights between women and men. Women who have a religious training are better equipped to deal with religious issues.

For example, *Payam-i Hajar*, edited by Azam Taliqani, the daughter of the late radical cleric Ayatollah Mahmoud Taliqani, was the first to publish an article (in 1992) refuting the legalization of polygyny and proposing a new interpretation of the *al-Nisa* verse:

> The analysis of the Quranic verse on polygyny shows that this right is rec-ommended in some specific cases and exclusively in order to meet a social need in view of expanding social justice.[9]

Specific cases are argued to be war periods during which the heads of house-holds were killed, leaving many widows and orphans with no financial resources. According to the author this phenomenon caused enormous problems for the community of Muslims. In the absence of social institutions to take care of widows and orphans this responsibility was delegated to Muslim men via polyg-yny. The author maintains, "God has recommended polygyny only in the case of a social need, and only if men can preserve equity between their wives."[10]

Combining her religious interpretation with the realities of the post-revolutionary Iranian society, the author rejects polygyny as a social necessity. "Contrary to the ancient time, the modern state and its social institutions are con-ceived to assist needy families. Therefore, polygyny has no social function to fulfill."[11] Referring to the data provided by the national census of the population and housing showing that the number of men is higher than that of women, the author argues that polygamy which only well-to-do men can afford (due to the high costs of *nafaqeh*[12]) deprives other men of marriage. The author concludes, "It has been shown that in reality it is pleasure rather than charity that motivates men to become polygynous."[13]

Nahid Shid,[14] a lawyer who has both a university and a religious education (she was a student of the late Ayatollah Najafi-Mar'ashi) and has initiated several amendments to the divorce law, especially *ujrat al-mithal* (principle that says when a man files for divorce his wife may ask to be compensated by her husband in return for the housework she has carried out during the marriage), maintains that:

> The bulk of the enforced laws can and should be changed because they are not divine orders. They are based on secondary orders. Blood money is one of them. It was determined when men were valued as warriors who contrib-uted to the expansion of Islam, while women were devoid of such social values. Times have changed and the law should reflect this change.... This law cannot be functional in a society in which women are medical doctors, university professors, engineers, and the like. Blood money should be the same for men and women.[15]

Shahla Sherkat, editor-in-chief of the influential women's magazine *Zanan* that was prohibited to publish in January 2008, argued: "Radical legal changes are needed to solve women's problems. Because many articles of the Civil Code are based on the *shari'a*, its reinterpretation proves necessary and women should be involved in this undertaking." She further maintained:

> The Qur'an has not banned women from becoming judges. This prohibition was initiated in the history of jurisprudence and in the opinions of the previous religious authorities, whose ideas on women probably were shaped by the examples of their own wives or female relatives whom they generalized to the entire female population.[16]

A few months following its publication, *Zanan* printed a series of articles written under a female pseudonym by Hojjat ol-Islam Mohsen Sa'idzadeh (who was imprisoned for several months in the summer of 1998 by the Special Court for the Clergy). These articles examined the obstacles toward women's authority in religious and judiciary institutions, and maintained that none of the main Islamic texts justified such prohibitions, that no consensus existed among religious authorities on the issue, and that in the past, several women in Iran and elsewhere in the Muslim world had attained the summit of religious authority. The author thus concludes: "a man has no natural or contractual privilege over a woman. If a man can become a judge so can a woman, and if a man can become a source of imitation, so can a woman."[17]

Secular women's contributions to these debates have been manifold. Through articles they published in women's magazines (especially *Zanan* and *Farzaneh*) or interviews, lawyers and jurists, sociologists and historians, political scientists, artists and writers, sportswomen, movie directors, and others – often considered as role models for the younger generation – have questioned the predominant ideological discourse on women. Several lawyers and jurists, including the 2003 Nobel Prize winner Shirin Ebadi, Mehranguiz Kar, Shadi Sadr and Nasrin Sotoudeh, have been particularly vocal. The first three individuals were forced to leave the country but continue to raise their voice against segregation laws; Sotoudeh was sentenced to 11 years in prison. In their writings, they have criticized Islamic laws from the viewpoint of the universal Declaration of Human Rights and other international conventions that the Islamic Republic has signed. Because they are well aware of the fact that Iran is a Muslim society, they too refer to Islam and the Qur'an to argue against gender inequalities. Thus, in their discourse, they argue that Islam is for the equality of rights between men and women, Muslims and non-Muslims. Based on this interpretation, they demand the reform of the Civil Code and the penal laws. Both Islamic and secular advocates of women's rights reject divine justifications for gender inequality through a new reading of Islam, which accommodates the equality of rights between men and women.

Women, politics and *shari'a*

Although women lost important parts of their civil rights, they maintained their political rights that the Shah had granted women in 1963 thanks to their collective political involvement during the 1977 to 1979 revolutionary years. This led

Ayatollah Khomeini to endorse women's political rights and to present an interpretation of Islam according to which not only the political and social rights of women would be guaranteed by an Islamic state, but women would gain true freedom, dignity and respect. He thus retracted his earlier stand to recognize women's political rights as lawful in Islam. Along with the leading clergy he had vehemently opposed the Shah's 1963 decision to enfranchise women, calling it an anti-Islamic measure. In a telegram sent to the Shah on October 9, 1962 he maintained: "By granting voting rights to women, the government has disregarded Islam and has caused anxiety among the *ulama* and the Muslims."[18] After the Revolution he encouraged Islamist women's activities in the public sphere. Women, however, were denied leadership positions in political, religious and judicial realms.[19]

Therefore, religious women also reinterpret the Qur'an and traditions to justify women's political and religious leadership.[20] Monir Gorgi, a renowned specialist of Islam, is one of the leading figures among them. She has a religious education and is Director of the Center for the Study and Research on Women's Problems in Tehran. Following Ayatollah Khomeini's order in the early 1980s, all religious seminaries for women in Qom were united and Ayatollah Mossavi-Ardebili appointed Monir Gorgi as Director of *Jamiat ul Zahra*. Gorgi's reading of the Qur'an refutes the position of the traditional jurisprudence that forbids women's access to leadership positions under the pretext that women are physically and morally weak. She analyzes the personality, opinion, and governance of the Queen of Sheba (Bilqiys) as reflected in the Qur'an. Gorgi argues:

> Although the Qur'an mentions only a few rulers, the Queen of Sheba is among them and she is depicted as one of the most just and rationalist rulers. This alone shows that the Qur'an accepts the capacity of women to manage and to lead. The Queen of Sheba is not an exception to the rule. She is a logical part of a global entity: women. She has shown that women are not weaker than men in matters of leadership and that they can be even better than men because the notion of justice was one of the peculiarities of the Queen of Sheba's rule.[21]

Concerning the biological differences between men and women evoked by conservative clerics to prohibit women's access to decision-making positions, Gorgi argues that in modern political systems the predominance of technical, technological and managerial knowledge has made physical force redundant in the exercise of power. Gorgi therefore questions the pertinence of Islamic political jurisprudence for which manhood is one of the preconditions of Islamic leadership.[22]

The Islamic constitution attributes religious and judicial leadership exclusively to men (articles 5, 107, 163), while remaining ambiguous as to the political leadership (article 115). Indeed, the word *rajul*, used to define the prerequisite condition for assuming the post of president of the republic, means both a man and a renowned personality, which by definition can also be a woman.

This ambiguity has led women activists to argue that constitutional law authorizes women to run for presidential elections. From among 238 candidates for the 1997 presidential elections, eight were women. Azam Taliqani was among them. She decided to run as a candidate in order to challenge the traditionalist views on women: "It is my legal right to run for presidency. Moreover, I want the meaning of the word *rajul* to be clarified in the constitution. If the Council of Guardians respects Islam, then there should be no problem with my qualification."[23] The number of women candidates increased to 47 in the 2001 presidential elections, and to 89 in 2005. They were 42 in 2009. Abbas-Ali Kadkhodayi, the Speaker of the Council of Guardians, then declared that there was no restriction for women's candidacy in these elections.[24] Nonetheless, the meaning of the word *rajul* remains ambiguous because all female candidates were disqualified by the Council of Guardians, which provided no reason for their disqualification.

As a result of women's struggles and their questioning of traditional gender roles and identities and advocating equal rights, the law on the condition of the choice of judges was reformed in 1996 leading to a better representation of women in the judiciary. According to the new law women judges may be appointed as examining magistrates, counselors in the administrative court, counselors in family courts, and counselors in the office of the protection of minors. The country had 300 women judges in early 2000 and many more women were being trained to occupy such positions.[25]

The conservatism of President Ahmadinejad and segregation policies implemented by his government on the one hand, and protest activities of Muslim and secular women on the other, led some traditional women including some members of the Parliament to criticize the low number of women in decision-making positions. On the occasion of legislative elections for the Eighth Parliament in April to May 2008, Maryam Behroozi, former member of the Parliament, member of the conservative Islamic Coalition Party, and President of the conservative Zeynab Association, declared: "Women should participate actively in decision making. There is no legal impediment toward women obtaining important numbers of seats in the parliament. It is the predominant patriarchal system that wants to thrust women aside from the public sphere."[26]

On the occasion of the June 2009 presidential elections, a large coalition of secular and Islamic women published a declaration demanding that the future president take measures to ratify the Convention on the Elimination of All Forms of Discrimination Against Women (CEDAW), promulgated by the reformist majority Sixth Parliament (2000–2004) but rejected by the Council of Guardians and the seventh and eighth conservative majority Parliament. They also demanded the change in discriminatory articles of the constitutional law and the Civil Code.

Following the contested results of the 2009 presidential elections and despite the repressive measures applied by the government against all opponents, and the imprisonment of many women's rights advocates, some vocal Islamic (and secular) women continue to struggle against conservative bills, laws, and perceptions that are to the detriment of women and their rights. Ashraf Boroujerdi from the Center for Research on Humanities and Cultural Studies is among them. A former deputy interior minister in charge of social affairs under President Khatami, she is a fine specialist of Islam and gender. She has argued that the Qur'an makes no difference in referring to men and women, and that sex is mentioned only when individual matters are discussed. She further argued that the Qur'an does not refer to sex but to humanity. Regarding woman's creation, Boroujerdi maintains that the Qur'an negates all the attitudes which consider her to be created from the left rib of man. "The Qur'an considers women's creation unique and does not recognize any essential difference between men and women except for the acquired characteristics."[27] For Boroujerdi, the Qur'an negates sex in attaining virtues, acquiring knowledge, preparing sound foundations for thinking, and selecting the best way available. She also maintains that Ayatollah Khomeini, the founder of the Islamic Republic, praised women's participation in the development of the society, saying that their role was no less than that of men.

In January 2010, when the Islamic Parliament was discussing the new Family Protection Bill prepared by Ahmadinejad's government, Ashraf Boroujerdi severely criticized its article 23 which concerns men's right to polygyny. She argued that the aim of the supporters of the bill is to normalize polygyny and to alter society's negative perception of it. Like Azam Taliqani and numerous other gender-conscious Islamic women, Boroujerdi believes that the Qur'an has emphasized the impossibility of polygyny and has recommended monogamy. She therefore maintains that "those who prepared the bill and those who support it are not propagating Islamic traditions, but the Arab traditions during the era of Arab ignorance (*jahiliyya*)." For Boroujerdi, this new Family Protection Bill targets those married women who pursue tirelessly their social and civil rights. "Conservative policy-makers have decided to launch a war against active women and their struggles and want to force women back to domesticity," she maintained.[28]

Contribution of reformist clerics

Faced with these intellectual endeavors and women's social struggle for equal rights, a new perspective has emerged among reformist clerics. They started to oppose the official and rigid interpretations of Islam that essentialize gender inequalities, and presented an evolutionist perspective, which attempts to adapt Islam to women's modern demands. Grand Ayatollah Yousef Sane'i, Ayatollahs Bojnourdi and Jannaati, and Hojjat-ol Islams Mohammad Mujtahid-Shabestari criticize "erroneous interpretations" of the Qur'an and the limitations set on women's rights in the name of Islam. Following Ayatollah Moqaddas-Ardebili's rules over four centuries ago, Grand Ayatollah Yusef Sane'i argued that Islam does not forbid women from becoming judges, political leaders or *mujtahids* and that they can deliver religious edicts (*fatwas*).[29] He also ruled that blood money should be the same for men and women.

Ayatollah Jannaati, a cleric who teaches at the Qom seminary, declared that over 50,000 fabricated *hadith*s existed, the majority of which are against women.

He argued that they are used to prevent women's access to higher positions and to obtain their social rights.[30] Hojjat-ol Islam Mohsen Sa'idzadeh also opposed the practice and legalization of polygyny. Regarding the Prophet's own practice of polygyny, Sa'idzadeh declared, "this is a personal position and does not constitute for Muslims a model to be followed."[31]

Mohammad Mojtahed Shabestari refutes the arguments of Islamic jurists who maintain that the family and society have a natural structure which finds its origins in the creation, and that rights and obligations of men and women as well as the division of labor within the family and the society should be established according to that structure. On the other hand, Islamic jurists considered the family as the main and the most important system of social life. They believed that political, economic or other systems should adapt themselves to the family system. Mojtahed Shabestari contextualizes and historicizes the reading and understanding of the Qur'an and traditions, and he argues:

> We should understand the Prophet's undertakings in the social and historical context of his time. He has modified certain rights and regulations, which he considered to be unfair to women. He established women's right to property, reformed women's inheritance rights and limited the number of wives for polygynyous men. He has thus advanced from injustice towards justice. If we accept this assumption, then we should also admit that the changes the Prophet made in the status of women are not ultimate. The main message of these changes carried out by the Prophet is that other inequalities which are imposed on women throughout history should be abolished.[32]

In the aftermath of the June 2009 presidential elections, several reformist clerics and intellectuals, including Abdolkarim Soroush, Mohsen Kadivar, and Hasan Yousefi Eshkevari who have denounced political Islam and instrumentalization of religion by the current leaders Khamenehi and Ahmadinejad, either were forced to leave the country or remained in exile. The conservative pro-Khamenehi Society of Qom Theology Teachers even declared that Grand Ayatollah Sane'i, one of the major high-ranking clerical supporters of reformist opponents, was not a source of imitation.

Conclusion

A masculinized construct of the Islamic state, essentialist discourses, and a gendered concept of citizenship have been challenged by women activists both Islamic and secular. In this process, Islamic doctrines and laws as well as patriarchal values and norms are contested and reinterpreted continuously by women activists, who have produced new discourses that have become part of public debates, interacted with political and religious processes and institutions, and created new meanings. Faced with those who use Islam to justify sex discrimination and perpetuate patriarchal logic and male domination, many Iranian women now refer to the same religion and, through their own interpretations and new readings, oppose gendered social relations. They contribute tremendously to the social construction of secularism and the emergence of a democratic system whose prerequisite condition is respect for human rights and the separation between religious and political spheres. These demands are increasingly uttered by Iran's Green Movement.

Notes

1 Khamenehi, A. (1995) *Cheshmeh-ye Nur*, p. 269.
2 Dabbagh, M. (1996) "Zanan va naqsh-e anan dar majlis" [Women and their role in the *Majlis*), *Neda*, 17–18 (winter), p. 9.
3 Kian, A. (2002) *Les femmes iraniennes entre islam, état et famille*, Paris: Maisonneuve et Larose.
4 Iran, *National Census of the Population and Housing, 1996*, p. 77.
5 Amini, F. (1994) Interview with the author, Tehran. 9 October.
6 Ibid.
7 Ibid.
8 http://english.aljazeera.net/focus/iran/2008/2008/09/2008922143119456556.html (accessed September 20, 2008).
9 Ebn-Eddin, F. (1992) "Lozoum-e eslah-e qavanin-e talaq, t'addud-e zojat va hezanat" [Necessity for the reform of laws concerning divorce, polygyny, and child custody], *Payam-e Hajar*, September 10, p. 28.
10 Ibid.
11 Ibid.
12 According to article1106 of the civil code, in permanent marriage the wife's maintenance [*nafaqeh*] should be provided by the husband. *Nafaqeh* includes housing, clothing, furniture, and food.
13 Ebn-Eddin, op. cit., p. 29.
14 Shid, N. (1996) Author interview, Tehran, February 22.
15 Ibid.
16 Sherkat, S. (1994) Author interview, Tehran, September 27.
17 Yadigar Azadi, M. (1992a) "Qezavat-e Zan" [Women's judgment], *Zanan*, 5 (May–July), p. 24.
18 Khomeini, R. (1989) *Sahifeh-e Nour*, Tehran, 9, p. 136.
19 Kian, A. (1997) "Women and politics in post-Islamist Iran: the gender conscious drive to change," *British Journal of Middle Eastern Studies*, 24 (1), pp. 75–96.
20 Kian, A. (2010) "Le féminisme islamique en Iran: nouvelle forme d'assujettissement ou émergence de sujets agissants?" *Critique internationale*, 46 (January–March), pp. 45–66.
21 Gorgi, M. (1993) "Zan va zamamdari: negahi beh hokoumat-e malakeh-ye saba dar Qur'an" [Women and leadership: a look at the Queen of Sheba's reign in the Qur'an], *Farzaneh*, 1 (autumn), p. 28.
22 Ibid., p. 29.
23 Taliqani, A. (1997) *Zanan*, 34 (April–May), pp. 6–7.
24 Kadkhodayi, A.A. (2009) [Online]. Available at: www.radiofarda.com/content/o2_women_iran_election/1606943.html.
25 Khabarnameh-ye Zanan (2001) Tehran, Center for the Participation of Women, 3 (March), p. 15.
26 Behroozi, M. (2008) Interview with Deutsche Welle [Online]. Available at: www.dwworld.de/dw/article/0,2144,3137038,00.html (accessed February 19, 2008).
27 Boroujerdi, A. (1995) "Women's position in Islam," paper presented to the First International Conference on The Role of Woman and Family in Human Development,

Tehran, Iran, May 22–24. Available at: www.salamiran.org/Women/News/The _Role _of_ Woman _and _Family_in_Human_Development.html.

28 Boroujerdi, A. (2010) Interview with *Khabar Online*, January 5; at: www.fardanews. com.

29 Sane'i, Y. (1995), Interview with *Payam*-e Zan, 63 (May), p. 6.

30 Jannaati, E. (2001) Interview with *Hoqouq-i Zanan*, March 19–20, p. 13.

31 Mir-Hosseini, Z. (1999) *Islam and Gender*, Princeton, NJ: Princeton University Press, pp. 263–264.

32 Shabestari, M.M (2000) *Naqdi bar Qara'at-e Rasmi az Din. Bohranha, chaleshha, rah-e halhâ* [A critique of the official reading of religion: crises, challenges and solutions], Tehran: Tarh-i Naw, pp. 503–504.

3 Women and social protest in the Islamic Republic of Iran

Fatemeh Etemad Moghadam

The highly visible presence and leadership of women during and in the protests following the June 2009 election has been widely reported in the media, newspapers, and blog sites. It is worth noting that women were also present in massive numbers during the Islamic Revolution of 1979. There are, however, distinct differences between the reasons for participation in social protest, as well as the types of demands that the participants have been articulating during the recent social protests versus the 1979 Revolution. In 1979, the primary articulated demands of female participants were largely similar to those of men. In 2009, however, women have been highly conscious of gender-based social and legal inequalities. Thus, equality of rights has been a primary objective for female participants. Indeed, many observers have noted the growing development of a strong feminist movement during the post-revolutionary period. This movement has been unparalleled anywhere else in the Middle East.[1] Many studies have pointed at two distinct trends in the legal rights, public presence, education, and labor force participation of women during the post-revolutionary period. In continuity with trends that began during the earlier part of the twentieth century, women's education, presence in public space, and participation in white-collar jobs have increased. In comparison to the pre-revolutionary period, however, discriminatory aspects of women's legal rights, in particular those pertaining to marriage, have been strengthened.[2] In this chapter I argue that the changes in the status and emancipation of women have been dichotomous and contradictory since the 1979 Revolution. Women have achieved greater autonomy, public presence, education, and economic power. At the same time, they are subject to increased legal subordination in marriage. I argue that the root of this legal subordination may be found in the strengthening of the medieval interpretation of legal commoditization of female sexuality in marriage.

In this chapter I will focus on the legal interpretations regarding the treatment of female sexuality in marriage and its implication for freedom of labor and autonomy of women. I will argue that a Muslim marriage is in essence a legal sale of female sexuality and reproductive labor. As such, it treats female sexuality as a commodity that is sold under regulated and specified conditions. This commoditizing aspect, however, is limited only to sexuality. The woman is not sold in marriage. This commoditizing aspect, however, opens up the possibility of interpretations ranging from near-complete legal ownership and control by the husband versus modifications and reduction to a symbolic aspect. I will argue that under the monarchy, the medieval legal interpretation of commoditization of female sexuality was treated as negotiable and modifiable. By contrast, the Islamic Republic has treated it as non-negotiable and has reinforced it through enhancement of women's entitlements in marriage. This reinforcement combined with a growing emancipation in economic, political, and social aspects has thus given rise to contradictions and female activism. Thus, women participate in social protests as agents aware of their own unequal rights who are aiming to eliminate gender-based legal discriminations.

Background

The origin and source of contention regarding legal commoditization of female sexuality and reproductive labor in marriage can be traced back to early Islamic society, the seventh century CE. From the start, Islamic tradition contained an ambiguity regarding the rights, position, and status of Muslim women in society and in the family. Islam was born in the merchant cities of Mecca and Medina. These were early and incipient merchant cities that had evolved out of, coexisted, and interacted with their surrounding nomadic tribal societies. Thus, the early Muslim society may be viewed as one that was undergoing a transition from nomadic tribal to urban mercantile. It was thus influenced by both traditions. Studies indicate that women in nomadic societies participated in all aspects of production, seasonal migration, and even warfare. Thus, compared to many other pre-industrial societies, nomadic women enjoyed public presence, autonomy, and power. By contrast, in pre-modern urban merchant societies, the presence of women was limited to their families and the private domain. They did not participate in trade. Most craft-related products were produced by men. In instances such as textiles and carpets where women participated in production, the products were traded by men. As such, even in instances where women were direct producers, they were not direct sellers of their products. As male populations were in excess of female, prostitution was prevalent in urban areas. As a result, distinct lines were drawn between 'honorable' and prostitute women. Family-oriented women were often veiled and secluded, and did not participate in public space. Their activities were limited to production for home consumption and bearing and rearing children. They were treated as properties of their families.[3] Thus, the transitional aspect of the early Muslim society and the coexistence of the dual and somewhat contradictory nomadic and urban merchant traditions created ambiguity in the rights, status, public presence, and labor force participation of women.

In essence a Muslim marriage, *aqd*, is a sale contract. The man makes the offer, *ijab*, and the woman accepts, *qabul*. The object of the sale is female sexuality and reproductive labor. The products of marriage, children, belong to the husband. At divorce, he has the right to child custody, and at the death of the husband, custody is given to male relatives. In exchange, the woman receives a

dower, *mahrieh*, and financial support, *nafaqeh*. If capable of meeting the financial obligations, a man may practice polygyny. The marriage contract may also
include additional provisions that should be agreed upon by the two sides. This
commoditizing contractual aspect may be attributed to the merchant tradition.
By contrast, the early tradition encompassed autonomous aspects that may be
attributed to the nomadic influence. A woman has the right to own and inherit
property independent of her husband. No prohibition exists regarding women's
labor force participation. In fact, the Qur'an states that working women should
receive fair wages.[4] Indeed, the Prophet's first and highly revered wife Khadijeh
was a merchant. Their marriage was monogamous, which suggests that Khadijeh
may have included the condition of monogamy in the contract.[5] The Prophet's
granddaughter, Zeynab, publicly challenged and condemned Caliph Yazid. For
Shi'i's succession is through the Prophet's daughter, Fatemeh). There were also
many other well-known and powerful women during the early Islamic period:
the Prophet's favorite wife A'yesha, another wife Salma, a grandchild Roqquia,
etc. Indeed, the version of veiling introduced in early Muslim society was limited
and moderate, and seclusion was not practiced in that society. The private house
of the Prophet in Medina was connected to his residence, and the apartment of
his favorite wife A'yesha was directly connected to the main mosque.[6] There are
ample examples of women who were economically and politically active, and
that women participated in public space and were not secluded. These autonomous and public participatory aspects may be attributed to the remnants of the
nomadic influence.

A woman and her sexuality, however, are not separate. Therefore, the theoretical sale of sexuality, the provision of autonomous rights, and the exemplary
lives of the revered women create ambiguity in the rights and autonomy of
women and allow for interpretations ranging from near-complete ownership and
control versus a purely symbolic treatment of ownership of sexuality, and
placing the emphasis on autonomy and public participation.

During the medieval period in Iran, the socio-economic conditions reinforced
the near-total ownership, seclusion, and excessive veiling of women in Iran.
Medieval Iran encompassed large urban centers with active craftsmen, trade and
merchant activities. Furthermore, from about the eleventh through the nineteenth
century most ruling dynasties were from a nomadic tribal origin. Within an existing nomadic tribal society women exercise autonomy and participation. As
pointed out by many historians, some elite aristocratic women from nomadic
tribal origins enjoyed power and wealth.[7] Superimposition of nomadic conquerors upon a settled population, however, created a different dynamic. Since the
main objective of the conquerors was to plunder the wealth of settled people,
women were also objects of plunder. Thus, the settled urban population tried to
hide their wealth and women, as evidenced by an architectural style that con-
ceals all signs of wealth inside walled houses, and a tradition of excessive veiling
and seclusion of women. Further, nomadic conquests and rule enhanced the
extent of seclusion, leading to male family ownership of the majority of urban
women. Under these conditions, the medieval Islamic law, the *shari'a*, made

interpretations that emphasized commoditization of female sexuality, and the legal and social mores amounted to near-complete control and ownership by the husband. At the outset of the twentieth century, when the Constitutional Revolution (1906–1907) and the rise of the Pahlavi Dynasty (1925–1979) marked clear departures from the medieval period. Nevertheless *shari'a'* continued to be based on medieval interpretations.

The Constitutional Revolution and the Pahlavi era (1906–1979)

Many of these medieval legal, socio-economic, and ideological characteristics have persisted in modern Iran. An important development of the modern era, however, is a growing tendency to perceive women as agents whose potential or actual labor positively contributes to society. For example, at the turn of the twentieth century, advocates of women's education stated that educated women can be better mothers.[8] The implicit assumption in this argument is that female labor productivity in child bearing and rearing is positive and can be increased through education. Reza Shah (1925–1941) expanded female public education and allowed women to enter Tehran University. Thus, women were perceived as having the potential ability to contribute positively to public life. Similarly, advocates of the removal of the veil argued that seclusion kept women away from public life and was a factor contributing to the backwardness of Iran. The controversial forced unveiling of women by Reza Shah (1936) is an example of this anti-seclusion perception and the belief that the absence of female participation in public space contributed to backwardness. The forced aspect of this policy may be criticized for being undemocratic. Veiling, however, implies that a woman only can be seen by her husband, or by male relatives who are sexually neutral to her. Consequently, a woman's physical appearance belongs to her husband. It thus may be argued that veiling is yet another dimension of a husband's ownership of his wife. Therefore, it may be argued that the unveiled presence of women in public space modified the extent of male ownership.

This perception of women as productive labor became pronounced in the 1960s and 1970s. Official government documents explicitly referred to women as "a relatively untapped supply of labor" that should be used for development. Therefore, the government policy aimed at removal and/or modification of the traditional barriers to education and labor market participation. In 1976, women comprised about 15 percent of the labor force and one-third of university students. During the 1960s and 1970s women were enfranchised and the minimum legal age for marriage was initially raised to 16 and then to 18, limitations were placed on polygyny, men's unilateral rights to divorce and child custody were terminated, and women's ability to obtain divorce improved. Civil courts were empowered to rule on divorce and parental rights to child custody. The basis of child custody was now the comparative suitability of each parent. Furthermore, upon the death of a father, a mother had precedent on child custody over the immediate male relatives of the deceased father.

The reforms thus modified the legal commoditization of female sexuality. Prohibition of child marriage as well as the equal parental rights in child custody undermined a father's ownership of his children and by extension, that of his wife's reproductive labor. Limitations on polygyny, modification of a man's unilateral right to divorce, and improvements in women's rights to divorce were modifications of commoditization of sexuality in marriage. Furthermore, the enfranchisement of women, their growing participation in public space, the labor market, and education were all trends toward the emancipation of women.[9]

Since the Constitutional Revolution and particularly after the 1930s, a division within the legal system was created. The Personal Status Law covering marriage, divorce, and inheritance continued to be covered by Islamic Law and largely under the control of the clergy. By contrast, all other laws were modernized, and settlements of disputes were transferred from religious courts to the secular courts under the jurisdiction of the Ministry of Justice, *Vezarat-e Dadgostari*. Thus, most aspects of the law were changed and modernized. By contrast, the laws pertaining to marriage and inheritance, the main legal sources of gender inequality, continued to be the medieval Islamic Law. However, the state did make partial attempts to change and modify the Personal Status Law. Each time the law was modified, however, the clergy viewed it as yet another intrusion by the secular state in the remnants of clerical power, control, and income.

Under Reza Shah there were no significant changes in the Personal Status Law. Reza Shah's aggressive attempt to bring women into the public space through forced unveiling (1936), however, created strong antagonism among the clergy and within many devout Muslim families. In contrast to the forced unveiling that was viewed by all members of the clergy as un-Islamic, the Family Reform Law of the 1970s was formulated in consultation with some members of the clergy. It was based on new interpretations of the law, and was not contradictory with the basic tenants of the *shari'a*.[10] Nevertheless, it faced a strong opposition from many segments of the clergy who viewed it as yet another intrusion of the secular state in legal matters that should be controlled by the clergy. It is worth noting that the reform removed the settlement of spousal disputes and the granting of divorce from the notary publics largely controlled by the members of clergy and their families, to the secular courts with secular judges who operated under the supervision of the Ministry of Justice. It thus deprived the clergy of a source of income.

In summary, the division in the legal system between modern secular and Islamic Law reduced the legal power and control of the clergy. Since attempts to reform Islamic Law were initiated by the secular state, the clergy were defensive and viewed the medieval Islamic Law as the legitimate interpretation. Factors that contributed to the Islamic Revolution (1979) are beyond the scope of this chapter. The dichotomy between Islamic and secular, however, was among the forces behind the social protests. One of the main aspects of this dichotomy was the modification in medieval legal commoditization of female sexuality.

The Islamic Republic and the post-election protests (1979–2009)

The 1979 Revolution created a government led by the clergy. As a result, the Personal Status Law was revised. Child custody was returned to the father and, in the event of the father's death, to the paternal grandfather or uncle. Child marriage was legalized provided that the girl had reached puberty, the father approved the marriage, and a judge asked the girl if she consented to the marriage. The obligatory limitation on polygyny was changed to a voluntary contractual condition in the marriage contract. A husband's unilateral right to divorce was reconfirmed and the difficulties for women to obtain divorce were increased. These reversals are all legal reinforcements of male ownership of female sexuality and reproductive labor. As compensation, however, new favorable provisions were introduced for women. Arguing that stipulation of a monetary value at the time of marriage in dower, *mehrieh*, is meant to reflect a certain real purchasing power and value, the law requires adjustments for inflation at the time of payment of the dower, usually at divorce or the death of the husband. Given the increased legal power of a husband over his wife, families of brides also insist on high dowers. It may thus be argued that the post-revolutionary legal system has resulted in increased commoditization, and a rise in the price of female sexuality and reproductive labor.

The Islamic Republic also applied a policy of forced veiling of women. In its undemocratic and repressive aspects, the policy was reminiscent of the forced unveiling of women. The extent of compliance to veiling is in many cases only minimal and veiling has not contributed to seclusion. On the contrary, veiling has brought into the public space women from devout Muslim and traditional families who otherwise would have been prevented from participation in the labor market and education by their families. Nevertheless, the implicit and ideological assumption of veiling is the monopoly control of a husband over the physical appearance of his wife thus increased male ownership.

The Islamic government also explicitly recognizes the productivity of female labor in production for family consumption and has introduced entitlements for household labor. Arguing that a marriage contract does not require women to perform household labor, that *mehrieh* and *nafaqeh* are compensations for female sexuality and reproductive labor only, and that child raising and household labor are the primary responsibilities of a married woman, new entitlements are introduced. The post-revolutionary marriage contracts include a stipulation of sharing at divorce of up to 50 percent of the wealth accumulated by the husband during the marriage. The acceptance of this condition by the husband is voluntary and the condition applies only if divorce is initiated by the husband. Furthermore, a judge will decide the appropriate share of wealth that should go to the wife. According to the testimony of women lawyers who have been involved in such cases, the approved amount is generally far below the 50 percent of the husband's accumulated wealth during marriage.[11] According to the law, if the condition of sharing wealth was not included in the contract, at divorce the woman is entitled to the wage equivalent, *ujrat al-mithal*, of the household labor performed during the marriage. Again, the entitlement to *ujrat al-mithal* applies only if a man initiates the divorce. Furthermore, there are no clear rules pertaining to calculation of the wage equivalent. The judge ruling over the case determines the amount which is generally far lower than the woman's wage equivalent. As justification, the ruling clergy argue that the traditional marriage contract does not provide financial rewards for household activities, and that such activities are the primary obligations of a Muslim woman and have precedent over participation in the labor market.[12] Therefore, the payment of wages for household labor at divorce has been introduced as a new reform to traditional divorce laws. It is worth noting that *nafaqeh*, and the new entitlements, are used as justifications for resisting the reversal of the law requiring the husband's permission for a married woman to work outside the home. While this law pre-existed the Revolution, its enforcement has been strengthened. It is argued that men pay *nafaqeh* and *ojrat-ol-mesl*, and are therefore entitled to have control over women's time.[13]

It is worth noting that the current legal interpretations of a man's ownership rights over the labor time of his wife go beyond the traditional medieval law. There are provisions in the Qur'an and the sayings of the Prophet that may be interpreted to mean that married women are entitled to compensation for child raising and household labor. There is a Qur'anic provision that a woman is not required to breast-feed her child, and if she does so can expect wages from the man.[14] There is also the advice that men who can afford to should hire domestic help for their wives. These may be interpreted to mean that women are not required but may perform household services and expect compensation for these activities. The traditional marriage contract makes no explicit reference to requirement of household labor. Indeed, the proponents of the new law have explicitly argued that the traditional contract does not require women to perform household labor. Thus, it begs the question: If women are not contractually required to perform household labor, why are such activities the primary responsibilities of a Muslim woman; and why should the husband have legal ownership claims over his wife's labor time? The new law thus extends a husband's legal ownership claims beyond sexuality and includes ownership over a woman's labor time. Thus, a married woman cannot freely choose to work outside the home.

The Revolution brought masses of women to the streets and encouraged them to be politically active. The initial attempts to force women out of the labor market proved impractical and were resisted. While secular women view forced veiling as an infringement of their freedom, veiling undermined family opposition to female participation in public space for many women from religious and traditional families. Today, the gender gap in education has been substantially reduced. In recent years, more than 60 percent of all university graduates were females. In comparison to the pre-revolutionary period, the official data do not show a significant increase in the share of females in the total labor force. However, the official data indicate that the participants have much higher education and skills and are involved in wide-ranging professional, managerial, and entrepreneurial activities.[15] There are also indications that the official data under-estimate the participation rates, and that there is a large unaccounted female informal economy that includes educated and professional women.[16]

In summary, in comparison to the pre-revolutionary period, Iranian women have substantially increased levels of education, economic power, political awareness and participation, and overall presence in public space. Legally, however, their subservience to male dominance within the family has increased. This contradictory dichotomous development has thus given rise to the development of a strong feminist movement in Iran. Since the inception of the Islamic Republic, women have been in the forefront of protests and quests for democratic and gender-egalitarian rights. The active presence and leadership of women during the protests against the contested presidential election (June 2009) was yet another manifestation of their quest for a democratic and gender-egalitarian society.

Another noteworthy aspect of current developments in Iran is the dichotomy within the clerical establishment concerning human rights and gender equality. The clergy is in power and is no longer in a defensive position vis-à-vis reforms imposed by a secular state. The dichotomy is now between the conservative and progressive segments of the clergy. Today, a segment of the ulama believe that even far-reaching and sweeping gender egalitarian legal reforms are not contrary to Islam. A number of leading clerics, such as Ayatollah Sane'i and Ayatollah Bojnurdi, have advocated in favor of a re-examination of the gender-based discriminatory laws and argued that the law has to be adjusted to the requirements of the time. Ayatollah Bojnurdi stated explicitly that Islam is supportive of human rights and does not value one sex over the other.[17] The discussion over the issue of gender rights is now very internal to the debates within the clerical community.

Conclusion

This chapter has argued that since the establishment of the Islamic Republic in 1979, the original Islamic ambiguity between women's autonomy and public presence versus husbands' ownership and control has evolved into a highly contradictory and inherently unstable evolution of autonomy and emancipation, as well as increased legal commoditization and subordination. It has been argued that this dual contradictory development has given rise to a strong feminist movement that manifested itself in massive women's participation and leadership in the social protests pertaining to the contested presidential election in June 2009.

Notes

1 Nikki Keddie, "Iranian Women's Status and Struggles since 1979," *Journal of International Affairs*, 60 (2007), pp. 6–38; Nayereh Tohidi, "Islamic Feminism: Perils and Promises," *The Middle East Women Studies Review*, 14, 3–4 (fall–winter 2001–2002), pp. 134–146; also available online at www.we-change.org.

2 Keddie, "Iranian Women's Status"; Fatemeh Moghadam, "The Political Economy of Female Employment in Post-revolutionary Iran," in Susan Slymovics and Suad Joseph (eds) *Women and Power in the Islamic Middle East* (Philadelphia, PA: Pennsylvania University Press, 2000), pp. 191–203; Valentine Moghadam, "Women, Work, and Ideology in the Islamic Republic of Iran," *International Journal of Middle East Studies*, 20 (1988), pp. 221–243; F. Nomani and S. Behdad, *Class and Labor in Iran: Did the Revolution Matter?* (New York: Syracuse University Press, 2006), pp. 126–134; Pavin Paidar, *Women and the Political Process in Twentieth-century Iran* (Cambridge: Cambridge University Press, 1997); and H. Sedghi, *Women and Politics in Iran: Veiling, Unveiling, and Reveiling* (Cambridge, MA: Harvard University Press, 2007).

3 Ester Boserup, "Economic Change and the Role of Women," in I. Tinker (ed.) *Persistent Inequalities: Women and Development* (Oxford: Oxford University Press, 1990), pp. 14–24.

4 This point was elaborated in an interview with Ayatollah Sayyed Mohammad Moosavi Bojnurdi, *Zan-e Rooz*, December 1993, p. 13.

5 There is no record indicating that the condition of monogamy was stipulated in the contract, but such contracts were not uncommon during the period. Since the Prophet did not practice polygyny during Khadijeh's life, it is possible to hypothesize that the condition of monogamy was stipulated in the contract.

6 Fatemeh Mernissi, *The Veil and the Male Elite: A Feminist Interpretation of Women's Rights in Islam*, trans. M. Lakeland (Reading, MA: Addison-Wesley, 1991), pp. 85–89, 115.

7 Nikki Keddie, "Introduction: Deciphering Middle Eastern Women's History," in N. Keddie and B. Baron (eds) *Women in Middle Eastern History* (New Haven, CT: Yale University Press, 1991), pp. 1–22; C. Hillenbrand, (2003) "Women in the Seljuq Period," in G. Nashat and L. Beck (eds) *Women in Iran from the Rise of Islam to 1800* (Urbana: University of Illinois Press, 2003), pp. 107, 114–115; C.F. Manz, "Women in Timurid Dynastic Politics," in ibid., pp. 121, 129–130; and Szuppe (2003), "Status, Knowledge, and Politics: Women in Sixteenth Century Safavid Iran," in ibid., p. 141.

8 Janet Afary, *The Iranian Constitutional Revolution, 1906–1911* (New York: Columbia University Press, 1996), pp. 172–207.

9 Fatemeh Moghadam, "Iran's New Home Economics: An Exploratory Attempt to Conceptualize Women's Work in the Islamic Republic," in E.M. Cinar (ed.) *The Economics of Women and Work in the Middle East and North Africa* (New York: Elsevier Science, 2002), pp. 339–360.

10 Statement by Mahnaz Afkhami who was Minister of Women's Affairs at the time.

11 From informal conversations with an Iranian woman lawyer who has been involved in many divorce cases.

12 This argument begs the question: If the traditional marriage contract does not require women to perform household labor, why are these activities the primary responsibilities of Muslim women?

13 Moghadam (2002), op. cit.

14 The Holy Qur'an (1988), verses 2:233; 65:6.

15 Roksana Bahramitash and Hadi Esfahani, "Nimble Fingers No Longer! Women's Employment in Iran," in A. Gheissari (ed.) *Contemporary Iran: Economy, Society, Politics* (Oxford: Oxford University Press, forthcoming).

16 F. Moghadam (forthcoming), "Iran's Missing Working Women," in R. Bahramitash and H. Esfahani (eds) *Veiled Employment: The Political Economy of Female Employment in Iran* (New York: Syracuse University Press).

17 *Zan-e ruz*, December 1993; available online at: www.we-change.org.

4 Exploring women's experience of higher education and the changing nature of gender relations in Iran

Goli M. Rezai-Rashti

The remarkable representation of women in higher education is a global phenomenon.[1] In Iran, since the 1990s, women's presence in higher education has grown significantly. The main objective of this chapter is to show the participation of women in higher education and to examine women's views of their interests and desires in obtaining a university education and how this increasing access to higher education is affecting the dynamics of gender relations.

This chapter has been adapted from a larger qualitative research project dealing with the participation of women in higher education in Iran.[2]

Introduction

In the post-September 11 2001 era, Muslim women's oppression came under more scrutiny. Indeed, the wars in Iraq and Afghanistan were partly legitimized on the basis of creating democracy and bringing more freedom to and liberating veiled women from such oppressive regimes.[3] The Islamic Revolution in 1979 and some of the legal, political and social changes in the lives of Iranian women did generate considerable research.[4] Until the early 1990s, most studies of women following the Islamic Revolution, including those of secular feminists,[5] focused on the negative aspects of these changes with little attention directed towards some of the dynamic and unexpected developments affecting the presence of women in almost all aspects of public life. As Afsaneh Najmabadi argues, despite discriminatory legal changes in Iran following the Islamic Revolution women have an unmistakable presence:

> Almost two decades after the 1979 Islamic revolution in Iran, against the deepest fears of many secular feminist activists of the revolution, not only have women not disappeared from public life, but they have an unmistakable presence in practically every field of artistic activities. It will be tempting for a secular feminist to claim that Iranian women have achieved all this despite the Islamic Republic, against the Islamic Republic, and even against Islam as the dominant discourse in the country.[6]

There are several interpretations for this unexpected increase in women's participation. Najmabadi argues that the Islamic Revolution brought women's issues to the forefront.[7] This was especially significant for those women who supported and sympathized with Islam and the Islamic revolution.[8] According to Parvin Paidar, the Islamic Republic's policies on women's education, employment and political participation were designed to reinforce women's continuing support for the revolution, thereby creating an image of stability both internally and internationally. However, the policies were based on the premise that women's participation outside the home would be countered with legal changes reinforcing the family (e.g., abolishing the pre-revolutionary Family Protection Law).[9]

Ziba Mir-Hosseini discusses the development of a set of complex circumstances after the revolution that made women's public participation more feasible. According to her, "paradoxically, the enforcement of *hejab* [head cover and loose clothing] became a catalyst here: by making public space morally correct in the eyes of traditionalist families, it legitimized women's public presence."[10] In other words, imposing the *hejab* allowed more women to participate publicly and freely because the public space became viewed as safe, 'sanitized' for all women, and no longer corrupt. In line with Najmabadi, Mir-Hosseini also discusses the important role of those who were sympathetic to the Islamic Revolution yet helped to create a feminist rereading of *shari'a* [Islamic legal] texts.[11] Discussion in women's journals (such as *Zanan*), women's groups and associations brought some of the patriarchal biases of *shari'a* laws into focus and made reinterpretation and rereading of the texts necessary. This helped form a new gender consciousness and made the new discourses about women possible. The understanding of these complex dynamics is significant for the assessment of women's achievement in higher education in post-revolutionary Iran.

Golnar Mehran believes that the interplay of tradition and modernity within a revolutionary context created a productive space in which women were able to become active participants in an educational terrain. She questions whether the Iranian educational system has been able to create its ideal female citizen:

> Could one conclude by saying that the Islamic Republic has failed to create the ideal female citizen – the New Muslim Woman? A more accurate assessment, in my opinion, would be to say that Iranian women have used the paradox of tradition and modernity to serve their own purpose, which is none other than empowerment.[12]

Keddie argues that the reforms undertaken by Mohammad Reza Shah Pahlavi (the previous royal regime), along with the contradictory policies of Khomeini's revolutionary regime, had a clear impact upon the presence of women in Iranian society.[13] Women were encouraged to participate in public life and have access to education, but at the same time the enforcement of *hejab* and the annulment of the Family Protection Law meant returning to polygyny, reviving temporary marriage, the right of unilateral divorce for men, and awarding child custody to fathers and their families. This created a situation that was strongly resisted by the women's press and women parliamentarians. Since the late 1980s, Islamic feminists have been able to advocate for a range of women's rights more openly and successfully, managing to encourage policy-makers to revise earlier restrictions on women's legal rights, though still within an Islamic framework. The area of education was one of the most successful issues on which Islamic feminists have campaigned. The most noted achievement was the lifting of restrictions placed upon women to access engineering, agriculture, and several related fields in universities.

It is important then to challenge the common-sense and generally accepted binaries of traditional/modern in the discussion of women and education in Iran. Access to education for women has been shaped historically by a combination of both modernist and Islamic discourses surrounding the role of women and their responsibilities as mothers and wives (modern and modest). Najmabadi argues that the role of mother and wife shifted significantly in the twentieth century, and it is erroneous to read the call for women's education as the reinforcement of their traditional role. She argues further that women's education entailed "two conflicting notions: one disciplinary, the other emancipatory."[14] These conflicting notions made women's presence in the nation possible and desirable, but at the same time it has regulated their presence in a productive way.

Pre-revolutionary Iran

As in other societies, the situation of women is connected to broader socio-economic and political developments. In the early twentieth century (1906–1911), the Constitutional Revolution shifted the power from an absolute traditional monarchy to Parliament, at least in theory, and the rule of law. This facilitated the protection of Iran's national interests vis-à-vis Western economic and political pressures through Western-style modernization. This type of induced modernity included women's issues, and created a link between national independence, progress, and women's emancipation. Najmabadi's research on the historical development of education for girls and women examines the early idea of women's education in the writings of reformers in the late nineteenth century when they traveled to Europe. She asserts that during this period the notion of being a mother and wife changed from its pre-modern concept. The father was the manager of the household, charged with the education and discipline of the children, and the mother was not necessarily the nurturer and caretaker of the child.[15] During the Constitutional Revolution, women's education was given special importance. In 1911, there were proposals for opening five elementary schools for girls to be subsidized by the government.[16] Najmabadi discusses the emergence of the new discourse of educated motherhood and nationhood in the constitutionalist journal which emphasized the importance of education for women:

> It is evident that the progress and prosperity of every country and nation are dependent in general on science and knowledge of men and particular on the education of women ... If our women [*pardagian*-the veiled ones] are not educated, how can they take proper care of our newborn, who are the

hope of our dear homeland? How can they know the correct rules of nursing a child, that is, the three ways of natural nursing, artificial feeding and the proper combination of both?[17]

In 1921, Reza Khan, the founder of the Pahlavi Dynasty (in 1926, when he became Reza Shah), came to power and initiated more than a decade of further modernizing reforms, including a ban on women wearing the veil (1936). The education system at primary, secondary, and university levels became open to women. In addition, opportunities were created for women's employment. In 1936, the traditional schools were abolished and replaced with state schools.[18] In 1941, the British and Soviets forced Reza Shah to abdicate in favor of his son, Mohammad Reza Pahlavi. Beginning in 1963,[19] he introduced a series of reforms under the banner of the "White Revolution," but in the 1970s his regime created a one-party system (the *hezb-e rastakhiz*) while enforcing political repression by creating a secret police (SAVAK), which became notorious for the arrest and torture of intellectuals and those who opposed the Shah's rule. The reforms introduced during this period included[20] the Family Protection Law, which restricted polygyny and gave women the right to sue for divorce and the custody of their children; earlier they also got the right to vote.[21] This period also witnessed a growing number of women attending several institutions of higher education.

Post-1979

With the Islamic Revolution of 1979, there have been many changes in the lives of Iranian women and men. The universities were shut down for three years, during which time the Islamic government introduced policies to change textbooks and the curriculum materials to reflect Islamic values. In addition, compulsory veiling for women was introduced and the Family Protection Law was repealed. Women were restricted from entering several fields of studies in universities, such as geology, mining, and agrarian science.

The reform introduced by the Islamic government may be divided into two distinct phases. From 1979 to 1989, the government became involved in removing the secular discourse that had been established by the previous regime and replaced it with an Islamic discourse. They tried to dismantle the symbols, institutions, and mores of Pahlavi regime.[22] In fact, most policies were actually formulated through a variety of ad hoc initiatives by a range of stakeholders in power, many with conflicting views.[23] The first phase focused on defining and regulating what was seen as the proper representation of Muslim women (i.e., women's appearance, behavior, and activities).

During the eight-year war with Iraq, women became active in the public domain, serving in war maintenance and nursing. Women who lost their husbands in the war gained custody rights, and received government funds for their children, even after they remarried.

Following the war and the death of Khomeini in 1989, a new phase in the Iranian socio-economic and political system emerged. This phase started with the institutionalization and development of the Islamic state. With the election of President Ali Akbar Hashemi Rafsanjani, a new era began in which free education, free healthcare, low income and cooperative housing started to erode.[24] The Islamic Republic's first five-year plan was launched in 1990. It promoted the neoliberal policies of privatization, deregulation, the modernization of the Tehran Stock Exchange, and the reintegration of Iran into the world economy:

> The clear message throughout the bureaucracy began to be: balanced economic growth and national development cannot take place in a situation of uncontrolled population growth and the economic, social, cultural marginalization of women. Shifts in gender policy also began to occur in areas of women and law and women and agriculture. After a decade of discouraging women from entering the law profession, the Iranian state reversed itself and deemed it advantageous to draw upon their experience and education.[25]

In May 1997, President Khatami was elected by a large margin and with the overwhelming support of Iranian women and youth. The political factions started to emerge, and the government became more heterogeneous with various positions leaning toward the conception of democratic participation and women's issues. During Khatami's first term in office, a woman became vice-president for environmental affairs and several other women became deputy ministers.[26] Khatami's reform, as Tazmini argues, was intended to enable a gradual evolution and development of the existing system rather than a radical shake-up of the system. It is important to understand Khatami's accommodation of the historical experiences of Western/Islam/modernity in the reform movement.[27] According to Tazmini, between 1997 and 2005, Iran saw evolutionary social changes that unfolded at a measured pace; however, this process neither imitated the West nor followed a rigid interpretation of the Islamic past. In fact Khatami's rhetoric accommodated historical, local, and national experience with an acknowledgment of the accomplishment of Western civilization.[28]

Educational policies

The underlying focus of education in the Islamic Republic, particularly at the outset, was its commitment and orientation to the development of an Islamic person. The High Council of Education laid out religious and spiritual goals first, followed by scientific, cultural, social, political, and economic goals. The key role and responsibility for women was seen as motherhood and the care and upbringing of children; while for men it was to provide economic support and to represent the family in other institutions.[29] Given these ascribed roles, men and women's education would be different:

> While the Constitution of the Islamic Republic establishes the government's responsibility for providing free education for all citizens up to the secondary level (Article 30), in discussing the rights of women the constitution

specifies that these rights will be assured 'in conformity with Islamic criteria' (Article 21).[30]

Several interviews and speeches by Ayatollah Khomeini reveal his unequivocal acknowledgment of women for their participation in the Revolution and at least lip-service to their freedom, their critical role in family and society, and their achievement in higher education, as long as no one "wants to do something against chastity or harmful to the nation."[31] In his words:

> Women have more right than men over this [revolutionary] movement. ... Women must be involved in the fundamental aspects of the country. Just as you had a fundamental role in the movement you must also have a share in the victory.... The country belongs to you. God willing, you must reconstruct the country.... Woman must have a say in her fate.
>
> The era of suppression wanted to turn our fighting women into disgraced beings, but it was God's will. They wanted to treat women like an object, like a commodity. But Islam has involved and involves women, like men, in every aspect of life. All people of Iran, whether men or women, must reconstruct this ruin which they have left us.[32]

The essence of his criticism was that during the previous regime, women were actually oppressed and encouraged to be treated as objects, rather than as active subjects for themselves, their families, and society. "It is woman who, with her correct education, produces humanity, who, with her correct education, cultivates the country."[33]

The second phase of the Islamic Republic's policies toward women's education changed. For example, the Women's Social and Cultural Council, responsible for studying the legal, social, and economic problems of women, decided, after numerous meetings and seminars that included university presidents, cabinet ministers, and in response to international pressure, to lift all restrictions on women entering any fields of study in the universities.[34] More

Table 4.1 Number of women admitted to universities based on fields of study, 1991–2002

Fields of study	1991–1992		2002–2003	
	Total admitted	% of women	Total admitted	% of women
Humanities	28,139	31	88,481	61.9
Sciences	10,305	37.9	22,296	78.2
Agriculture and Vet	4,101	2.5	14,499	51.1
Technical and Engineering	13,392	6.6	56,240	20.9
Medicine	14,347	46.1	24,098	73.7
Arts	1,149	38.1	10,422	74.5

Source: Adapted from Kazemipour (2004).[35]

Table 4.2 Number of students (male and female) admitted and graduated from higher education institutions, 1979–2002

	Sex	1979–1980	1991–1992	2001–2002	% of increase 1979–1991	% of increase 1991–2002
Admitted	Male	26,542	50,765	104,109	5.5	6.7
	Female	11,875	20,668	116,927	4.7	17.1
	Total	38,417	71,433	221,036	5.3	10.8
Students in universities						
	Men	120,646	247,076	396,719	6.1	4.4
	Women	53,571	96,969	412,848	5.1	14.1
	Total	174,217	344,045	809,567	5.8	8.1
Graduates	Men	30,714	35,777	71,080	1.3	6.4
	Women	12,507	16,576	56,370	2.4	11.7
	Total	43,221	52,353	127,117	1.6	8.4

Source: Ibid.[36]

recently (since 2000), women's admission to universities has reached more than 60 percent of the total student population at the undergraduate level. Since the 1990s, there has been a significant increase of women at all levels in universities (see Table 4.1 and Table 4.2). The participation of women in all fields of study is significant. Although the rate of their participation in the technical and engineering fields was much less than male's participation (but three times more than in earlier decades), women did well in all fields of basic sciences, arts, and medicine.

The participation of women shows a significant shift in the gendered structures of the academy. The distribution of female students in the fields of sciences, agriculture, and medicine indicate a clear change and does not reflect the historical pattern of gendered disciplines (except in engineering). This pattern is also in contrast with the statistics from developed countries such as Canada which show that the increasing presence of women in higher education institutions did not shift the gendered nature of the academy: As Drakich and Stewart assert:

> Women crossed the magical threshold of 50 per cent in 1988 not to accolades but to concerns of equity for men and feminization of universities. Eighteen years later, women continue to enter universities in large numbers, but their numbers have not produced a significant shift in the gendered structures of the academy.[37]

Table 4.3 Number of students' applications based on sex for university admission exams, 1983–2001

Year	Women	Men	Total	% women	% men
1983	131,427	181,240	312,667	42	57
1984	133,066	218,197	351,263	38	63
1985	143,350	254,274	397,624	36	64
1986	202,841	383,245	586,086	35	65
1987	184,532	310,280	494,812	37	63
1988	159,783	249,420	409,203	39	61
1989	161,350	279,549	441,184	37	63
1990	301,992	488,998	790,990	38	62
1991	317,720	513,459	831,179	38	62
1992	357,430	554,821	912,251	39	61
1993	397,479	621,391	1,018,870	39	61
1994	456,745	656,064	1,112,809	41	59
1995	558,531	718,651	1,277,182	44	57
1996	582,535	676,493	1,259,028	46	54
1997	665,411	684,292	1,349,703	49	51
1998	739,665	696,739	1,436,404	51	49
1999	788,448	672,367	1,460,815	54	47
2000	818,972	640,560	1,459,532	56	44
2001	913,305	680,185	1,593,521	57	43

Source: Adapted from Karnameh-Haghighi and Akbari (2005).[38]

It is also important to note that the distribution of women and men admitted to universities closely corresponds to the percentage of applications to universities (see Table 4.3).

Methodological considerations

The main objective of this research is to investigate how women and men perceive this increased participation of women and what they think about their future, family, and employment, as well as how this increasing participation of women is affecting the dynamics of male–female relationships and the nature of the gender regime in Iranian society. This research is based on interviews with students in five universities in Iran. The aim in conducting this research was to produce further knowledge about women's and men's views of their participation and experience in higher education as a basis for examining questions of agency, gender relations, and participation in Iranian society. It also involves their perception of employment opportunities, relationships, and attitudes toward marriage. Male students were interviewed in order to show the significance of gender relations as well as the relational aspects of gender regimes in Iran. In total, 51 interviews (individual and focus group) were conducted. The research used a qualitative case study method. Patton argues that individual cases "selected purposefully ... [p]ermit inquiry into and understanding of a phenomenon in-depth."[39] He argues further that the "logic and power of purposeful sampling derive from the emphasis on in-depth understanding. This leads to selecting information-rich cases for study in-depth."[40]

In addition, Creswell argues that "we use qualitative research to develop theories when partial or inadequate theories exist for certain populations and samples or existing theories do not adequately capture the complexity of the problem we are explaining."[41] Stake states, "Case studies are of value for refining theory and suggesting complexities for further investigation, as well as helping to establish the limits of generalizability."[42]

It is important to state that the political climate in Iran has not been conducive to research especially in the fields of humanities and social sciences. This research also encountered several challenges in the initial phases of obtaining permission and ethical considerations. In fact, without having an Iranian collaborator and establishing a cohesive network of professionals in several institutions, this research would not have been possible. This connection was important to gain access to universities and students. I also accepted invitations from several faculty members to be a guest lecturer in university classes and participated in several panel discussions. In addition, being an Iranian who speaks the language and is familiar with the culture and university system was certainly an asset in conducting this research. The research included several universities with institutional variations. For example, these included one technical and engineering university, an all-female university, two universities with a women's studies program, and a university for medical education.

Findings

Preliminary findings suggest that there are some significant changes in the lives of men and women, and the nature of the gender regime in Iran. One of the main findings of the research is that there is a need to focus more attention on the significance of gender relations and the relational aspect of gender. Issues of masculinity and femininity were discussed over and over by the participants in this study. It seems that access to higher education is gradually transforming the nature of gender regimes in Iran. In this section, there will be several examples of these changes discussed by the participants.

Choice/masculinity and femininity

Women who were interviewed discussed their admission to universities and the institutions of higher education because of their own interests and also a lack of choice in obtaining good jobs with a high school diploma. They stated predominantly that their admission to universities makes them more employable and will improve their earning potential, social status, and the possibility of accessing better positions, while as high school graduates the only position open to them would be secretarial work which is badly paid and not valued.

Most students indicated that there are more positions open to men. For example, men can work as taxi drivers, in factories and/or construction sites, as security guards, or in restaurants. Some indicated that employers often do not hire women because they know that women's authority might be challenged by male employees:

> There are jobs like, for example, supervising or managing a restaurant. It is not necessary to be a man to be able to perform these jobs. But they prefer to hire men because they think other employees in the restaurant would not accept women's authority and would challenge them.

A male Ph.D. student asserted that "there are not enough incentives for boys to come to university because after completing their education they might not be able to obtain employment or they may end up in jobs that do not pay well." For women, it is not so important to think about employment because traditionally men are obligated to support their families financially. For example, this student stated that as a high school math teacher, he was earning much less than someone with a high school diploma who works in a trade. He made a lot of negative comments about working as a teacher because of its low financial rewards.

One of the female students discussed the reasons why her brothers did not go to university but instead became involved in trade and family business:

> My brothers did not go to university because they thought if they go to university they have to spend 10 years of their lives studying, just to obtain a

BA or B.Sc. degree. They cannot find employment and for this reason they are in trades and work in our private/family business.

Issues of masculinity and femininity were discussed by both women and men as an important indicator of men's lack of interest and desire to gain a university education. Most participants argued that the lack of choice for women encouraged them to gain a university education while for men there are more options:

> For boys there is a lot of entertainment in our society and it prevents them from studying while for girls, there are only a few options. For girls, many of them love to study, but there are also some who study because they have nothing else to do. I have seen these kinds of people.

Social class and access to university education

Several graduate students talked about their access to higher education because of their own interests. Their families' lack of education, wealth, and/or conservative ideas did not prevent them from accessing university education. One male student asserted:

> My parents are not educated. My parents gave me some financial support when I was in high school. Their financial support was helpful, but they could not provide me with much intellectual or moral support. I found the way all by myself.

This statement corresponds with Mehran's observation that after the Revolution an increasing number of men and women from the lower-middle class and some from rural origins became increasingly visible in the public sphere.

> In fact, the process of revolution had widened the circle of women who have left their marginalized existence. It has opened the door for women other than the formerly empowered members of the urban elite whose high levels of education, wealth and family status had enabled them to break through many visible and invisible ceilings that kept their lower-class sisters "in their proper place."[43]

Higher education and gender relations

All the participants interviewed discussed the positive impact of attending higher education institutions. They believed that universities are creating an environment that raises male's and female's consciousness and provide an opportunity to meet each other which would not have been possible in any other social situation. Women in general discussed how the university created a safe space for them to become more confident. This is especially true for those women who performed well academically:

> I think there is no difference between women and men. I experienced this myself. When I came to university, I was staying away from interacting with men at first but gradually because I was a very good student during my Bachelor degree, my confidence improved and this affected my relationships. Now, I don't see any difference between men and women and I can become friends with them and feel comfortable and equal.

One male student, Hamid, who is in the engineering field, talked about how the relationship between men and women is changing and how women's increased participation in university is having a positive impact upon men's attitudes toward women:

> For our generation, we are starting to believe in women's abilities.... For example although in my department there are 75 percent men and only 25 percent women, in the last few years I have noticed that some of the girls are far superior in terms of their intelligence ... Girls are making more effort and the best student in our faculty is a woman with the highest mark in our class of fourth-year engineering.

Education, marriage and change of gender regime

One of the main aims of this research was to explore the impact of higher education upon men's and women's lives. Further, it sought to understand how they see their future in terms of employment, marriage, and having children. An important phenomenon is the increasing age of marriage for women. Many men and women believed that owing to cultural norms, highly educated women have difficulty getting married. This is because men have traditionally been more educated and have better earning power. With the significant increase in the percentage of women with higher education degrees, they argued that men are hesitant to be involved with a woman with a degree in higher education because it is uncommon for men and they do not want to be equal or inferior to their partners. For example, Meena, a 42-year-old university professor who had just been promoted to the rank of full professor, explained:

> While I was studying for my Bachelor degree, I had many proposals for marriage. After entering the Master's degree, the number of proposals decreased and by the time I entered Ph.D. program, they became non-existent.

Leila, who is in the Ph.D. program and married to someone who just entered a doctoral program, also believed that this is becoming an issue for both men and women. It is not only men who do not intend to marry someone who is more educated, but women themselves are reluctant to marry someone who is less well educated. She describes her own situation:

I wanted my husband to be accepted in the Ph.D. program. He wanted it too. We both liked it.... One of my conditions for the marriage was for him to get accepted. I wanted my husband to be at the same level of education.

Another female student in the graduate program discussed her anxiety as she was gaining more education:

The more education I had, the more worried I was getting. First of all, there would be fewer cases of men who would propose to me. Some men might even be afraid to approach. I think men have trouble being involved with someone who has higher education than them. It rarely happens.

Another female student discussed her observation of other female graduate students' views living in the same university dormitory:

Higher education definitely has an impact on marriage. Now, most of the female students whom I see in the dormitory have this problem. They are single and they are feeling hopeless. They do not think about marriage anymore because they don't think they ever would be able to find someone suitable. Many of these women do not accept anyone with a lower level of education than what they are obtaining.

These examples clearly show the changing nature of gender relations owing to women's increased participation in higher education.

Mehrieh

Mehrieh is a price that is normally specified in the marriage contract and is payable to a woman by the man after the consummation of marriage. The woman can claim her *mehrieh* any time during the marriage, but traditionally woman's *mehrieh* was paid upon divorce. One issue that is becoming very interesting in terms of gender relations is *mehrieh*. Prior to the Revolution, *mehrieh* was rejected by many young, educated women as a sign of their modernity. In recent years, many educated women have been asking for a very high amount of *mehrieh.* The findings of this research show that the use of *mehrieh* should not be seen as a sign of a return to tradition but, as one of the participants put it, "it is a modern phenomenon" that enables women to minimize the impact of discriminatory family laws that were established following the Islamic Revolution.

Two female professors compared the rise of *mehrieh* with discriminatory laws in the country. One of the faculty members described it as an 'historical revenge,' because women historically were oppressed and have now found the opportunity to seek vengeance. She asserted:

This is dangerous. I think women are playing a game in order to change the family law. If we want women to stop this game, we have to change the law.

> For example, these days, there is the possibility of pre-nuptial agreements which give women the right to divorce, dividing the property, housing and others.... But an educated woman usually does not see it at their level to fight for these rights before marriage. She fights for high *mehrieh*. I think she should fight for her legal rights.

Many participants in the research discussed the discriminatory laws following the Revolution as the main cause of increasing *mehrieh*. For example, one of the female participants stated:

> My family wanted a very high *mehrieh*. For example, my brother's wife had a dowry of 714 gold coins. My brother was asking a higher *mehrieh* for me and his argument was that his own wife who is a high school graduate was given 714 gold coins, while his sister (me) with a doctorate should ask for at least 2,000 gold coins. I had to intervene and tell them I don't want to have a high *mehrieh* and we settled for 750 gold coins.

In this case, one can see that there is a relationship between *mehrieh* and education. This participant discussed her financial security and her lack of interest to get into debate about the amount of her *mehrieh*.

Another woman professor also observed that, although the discriminatory laws had created a situation in which women are asking for a high dowry, there is a sense that this has become normalized and institutionalized, and is now a source of competition among families:

> It is also competition among families (*cheshm ham cheshmi*). For example, if my cousin has this much *mehrieh*, I should have the same or more.

One female participant who was married and divorced and had a personal experience with the family laws was a strong supporter of *mehrieh* for women. She discussed the importance of *mehrieh* in the context of current family laws in Iran:

> For myself, I am a strong believer in *mehrieh* for women. *Mehrieh* should not be seen in the traditional sense. In this country women cannot negotiate their civil and legal rights through legal means. I was married for five years and found out that I could not live with my husband any longer. We discussed divorce but he said no. My *mehrieh* was 1,370 gold coins [*sekeh-ye azadi*]. I threatened that I would litigate for my *mehrieh*. This was the only way that I could secure my divorce. I am absolutely sure that because of this high *mehrieh* he agreed to divorce.

Listening to the voice of women, it appears that culture is both a problem but also a solution. It certainly shows a sense of agency at least among educated middle-class women. The *mehrieh* has provided a productive cultural means in which women have been able to claim their legal and civil rights that had not been granted to them by the constitution of the Islamic Republic.

It is interesting to see the views of male respondents. Most male students who were interviewed discussed *mehrieh* as a means of competition among girls and their families. They rarely acknowledged that the family laws are discriminatory toward women. Hamid stated, "Unlike what is in our religion and tradition, the *mehrieh* has been misused. This is becoming a tool in women's hands to further control men. This makes women more powerful and it can lead to the oppression of men." When asked if it would be possible to think that this is because of the discriminatory laws, he responded:

> I don't know much about these laws. I cannot give you my opinion. But it appears that women are just in competition (*cheshm ham cheshmi*) over the *mehrieh.*

Conclusion

These preliminary data show that men's and women's relationships are going through some fundamental changes. Women's participation in higher education is changing their expectations, making them more aware of inequalities, and affecting their ideas about marriage and family. They are becoming more conscious about their rights as women and actively participating in changing their social landscape. They are discovering that one tool to achieve this transformation is through their participation in higher education, which will give them the possibility of better employment. Men who were interviewed seem to have anxieties about the current state of gender relations. On the one hand, there is a desire to interact with more educated women, but on the other hand, they are anxious about losing their authority in the family and competing in a labor market where jobs are scarce.

Notes

1 For example, Nozaki, Y., Aranha, R., Fix-Dominguez, R., and Nakajima, Y. (2009) argue that "one of the most significant worldwide transformations in education over the past several decades has been the drastic increase in women's access to colleges and universities." See their "Gender gap and women's participation in higher education: Views from Japan, Mongolia, and India," in Wiseman, A.W. and Baker, D.P. (eds) *International Perspectives on Education and Society*, Vol. 10, *Gender, Equality, and Education from International and Comparative Perspectives*, Bingley, UK: Emerald Group Publishing, (p. 217).

2 The research project has been supported by the Social Sciences Research Council of Canada (410–2006–1426).

3 Lila Abu-Lughod in an article focusing on this issue of saving the Afghani women discussed how the issue of the veil and saving Afghani women became a dominant discourse during this time. For example, in 2002, Laura Bush remarked: "Because of our recent military gains in much of Afghanistan, women are no longer imprisoned in their homes. They can listen to music and teach their daughters without fear of

60   *G.M. Rezai-Rashti*

punishment. The fight against terrorism is also a fight for the rights and dignity of women" (cited in Abu-Lughod, *American Anthropologist*, p. 784).

4 Afary, J. (2009) *Sexual Politics in Modern Iran*, New York: Cambridge University Press; Najmabadi, A. (2005) *Women with Mustaches and Men without Beards: Gender and Sexual Anxieties of Iranian Modernity*, Los Angeles: University of California Press; Moallem, M. (2005). *Between Warrior Brothers and Veiled Sisters: Islamic Fundamentalism and the Politics of Patriarchy in Iran*, Los Angeles: University of California Press; Mir-Hosseini, Z. (1999) *Islam and Gender: The Religious Debate in Contemporary Iran*, London: I.B. Tauris; Bahramitash, R. (2003) "Revolution, Islamization, and Women's Employment in Iran," *The Brown Journal of World Affairs*, 9, 2, pp. 229–241; Moghadam, V. (2003) *Modernizing Women: Gender and Social Change in the Middle East*, London: Boulder; and idem. (2000) "Women's Socio-economic Participation and Iran's Changing Political Economy," in Alizadeh, P. (ed.) *The Economy of Iran: Dilemmas of an Islamic State*, London: I.B. Tauris, pp. 233–260.
5 Afshar, H. (1985) "Women, State and Ideology in Iran," *Third World Quarterly*, 7, 2, pp. 256–273.
6 Najmabadi, A. (1998a). "Feminism in an Islamic Republic: Years of Hardship, Years of Growth," in Haddad, Y. and Esposito, J. (eds) *Islam, Gender, and Social Change*, New York: Oxford University Press (p. 59).
7 Najmabadi, A. (1998a). "Feminism in an Islamic Republic: Years of Hardship, Years of Growth," in Haddad, Y. and Esposito, J. (eds) *Islam, Gender, and Social Change*, New York: Oxford University Press.
8 Prior to the Revolution the women's question was mostly subsumed within political and economic issues. The priority was set around changes the structural condition before dealing with women's issues. This is especially true among the leftist group.
9 Paidar, P. (1996). "Feminism and Islam in Iran," in Kandioti, D. (ed.) *Gendering the Middle East*, London: L.B. Tauris (pp. 51–68).
10 Mir-Hosseini, Z. (1999). *Islam and Gender: The Religious Debate in Contemporary Iran*, London: I.B. Tauris (p. 7).
11 Ibid.
12 Mehran, G. (2003) "The Paradox of Tradition and Modernity in Female Education in the Islamic Republic of Iran," *Comparative Education Review*, 47, 3, p. 286.
13 Keddie, N. (2000) "Women in Iran since '79," *Social Research*, 67, 2, pp. 435–438.
14 Najmabadi, A. (1998b) "Crafting an Educated Housewife in Iran," in Abu-Lughod, L. (ed.) *Remaking Women: Feminism and Modernity in the Middle East*, Princeton, NJ: Princeton University Press (p. 113).
15 Najmabadi, A. (2005). *Women with Mustaches and Men without Beards: Gender and Sexual Anxieties of Iranian Modernity*, Los Angeles: University of California Press (pp. 183–184).
16 Until then the dominant ways of schooling for girls and boys were traditional *maktabs* or they were tutored at home.
17 Najmabadi, A. (1998b) "Crafting an educated housewife in Iran," p. 106.
18 Najmabadi, A. (2005) *Women with Mustaches*.
19 In 1953, the Shah was restored to power by a military coup (supported by the American government), which overthrew the government of Prime Minister Mohammad Mossadegh, and which had nationalized Iran's oil resources.
20 It is important to note that many of the reforms' beneficiaries were upper- and middle-class urban women.
21 Keddie, N. (2000) "Women in Iran since '79," *Social Research*, 67, 2, pp. 435–438.
22 Farhai, F. (1998) "The Contending Discourses on Women in Iran," *Third World Resurgence*, 94. Available online at www.twnside.org.sg/title/iran-cn.htm (accessed September 11, 2000).
23 Paidar, P. (1996) "Feminism and Islam in Iran," in Kandiyoti, D. (ed.) *Gendering the Middle East*, London: L.B. Tauris (p. 61).

24 Bahramitash, R. (2003) "Revolution, Islamization, and Women's Employment in Iran," *The Brown Journal of World Affairs*, 9, 2, 229–241 (p. 235).
25 Farhai, F. (1998) "The Contending Discourses on Women in Iran" (pp. 5–6).
26 Farhai, F. (1998) "The Contending Discourses on Women in Iran."
27 Tazmini, G. (2009) *Khatami's Iran*.
28 Ibid., p. 5.
29 Higgins, P.J. and Shoar-Ghaffari, P. (1994) "Women's Education in the Islamic Republic of Iran," in Afkhami, M. and Friedl, E. (eds) *In the Eye of the Storm: Women in Post-revolutionary Iran*, London: I.B. Tauris (p. 20).
30 Ibid., p. 21.
31 Khomeini, R. (1982) "The Question in Women," in Tabari, A. and Yeganeh, N. (eds) *In the Shadow of Islam*, London: Zed Press, p. 98.
32 Ibid., p. 99.
33 Ibid., p. 101.
34 Boozari, S. (2001) "Jaygahe zanan dar amoozesh aly az didgahe ammar" [Development of Women's Participation in Higher Education], *Cultural and Social Studies, Women Studies, 2*, Tehran: Scientific and Cultural Publications, vol. 2, pp. 93–113.
35 Kazemipour, S. (2004) *Investigation and Discussion about Women's Increased Participation in Higher Education, Ministry of Science, Research & Technology*, p. 34 (in Persian).
36 Kazemipour, S. (2004) op. cit.
37 Drakich, J. and Stewart, P. (2007) "Forty Years Later How are University Women Doing?," *Academic Matters*, p. 6.
38 Karnameh Haghighi and Akbari, N. (2005) *Pezhohesh Zanan*, 3, 1, p. 81.
39 Patton, M.Q. (2002) *Qualitative Research and Evaluation Methods* (3rd edn), Thousand Oaks, CA: Sage (p. 46).
40 Ibid.
41 Creswell, J.W. (2007) *Qualitative Inquiry and Research Design: Choosing among Five Approaches* (2nd edn), Thousand Oaks, CA: Sage (p. 40).
42 Stake, R.E. (2000) "Case Studies," in Denzin, N.K. and Lincoln, Y.S. (eds) *Handbook of Qualitative Research* (2 edn, pp. 435–454). Thousand Oaks, CA: Sage (p. 448).
43 Mehran, G. (2009) "Doing and Undoing Gender: Female Higher Education in the Islamic Republic of Iran," *International Review of Education*, 55, p. 547 Dr. Golnat Mehran was instrumental in facilitating this research. I am enormously grateful to her for all her support.

5 Exclusionary cartographies

Gender liberation and the Iranian blogosphere

Niki Akhavan

On July 18, 2003, the *Wall Street Journal* ran an editorial entitled "The Blog Shall Make You Free." With this bold announcement of the liberatory power of blogs, the editorial lauded Iranian blogs for allowing women "to talk about dating, sex and other taboo subjects," for "playing a real role in Iran's democracy movement," and for "giving Iranians a new free-speech outlet." The editorial also credited English-language Iranian bloggers outside of Iran as the main reason why "Westerners" know about the then newly inaugurated Iranian governmental campaign of punishing bloggers.[1] In 2005, similar ideas reappeared in the work of Nasrin Alavi, who published a book of translated blog excerpts under the title *We Are Iran*. Although the pseudonymous author provides no information on his or her selection process, Alavi maintains that the passages chosen for publication – almost all of which variously critique the current government and express dissatisfaction with those aspects of their lives that are most impacted by its policies – reflect "today's real Iranians."[2]

From 2002 to 2007, blogs dominated as the primary online site for Iranian cultural and political production. During this time, proliferating sets of discourses continually glorified the Iranian blogosphere – or *weblogistan* (the land of the blogs), as it is known among the Net savvy – as a site of resistance where women in particular find liberation from the state as well as from social and cultural restrictions. These prevailing accounts of the broader Iranian blogosphere operated upon several problematic assumptions. In addition to uncritically reproducing celebratory claims about the possibilities of the internet,[3] they ignored the nuances of the Iranian blogosphere, state, and society. In other words, these narratives tended to reduce the contradictions and contested nature of the Iranian state and contemporary politics down to a monolith captured by the signifier Islamic Republic of Iran (IRI) against which an equally homogenized blogger community is understood as subversive. Similarly, they assumed an easy binary between Iran's "people" (depicted as "pro-Western") and the Iranian government (presented as "anti-Western"), thus excluding an examination of the complexities of both.

Within this framework, the Iranian woman figures as being defined primarily by her status as victim and her oppression most often is articulated in terms of her physicality such as restrictions on her dress and sexuality. Furthermore,

Iranian women only appear as though the scope of their actions is limited to the cybersphere: the continuities between their expressions of dissent through blog-ging and their lived experiences are unaddressed, thereby eliding the numerous arenas in which Iranian women have been active in pursuing a number of projects aimed variously at bringing about change. Similarly, dominant accounts rarely include an investigation of how bloggers themselves conceive of their aims, instead projecting narratives of liberation that are more in tune with long-distance imaginations of Iranian women than with the specificities that shape their lives and, in turn, their blogs.

The fixation on the bodies and physical condition of women from the Muslim world, of course, has a long history with contemporary manifestations that have not been limited to discourses about the internet. Focusing on the rise of the genre of memoirs by Muslim women – specifically Iranian women – that are published in the non-Muslim world, Farzaneh Milani has described them as "hostage narratives" that portray the Muslim woman as a "victim of an immobi-lizing faith, locked up inside her mandatory veil – a mobile prison shrunk to the size of her body."[4] Similarly, Roksana Bahramitash has employed Parvin Padi-ar's category of "Orientalist Feminism" to identify the racist and classist assump-tions underlying such works,[5] while Hamid Dabashi has pointed out their ideological and material function.[6] As Bahramitash, Dabashi, and Milani all make clear, the themes and depictions of Muslim women as they appear in the memoir genre are intertwined with broader historical and contemporary dis-courses that have failed to adequately capture the rich scope of women's experi-ences in the Muslim world.[7]

In short, dominant narratives regarding Iranian women's blogging activities during the heyday of the blogosphere fell within long-standing frameworks for speaking about women in Iran and the Muslim world more generally. Since such accounts considered Iranian women as always already trapped, victimized, and disenfranchised, they take the appearance of women bloggers as in itself radical, leaving little room for further investigations. Furthermore, since blogging is taken as resistance, the Iranian blogger is figured as secular, and hence by exten-sion opposed to the current religious-based government. Women bloggers whose personal backgrounds or online activities do not fit this profile are excluded from consideration.

To counter these exclusionary tendencies, this chapter aims to challenge critically the growing chorus on the political significance of the Iranian blogo-sphere that overlooks its nuances by examining often ignored dimensions of *weblogistan*. To begin with, this chapter will show that Iranian women's blog-ging is not an exceptional mode of expression or activity: Iranian women blog-gers exercise their agency both online and off; the lines between the two realms of the virtual and offline are not sharp and distinct, but rather are con-tinuous and interlinked. In addition to leaving out entire groups of women (and men) online, dominant narratives have also erased the complexities of those bloggers who are deemed worthy of inclusion. In response, the chapter takes steps toward reviving both with the aim of revealing the contradictions and contestations of the blogosphere as well as the broader socio-political contexts in which it is embedded.

Approaches to the Net as a site of research

In addition to building upon the insights of works that have traced and challenged the troubling frameworks applied in speaking about Iranian and Muslim women, this chapter's methodology is informed by the work of scholars who stress the importance of integrated approaches to the study of Net-based phenomena. Steven Jones was among the first to disrupt celebratory assessments of Net phenomena by calling for their contextualization in pre-existing frameworks for understanding media and social formations.[8] Urging an ethnographic methodology, Daniel Miller and Don Slater suggest that cyberspace must not be understood as "an experience of extreme 'disembedding' from an offline reality."[9] Instead, they call for methods that explore the continuities and connections between the virtual and non-virtual worlds. Also supporting an ethnographic approach, Christine Hine suggests that reifications of the internet can be avoided if cyberspace is understood as arising out of and changing within particular contexts of production.[10] Toward this end, she suggests approaching the Net as both culture and cultural artifact; in short, the Net contains spaces where culture is produced, but those sites are themselves products of culture.

Taking cues from such works, my investigations here into what is categorized as "women's liberation through blogging" will similarly take care to situate Iranian women bloggers within the context of their larger presence and participation in offline public spheres. While I address some of the ways in which resident and diasporic Iranian women have deployed the Net in destabilizing and transgressing various social and legal taboos, I will argue that such cases of online resistance are in continuity with – rather than in contradiction to – the activities that women historically have carried out offline. In other words, contrary to the implications of popular accounts, Iranian women's blogging by itself does not necessarily constitute a radical departure from their lived experiences. The discussion of bloggers completely excluded from mainstream narratives will also situate their online activities in the broader socio-political contexts which both give rise to and in turn are shaped by them.

Women in *weblogistan*: contexts for consideration of gender and the narrative of liberation online

Although no systematic attempts have been made to discern the gender ratio of bloggers, it is apparent that both diasporic and resident Iranian women make up a heavy share of the *weblogistan*. In contrast to men bloggers who tend to take their gender for granted as the norm that need not be spoken, Iranian women bloggers are often explicit in identifying themselves as such. This foregrounding of one's gender is apparent at first glance in structural features such as graphics, title, and/or url addresses. These practices of marking one's gender traverse language and location: whether they are in English or Persian, blogging from within Iran or in diaspora.[11]

In terms of blog content, the trend is similar: women bloggers are often vocal about a focus on gender, and their engagement with such issues is manifest in various ways, much of which pushes boundaries that cannot be traversed easily in offline spaces that are more closely policed by political and social restraints. However, the two spheres of on- and offline are not strictly delineated, nor is it the case that women have no agency as public actors outside the blogosphere but have complete autonomy within it. On the contrary, despite certain legal and social constraints, Iranian women are integrated into various segments of Iranian society and have taken lead roles in addressing a number of pressing issues. In many cases, such as those involving the state-sponsored charity establishment known as *bonyads*, largely conservative women, generally aligned with the hard-liner elements of the Iranian government, are variously active as both particip-ants and beneficiaries.[12] Those who do not choose to work directly with state-sponsored establishments have increasingly turned to the civil society sector where women have had leading roles in establishing and running non-governmental organizations.

Despite this, narratives of Iranian women's liberation, particularly when they are produced and disseminated by diasporic and other sources outside of Iran, tend to take for granted a unidirectional shift for the worse in the position of women following the 1979 Revolution. While it is indeed the case that imposed changes in state-enforced moral and legal codes have had variously detrimental consequences, the impact of such changes has been neither categorical nor uncontested. Furthermore, it is not the case that the blog has created a heretofore missing opportunity for women's public participation. Both before and after the 1979 Revolution, women have held positions in the government and other public sectors, and their numbers on university campuses have been comparable, and in recent years have surpassed, those of male students.[13] In addition, women have continued to be active as cultural producers, working as artists, journalists, and public intellectuals.

Thus while the conditions under which they could become visible and be influ-ential may have changed, women did not disappear from the public sphere after the formation of the Islamic Republic. The government's imposition of the manda-tory *hejab* in spite of widespread protests on the part of women and women's groups, for example, initiated a shift in the literal and figurative face of Iranian women.[14] On the other hand, enforced codes of public morality exemplified by the veil have also benefited many women: those from religious backgrounds, for example, who tended to be marginalized within public spaces both because of family pressures and prejudices against the inclusion of veiled women, could now more actively participate in spheres from which they were previously absent. In short, the newly formed Islamic Republic embraced women who – in both appear-ance and ideology – met the self-image it was attempting to build.

Furthermore, addressing changes for women in terms of a framework of before and after the Revolution tends to obscure the developments that have occurred during the tenure of the IRI. The founding years of the new government, during which it consolidated its power while also fighting an eight-year war with Iraq, are usually identified as the most repressive for political and social expression in general and for women in particular.[15] For a variety of reasons, the socio-political environment has become more malleable following the death of Ayatollah Khomeini, with the first significant shifts developing under the rule of President Ali Akbar Hashemi Rafsanjani, whose projects of economic liberalization envisioned a pragmatic-Islamic-capitalist state (which needed women's participation in the workforce, stable fertility rates, etc.).The 1997 election of Mohammad Khatami and his support for the cultivation of a civil society built on dialogue also required the inclusion of women. Of course, none of these changes have gone unchallenged by hardliner elements among the institutional power structure and the population groups who support them.[16] However, even the most conservative components of the IRI – including the administration and supporters of President Ahmadinejad – rely on the mobilization of women within their ranks, so the myth of "women" vs. "state" that is the bedrock of popular accounts about the Iranian internet does not reflect the complexities on the ground. At the same time, it is clear that the role of women in Iran is a greatly contested one, and it is in light of these struggles and the ways in which they have become articulated in discourses of liberation that I now turn to some examples of women in *weblogistan*.

Ambiguities on the blogosphere and beyond

Since many bloggers, especially those writing from inside Iran, maintain anonymity, one is often left to rely on the online texts to discern how and whether their blogging is intertwined with their lived experiences. Thus, the blogs serve as the main source from which the continuities with and reciprocal impacts on the ideological and material spaces offline can be examined. It is useful, therefore, to begin with examples of how bloggers themselves articulate their relationship with the practices of participating in the blogosphere, particularly since self-conscious statements such as these tend to be elided in favor of broader statements which generalize about the "freedoms" that the space of the blog provides for women.

Previously, a journalist for a now banned reformist paper, Parastoo Dokoohaki, was an Iran-based activist and feminist who kept a well-known blog called *Zan Nevesht (Written by a Woman)* since 2002. Like many bloggers, Dokoohaki covered a variety of subjects ranging from musings about her personal life to comments on the state of journalism, politics, and social affairs. Her site included an entire category of posts organized under the heading "Women's Issues" and which focused on cases highlighting social and legal difficulties facing women in Iran. In her first post dated June 6, 2002, she explained her choice of blog title and her motivations for writing as follows:

> Now why the "Writings of a Woman"? Why not? In my opinion the world from the view of men and the world from the point of view of women is

quite different. It appears that women have not really had the opportunity to record their point of view and the handful of women who have recorded anything have chosen to do so mostly from the point of view of men. [Poets] Forough Farokhzad and from the new generation Geranaz Mousavi are the exceptions in this regard. These things are said by feminist critics by the way, not by me! And these critics of course are not familiar with the world of weblogging because if they were, they would have surely reconsidered their view.[17]

At least two points are worth noting in the above entry. The writer refers to women and men in general terms, but it is clear that her frame of reference is discourses in the Iranian arena. While the post begins as a lament about the dearth of material written by women, the reader soon becomes aware of a sleight of hand: the author has pulled one in with the familiar only to reverse herself in declaring that the *weblogistan* has made a decisive intervention in this trend. In addition, by beginning her blog as such, she locates herself within the very movement whose power she is announcing. At least for this writer, then, the blog is a space for making various self-conscious disruptions in lopsided power structures. The author does this not only by providing commentary on the world from the "point of view of woman," as she says, but also in using the space of the blog for mobilizing her readers around on-the-ground events that have consequences for women as individuals or as members of a constructed group. What becomes clear in tracking her blog, in short, is that the ideas and philosophies she espouses online are reciprocally integrated with the causes she promotes in her offline activities.

Furthermore, the blog is not an exceptional space for her to exercise agency, but is rather an extension of her offline work. Dokoohaki makes sure that her audience is kept abreast of the range of activities with which she is involved, and she often uses the blog for engaging her readers in thinking through problems she faces in her personal life and career. Updates about her journalistic projects and her activities with women's rights organizing make up a significant portion of her writing. These posts function as an important information source not just for readers who have an interest in Dokoohaki herself, but for those who wish to engage with the bigger political and social issues she addresses. In March 2007, for example, after she and more than 30 of her colleagues were arrested and later released on heavy bails as part of a government crackdown on women campaigning to reform discriminatory laws, Dokoohaki's site became one of the major focal points for transnational activists who relied on her blogs for updates and for getting a sense of what kind of solidarity organizing would best suit the needs of the women activists.

The continuities between the online expression of bloggers' desires and the pursuit of concomitant goals offline are even apparent in the case of the pseudonymous author Zeitoon, excerpts of whose blog is a staple of popular discourses on the Iranian blogging phenomenon. Zeitoon exemplifies the disgruntled young, educated, middle-class woman whose experiences are privileged not only in mainstream narratives about the phenomenon of blogging but in the earlier noted accounts concerning Iranian women in general. Writing from the suburbs of Tehran since September 2002, critiques of the government and societal ills have formed a consistent part of her entries, and these commentaries are usually couched in terms of her daily activities and projects. Yet despite her at times tiresome and repetitive expressions of distaste for governmental policies, Zeitoon's blog is also filled with contradictions and contestations, a fact that is not apparent in the popular narratives that cite her writings in pushing the thesis that the Net is the domain of straightforward resistance to and wholesale rejection of the ruling establishment.

During the presidential elections of 2005, for example, when transnational debates over candidates and the question of whether to participate in the electoral process consumed much of the *weblogistan*, Zeitoon originally came down in favor of non-participation. In the month before the elections, she not only repeated her conviction to boycott the elections several times, but she ridiculed those who were willing to go the polls out of fear that not having the stamp of having voted in their national ID papers might later result in negative consequences:

> It's interesting that some people think that you have to have a stamp on your ID papers so that you can breathe in this country. Dear sirs, that is an old story. And some people say that they will cast a blank ballot. I think a blank ballot is much worse than voting for the worst of them! Because it is a sign of fear! Even a blank vote will make them happy.[18]

Despite her seemingly steadfast decision against voting and engaging in any act that the ruling establishment may interpret as a gesture of support, Zeitoon surprised her readers when she announced on the day of the elections that she had voted for a Reformist candidate.[19] This unexpected change of heart was met with much hostility on the part of many of her readers who expressed their anger either in her comment section or on their own blogs. Zeitoon herself summarized the insults she received as including "Traitor, spy, criminal, betrayer, deceiver, two-faced, country-seller, misogynist (!), complicit in crimes of regime, giver of legitimacy to regime."[20] In citing her dismay at the various attacks against her, Zeitoon seemed shocked at the willingness of certain readers to cast her in black-and-white terms that left no room for the nuances behind making on-the-ground decisions about one's political participation.

The mini-scandal that erupted on the *weblogistan* in response to Zeitoon's seemingly sudden change of heart vis-à-vis the elections is significant for a number of reasons. While it is true that Zeitoon, like many other women bloggers, uses the space of her website to engage in discussions that may push the limits of legally and socially permissible speech offline, her virtual existence is very much intertwined with her offline one. Furthermore, the fact that even Zeitoon – one of the most cited figures in the mainstream narrative about resistance on the Iranian blogosphere – does not easily fit into the reductive frameworks used in assessing the *weblogistan* and Iranian society more broadly is indicative of the severe shortcomings of such discourses.

Looking at women's pages – whether they fall under the much-used and inadequate category of oppositional sites or whether they are among the diverse blogs that are unnoticed by popular accounts – shows that Iranian women's blogging activities were interlinked with their experiences offline. Dominant narratives about the *weblogistan* do not entirely deny women's agency, but they do limit it to the virtual sphere. The inaccurate assessment that women's expression of their goals and desires is restricted to their online activities undercuts their widespread contributions to Iranian society at large and their achievements in advancing personal or social projects. Whether they were explicitly involved in campaigns of social reform as is the case of Dokoohaki or whether they limited their open declarations about their political activities to descriptions of their voting as Zeitoon did, Iranian women bloggers have shown that they exercise their agency both online and off.

As will be clear in the ensuing section, this is also true for women bloggers who are politically oriented toward the most conservative elements of the ruling establishment. Blogging may complement their offline activities, provide them with an additional arena for expressing their views, and enable connections with geographically dispersed interlocutors – all of these features may account for the activity's popularity with Iranian women and men alike. But as the above examples and the earlier discussion about women's role in Iranian society show, it is not the case that the blog is an exceptional space of freedom for women who have no other outlets for expression or activism.

Before moving on to examining the often overlooked elements of *weblogistan* such as the governmental and/or conservative deployments of the blogosphere, a final point speaking to the shortcomings of the mainstream narrativization of Iranian women should be addressed. As exemplified in the earlier noted *Wall Street Journal* editorial, online expressions of women's sexuality are often cited as evidence of the Net's liberatory power. In fact, one of the very first women's blogs to gain widespread attention in the non-Persian language foreign press was the now-defunct site of *Faheshe* (Whore), which claimed to be the diary of an Iranian prostitute whose entries highlighted the corruption and gender bias of the legal system.[21] While it is clear that many women's sites, including the blogs noted above, contain discussions of sexuality and may broach topics that are not easy to raise offline, the topic is not a major focus of most of the sites authored by women. Of course, there are Iranian blogs devoted to sexuality, but their numbers are not particularly noteworthy as compared with sites of the same kind among bloggers of various other national backgrounds and geographical locations. In short, there is nothing remarkable about Iranian women's discussions on sexuality unless one takes for granted that their condition is one of long-repressed desires. Again, my contention here is not to deny the constraints on women's sexuality within the framework of Iranian law or society, but to question how the lopsided focus on the online expressions of sexuality figures into narratives that de-link the online from lived experiences thereby eliding the scope of women's agency, fetishizing the space of the Net, and uncritically reproducing tropes of cloistered Muslim women for whom liberation from sexual and gender oppression is a, if not *the*, core concern.[22]

Other weblogistans: marginalized sites of the blogosphere

The technophilic discourses about the Iranian Internet in general and blogging in particular – perhaps because they often rely on a tradition/modernity binary – tend to overlook the deployments of the Net by religious sectors of the populace and/or by the government and its supporters. In this framework, the Iranian government, due to its theocratic underpinnings, is cast on the side of "tradition," as are its supporters and religious Iranians in general. If the implicit logic behind these accounts is that the religiously inclined, in particular fundamentalists, are understood to be contrary to modernity and its presumed technological accoutrements, then it follows that the Net would be antithetical to these elements and better suited for their opposition.[23] Such frameworks continue to hold sway despite mounting evidence to the contrary. Fundamentalist militant groups such as Al-Qaeda, for example, have relied heavily on the web for propaganda use and recruitment. In addition, prior to the advent of the internet, scholars addressing the Iranian Revolution outlined the technological savvy of Ayatollah Khomeini and his supporters.[24]

Similarly in the context of the blogosphere, the *weblogistan* is not the exclusive domain of the secular and/or oppositional: whether for official or personal use, individuals and groups variously associated with the government have successfully claimed a substantial corner of the blogosphere, as have a range of religiously rooted bloggers. In the case of the latter, it is important to note that the proclivity toward religion does not guarantee a particular stance for or against the government as a whole or in part.

The most prominent blogger defying the easy categorization of the Iranian blogosphere is Mohammad Ali Abtahi, a ranking cleric whose official posts in the Iranian government included being vice-president and presidential advisor during the tenure of Reformist Mohammad Khatami.[25] Abtahi began his personal blog while still a member of the cabinet; given the high level of his position and the casual nature of his blog, Abtahi's site garnered much interest and readership. In fact, despite their penchant for ignoring the online activities of clerics and governmental officials, mainstream accounts of the Iranian blogosphere occasionally include a nod to Abtahi's blog. However, even in cases where his contributions are recognized, he is treated as an exception.Furthermore, given the power struggles between the Reformists and the Conservatives during the period under consideration, Abtahi was treated as broadly oppositional, and for that reason his inclusion did not greatly disturb the overall narrative about the function of the blogosphere vis-à-vis the government.[26]

If Abtahi's critiques of aspects of the political establishment and developments allowed his blog to be categorized as broadly oppositional, there were many bloggers – ranging from officials to private citizens – who left no doubt about their full allegiance to the most conservative elements of the ruling government. Thus while individuals and officials sympathetic to Reformists may have been among the *weblogistan's* initial, enthusiastic, and most active members, their political opponents were not far behind in taking to the medium.

In addition to his official site pertaining to the office of the presidency, for example, President Mahmoud Ahmadinejad keeps a personal blog site which he has used to note his reactions to public meetings, to post open letters, and to comment on various issues.[27]

The sites of current or former officials from the range of political alliances are few as compared with the sites of the large number of private citizens from the corresponding parts of the political spectrum. Unlike the blogs of officials, who may be restrained by professional duties and considerations, these sites tend to be more active in terms of the frequency of posts and intensity of interactions via links and/or comments sections. One of the more prolific bloggers closely self-identifying with the Supreme Leader and the more conservative components of the Iranian government is Abuzar Montazer-Alqaem, who has been writing since December 2003. His blog is named after the Pasdaran (known as the Revolutionary Guards in English), which is a paramilitary force initially created by Ayatollah Khomeini to protect the post-Revolution victories. The Pasdaran are ultimately under the command of the Supreme Leader and continue to espouse the rhetoric of safeguarding against what are deemed counter-revolutionary forces from inside and outside Iran. The Pasdaran also are linked to the Basiji (which literally translates into the mobilized), a people's militia which they organize and oversee. The Basiji forces are best known for their role in carrying out the human wave attacks on the battlefields of the Iran–Iraq war, and historically have comprised mainly young men from religious families.[28] The Basiji are organized in various levels and locations, and have members who are active within the charity organizations and/or in high school and university campuses. During moments of social and political upheaval, such as the student demonstrations of 1999 and 2003, Pasdaran and Basiji have been known for stepping in and at times violently suppressing expressions of dissent.

Identifying himself with the Pasdaran, the author of this blog sends his readership a clear signal about his social and political leanings.[29] Therefore, the content of his blog provides a good indication not only of internal power struggles in Iran in what at that point may be described broadly as antagonisms between the Reformists and Conservatives, but it also allows insight into the positions of the latter vis-à-vis Iranian and international developments during that time. Before addressing the general gist of his regular posts, it is important to note that Abuzar Montazer-Alqaem conceives of his audience as a trans-national one that does not necessarily share his socio-political outlook and for whom he is providing a much-needed service. One can see this explicitly in his response to a friendly reader who had critiqued the content of his site as providing too much repetitive information similar to that which is already contained in the Iranian press:

In the name of God. Others have brought up this issue too. But you don't know the whole story. The story is that a huge part of my friends, acquaintances, and readers are outside the country such as in the U.S., and they confirm that since they are not familiar with the various news sources and the differences in opinion and tastes in Iran, an important portion of the news and debates they read about is from my blog. And so I have to make-up for this by putting some of the more important news stories here. The second issue is that the audience of my blog is not just religious and polit-ical folks like you guys. There are some poor people who once in a while end up on my blog via random clicks and reading a top news story is an event for them. The issue is that I put here some of the news that others online and offline may want to censor. The core concern is to reach, address, and publish certain topics. My brother, most people don't go scouring the news services! Go look at webgozar [a site ranking web pages by popular-ity],[30] see what are the most popular sites! People are after a bunch of crap! Go see which one of the sites of Persianblog[31] are the most popular. You can see what kind of crap gets the biggest audience. The most popular site on Persianblog is a site that takes vulgar photos of movie stars and turns them into wallpapers that the readers can download. This has become the way to gain an audience for your blog. Well these people are deprived of news and information. One should think about them too. That is why I put these things here on the first page.[32]

It is noteworthy that someone identifying himself with the most conservative elements of the Iranian government and society and whose blog content does not reveal flexibility in deviating from the official line nonetheless takes his audi-ence as being transnational and transcendent of particular ideological and phys-ical locations. Montazer-Alqaem's site also reflects that he is tuned into what is happening in the broader blogosphere, and he often cites the claims of well-known bloggers such as those mentioned in mainstream discourses.[33] Despite the evidence that this blogger and others like him both engage a transnational audi-ence and participate as a reader of a range of blogs, such interconnectivity is not acknowledged in dominant discourses. In popular, academic, and intelligence discourses, if Iranian right-wing groups such as the Pasdaran are granted any transnational activity at all, their connectivity is articulated in terms of the trans-fer of funds and/or arms to groups that share their ideologies. Given the heavy deployment of the Net by groups such as Al-Qaeda, an increasing number of accounts have considered such phenomena in terms of their transnational implications.[34] Similar recognition, however, has not yet been granted to the Iranian Internet, which continues to be predominately mapped in terms of earlier noted binaries that account neither for Iranian virtual nor offline realities.

As a devoted follower of the Supreme Leader Ali Khamenehi, Montazer-Alqaem's site routinely included posts dedicated to covering the Leader's speeches, meetings, and various public appearances. The entities, groups, and individuals he singled out for critique and ridicule are those that are perceived to be the opponents of Khamenehi and his followers. Thus, in addition to address-ing issues and figures such as those pertaining to U.S. foreign policy or UN reso-lutions against Iran, the Pasdaran blog took up the role of identifying and berating Iranian "enemies," be they inside or outside Iran. As such, his site provided insight into the complexities of internal Iranian ideological and power struggles. His repeated attacks against the earlier mentioned Reformist former vice-president and fellow blogger, Mohammad Ali Abtahi, for example, high-lights tensions among the various factions inside Iran.[35] In addition, Abuzar Montazer-Alqaem's criticisms of Reformists was not limited to electoral politics but was applied as well to spheres of cultural production, including that of the blogosphere.

For example, Abuzar Montazer-Alqaem condemns Persianblog's director, Mehdi Butorabi, for collaborating with foreign and diaspora websites in drawing mass attention to the filtering of his blog service provider site. According to Montazer-Alqaem, Butorabi's reaction was a disproportionate one which placed the movement's grudges and agendas above what Motazer-Alqaem deems are the interests of the nation:

> The political manifestations of this so called Reformism are truly irritating ... I saw that Butorabi intensely worked on creating an atmosphere counter to that which is in the national interest, and all because Persianblog was accidentally filtered.... It is us who are the investments of Persianblog and in actuality it is us, our weblogs, that give Persianblog its identity and bring it into existence. Dr. Butorabi, because of one technical, administrative, or judicial mistake, accuses the entire regime of limiting a blogging service of thirteen million posts.[36]

What the above post reflects is the recognition that technologies such as blog service providers are imbricated with the political and particular situations of those who administer them. It also shows the micro-dynamics behind both the technical aspects and the content of blog production. As such, it highlights the reciprocal relations between the online and the offline and indicates the com-plexities of the *weblogistan* as a site that reflects the factional power struggles of the realities in which it is embedded

While he is among the most prolific and at times abrasive of the bloggers associated with the more hardliner elements of the government, Abuzar Montazer-Alqaem is but one of the more well known of many bloggers with similar social and political leanings. Merely examining the blogs he has linked to and repeating this process on each blog reveals a widespread and transnation-ally dispersed web of pro-conservative political and religious sites rivaling that of the secular and/or oppositional *weblogistan*. In addition to tracing such blog-gers via their interconnectedness through hyperlinks, one also can find unions or networks that have been created with the express purpose of drawing together similarly minded writers. In addition, group pages may be found that include the contributions of several bloggers. The Association of Muslim Bloggers, the group site of Basiji Students, the Followers of Mahdi Bloggers, and Hezbollah Bloggers are examples of such networks.[37] The interlinking of sites via unions and/or the creation of joint blogs reflect that bloggers who share similar political outlooks as Abuzar Montazer-Alqaem have an active presence online, are aware of one another, and have attempted to enhance their connectivity via conscious efforts at networking.

While many of the blogs aligning themselves with conservative elements of the Iranian government were rife with masculinist expressions of religiosity and militancy, these sites were not the exclusive domain of men; nor were women exempt from engaging in similarly militaristic expressions. As an example, the blog entitled *Majnoon-e Velayat*, which translates into Crazy for the *Velayat*, a reference to the *Velayat-e faqih*, the current system of religious rule in Iran, is written by a woman under the pseudonym of *Beyt al-ahzan* (House of Misery).[38] The site was listed with the ring of Hezbollah Bloggers and often engages with the history and theology of Shi'ism. Her concern with religious history and doctrine, however, is often expressed in militaristic terms that draw on recent and contemporary events such as the Iran–Iraq war and the current conflicts in the region. Similarly, the blog *Laleley-e Basiji* is another site that incorporates Islamic history and doctrine with her discussions of current issues of political importance.[39] Despite the fact that *Laleley-e Basiji* often foregrounds her gender in taking up the issues she discusses, sites such as hers were entirely absent from the popular – and largely Western – accounts which expressed much enthusiasm about the category of "Iranian women bloggers."

Parinaz, the author of *Dar Ouj-e Tanhayee* (At the Peak of Loneliness), is another example of the kind of woman blogger overlooked in such accounts. Writing since August 2002, Parinaz's posts are a mixture of poetic prose and poetry. In addition to listing the page sites of fellow bloggers, Parinaz has a number of links to other sites which indicate her interwoven interests in poetry, literature, and religion: included are *Anjoman-e Shaeran Iran* (Iranian Poets Society),[40] *Loh Paygah-e Farhang va Adab-e Farsi* (Slate, Base for Persian Culture and Literature),[41] as well as sites devoted to Imam Mahdi, the last Imam of Twelver Shi'ism whose return is anticipated by observant followers.

While her posts are consistently religiously themed, often specifically around messianic tropes pertaining to Imam Mahdi, the blog also appears to function as a platform for the author to experiment with and share her poetic works; furthermore, the contents of her poems do not always explicitly specify a religious subject, thus leaving room for layers of interpretation:

Alas
The Sorrows of this heart
are not one or two!
It must
sit
count
the days without you!
And then
as always
it must give these sorrows
like the balloons from times without worry

to the sky for safekeeping.
This sorrow too
will pass...
And your sorrow will remain
Because the balloons of your heart too
Are the prisoners of the sky?![42]

A few of those who chose to comment on the blog indicated a messianic reading of the poem; however, the majority wrote in general but encouraging terms about the poetry itself. The range and number of poems Parinaz has written on her site over the years, despite their often explicit religious subject, leave room for multiple interpretations, including those with sensual and romantic overtones:

'If My Heart Were to Break, it is Worth the Sacrifice for Your Drunk Eyes'

I did not deserve so many wanderings
In the place where I was lost seeking the minutes in the death of seconds
You did not tell me that it is the hour where you have left the circle of will
When I planned in the corners of the trapezoid and spun from the intensity of the emptiness of my wanderings
You did not tell me that you no longer approve of my madness, in this hidden darkroom
Your silence cast me to the rays of the eclipsed sun.
And your patience became a weightless cloud on the boundary of my heart.
If it wasn't for your sweetheart's mediation,
say that you would try my doubts in the algebra of the court of justice,
and you would forever exile me from the circle of your will to the law of eternal punishment!
I did not deserve so much kindness.[43]

In addition to using her blog as a site for expressing her spiritual devotion and the poetry that it inspires, Parinaz also occasionally writes about her life activities such as various religious pilgrimages. The poems she writes to variously commemorate such trips, religious and political anniversaries, or even her own birthday, show that her blogging activities are integrated with her offline involvements: the blog may provide the space for her to creatively engage and publicly share aspects of her lived experiences and concerns, but the site is clearly not an exceptional space where she has the agency to pursue interests that she cannot follow elsewhere.

Despite the heavy focus on politics and the religious underpinnings of their views, the blogs that may self-identify as adhering to conservative elements of Iranian society share with bloggers from differing backgrounds the tendency to incorporate their own daily lives and thoughts into the content of their sites. Just as was the case with the earlier examined blogs that were critical of the government and its policies, the blogs of the type addressed in this section clearly reflect their imbrication with the lived realities of the authors; the continuities and reciprocal relations between their activities and expressions offline and online are apparent on various blogs regardless of their particular political and/or geographical locations. Another example (see below) from a religious blogger, this time one that explicitly claims allegiance to conservative elements of the state, is helpful in further illustrating this point.

Khale Zahra is a fairly prolific blogger who began writing in 2006. She asserts herself as a religiously devout supporter of the more conservative tendencies in the Iranian government. She regularly includes religious material, engages with local and global politics, and relays her personal experiences and musings. The following post from her blog is a highly personal message drawing from her lived, daily experiences while also making a point with broader social and political issues. The post is addressed to her father, a veteran of the Iran–Iraq war and who still is suffering from and undergoing treatment for having been exposed to the chemical weapons used by Iraq during the eight-year war:

> By the way, dad, a few days ago I was in the taxi with a guy who was a chemical victim like you and he was feeling really bad because of the change in the seasons; his symptoms had suddenly appeared and the palms of his hands were covered with deep cuts. He was really frustrated because the *Naser Khosrow* [clinic] has been shut and he can't get his medicine. He said the *bonyad* had told him that his turn would come within a few months and he then could come to use their facilities. He was in much pain when he said: "How can I afford to get these expensive and hard to find drugs for the next four or five months. Maybe I won't even survive until then." Then he started crying and got out of the taxi a little further down the road. Yeah, dad, you went [to the frontlines] for God and for your honor, which is the soil of your homeland, but as God is your witness, what percent of your due have they given you? Don't be humble, maybe 20%? You know what, let us list your souvenirs from the war: tearing in your stomach and intestines, broken ribs that have healed into your flesh, being exposed to chemical weapons, being shell shocked, having more than a hundred shrapnel of different sizes throughout your body, ripping of your ear drum as a result of blasts, and a few more symptoms that will show up in the coming years. Dad I love this regime but more than it I love you so I have a right to be frustrated.[44]

For this blogger, the aftermath of the war and the current lack of care for veterans is part of her lived experiences, a fact her post shows is true for other Iranians still suffering the consequences of the eight-year war with Iraq. From what she reveals in her posts, her family has a history of participating in and supporting various government-sponsored activities and policies. Yet even this most devoted believer in the Revolution is not uncritical of certain aspects of the Iranian society or polity. Through her emotionally charged post, she pinpoints the government's shortcomings in providing for the same war veterans to which it claims to be indebted. In short, just as the examinations of blogs generally cited to argue for the oppositional nature of *weblogistan* revealed that they are not monolithic or dogmatic in their expressions of dissent, the investigations in this segment show that the kinds of sites elided from mainstream narratives are also clearly engaged with the material conditions that give rise to them and reveal nuances in their analysis of online and offline activities.

Zahra Ghadyani, the author of *Donya-e Se Khahar* (The World of Three Sisters), is another self-identified hardliner and devoutly religious blogger who routinely incorporates her daily life into her blog, beginning with her inaugural post, organized into three parts under the subheadings "Why a Weblog?," "Why Three Sisters?," and "What does your Longing Heart Wish to Say?":

> "Why a Weblog?"
> The story started when exams were over and I fell. Off my bike, that is. Don't think I don't know how to ride a bike, no. ... The bikes of the dorm are all crooked because of how many times kids have fallen off of them and so naturally when one wants to make a turn like I wanted to, one falls down. I landed on my elbow with my full weight, and naturally was hurt badly and bled a whole bunch and this is how I rolled in my own blood and my pure blood flooded the thirsty ground of the dorm. But since the grounds of the dorm have been covered with asphalt, it wasn't possible for tulips to bloom from the blood of the youth of the nation. It was as a result of this incident that I decided to start a blog. There must be some relationship between these two events, otherwise, how come I never thought of blogging before?[45]

Light-hearted in tone, the initial post engages a personal incident and points out the seeming randomness of her decision to begin blogging. Yet the dark humor about bleeding profusely and the absence of blooming flowers is also a bold and risky move: the themes she is toying with are central to the post-revolutionary discourses of martyrdom. Government-sponsored murals, posters, songs, often dating to or referencing the eight-year Iran–Iraq war, are filled with slogans and images of red tulips bursting from the land where the blood of Iran's young defenders has been spilled. In joking about her fall in terms of "pure blood flooding the land" and the "bloom of tulips from the blood," Ghadyani is unmistakably and brazenly playing with tropes that are sacred to the State and to its hardliner supporters such as Ghayani herself.

The second part of her initial post is also potentially subversive, although more subtly so:

> "Why Three Sisters?"
> The philosophy of why there are three of us sisters, I don't know. One must ask the single creator the wisdom of giving my mom and dad three daughters. But the reason for naming the blog as such, I know. Have you heard this song before: "us four brothers (dam daram dam), along with three sisters (dam daram dam), we flutter around her, around our flower of a mother (dam daram dam)." The three of us sing this song with a few

changes and acting in a way that such songs require, we sing for our mom: "Us three sisters, without any brothers, we flutter around her." Of course there is another version "Us zero brothers, along with zero brothers, we flutter around her." And so this whole thing became the inspiration for the name of this blog.[46]

As she did in giving the reason for beginning her blog, Ghadyani relates the name of her blog in very personal terms. Perhaps more importantly, the post shows engagement with spheres generally considered alien to the religious classes or the fervent supporters of the Iranian government. Ghadyani not only makes direct reference to a song by diasporic Iranian singer Serjik, but credits his music and the family revelry it gave rise to as the direct inspiration for the name of her blog. In this and subsequent posts, Ghadyani shows that far from being unaware or uncritically hostile to the cultural products of "the West," she is able variously to enjoy, criticize, or draw inspiration from them.

Indeed, all of the above posts from the invisible women bloggers of *Weblogistan* challenge both the dominant accounts of the Iranian blogosphere and the vast array of assumptions that undergird them. Vastly differing in their styles and approaches to blogging, the women cited in this section share an inclination toward religion and the current government. Yet they also show a willingness and ability to push boundaries, whether those boundaries are stylistic, social, or political. In other words, they cannot be dismissed as "tools" of the system who merely parrot its official stances; on the contrary, they reveal courage in engaging even the most sensitive topics and symbols of post-revolutionary Iran.

Conclusion

As the above discussions have shown, Iranian women were a significant part of the blogosphere during the height of its popularity from 2002 to 2007. They deployed their blogs variously to interrogate issues of gender, question governmental policies, and organize to bring about social change. Yet dominant accounts during this period adequately address neither the complexities of Iranian women's blogging nor that of the socio-political contexts in which they appeared. Instead, they produced formulaic narratives that consistently privileged the viewpoints of largely middle- to upper-class and self-identified secular women while completely ignoring, and thus erasing, the voices of women who did not appear to fit these prescribed criteria.

Since dominant accounts eroded the complexities of the blogs they addressed, even women bloggers who fit the unspoken formula and were included in the mainstream narratives were undermined by the same discourses that claimed to celebrate them. In addition, by framing women's blogging in terms that limited their agency to the virtual arena, such accounts endorsed assumptions of male-only Muslim public spheres and elided women's active, multi-leveled participation in a number of areas.

The examples of women's online activities covered in this chapter show that critical stances toward the state and society were found among both self-identified supporters and opponents of the government; Furthermore, regardless of their political orientation, women's blogging activities were an integral part of their on-the-ground career, social, or political involvement. This latter point indicates that the *weblogistan* can function as a tool for challenging misconceptions about the lives of Iranian women, wherever they may fall on the social and political spectrum.

In the end, much remains to be explored about Iranian women's participation on the blogosphere and the net in general. If women's participation in the blogosphere is grasped in ways that ground it in their offline contexts, it becomes possible to see that Iranian women assert their agency in a multiplicity of ways that are neither limited to the online nor restricted to individuals with particular political dispositions. Furthermore, expanding assessments of the Iranian blogosphere to include integrated analyses of heretofore disregarded bloggers provide opportunities for moving beyond the clichéd frameworks that have continued to dominate discourses about the Iranian blogosphere and Iranian subjects more generally.

Notes

1 "The Blog Shall Set You Free" [editorial] (2003) *Wall Street Journal*, July 18.
2 Nasrin Alavi, *We Are Iran*, Brooklyn, NY: Soft Skull Publishing, 2005, cover.
3 As early as 2000, David Silver pointed out in his review of a decade of cyberculture studies that by the late 1990s, accounts of cyberculture had moved beyond celebratory musings to include diverse methodologies that consider the complex social, cultural, and economic components of online phenomena. Despite the shift toward more nuanced analysis of the Net as a site of cultural and political production, dominant accounts of the Iranian Internet seem lodged in an earlier time when Net enthusiasts prevailed. David Silver, "Looking Backwards, Looking Forward: Cyberculture Studies 1990–2000," in David Gauntlett (ed.) *Web Studies: Rewiring Media Studies for the Digital Age*, Oxford: Oxford University Press, 2000, pp. 19–30.
4 Farzaneh Milani, "On Women's Captivity in the Islamic World,"*Middle East Report*, 246 (2008), pp. 40–46.
5 Roksana Bahramitash, "The War on Terror, Feminist Orientalism and Orientalist Feminism: Case Studies of Two North American Best Sellers," *Critique*, 14, 2 (summer 2005), pp. 221–236.
6 Hamid Dabashi, "Native Informers and the Making of the American Empire," 2006, *Al-Ahram Weekly*. Available online at: http://weekly.ahram.org.eg/2006/797/special.htm.
7 For accounts that further consider the function of popular constructions in eroding the agency of Muslim women, see Lila Abu-Lughod, "Do Muslim Women Really Need Saving? Anthropological Reflections on Cultural Relativism and its Others," *American Anthropologist*, 104, 3 (2002), pp. 783–790; and Kevin J Ayotte and Mary Husain, "Securing Afghan Women: Neocolonialism, Epistemic Violence, and the Rhetoric of the Veil," *National Women's Studies Association Journal*, 17, 3 (2005), pp. 112–133.
8 Steve Jones, "Understanding Community in the Information Age," in S. Jones (ed.) *Cybersociety: Computer-mediated Communication and Community*, Thousand Oaks, CA: Sage, 1995, pp. 10–35; and Steve Jones, "The Internet and its Social Landscape,"

in S. Jones (ed.) *Virtual Culture: Identity and Communication in Cybersociety*, London: Sage, 1997, pp. 7–35.

9 Daniel Miller and Don Slater, *The Internet: An Ethnographic Approach*, Oxford: Berg Publishers, 2000, p. 5.

10 Christine Hine, *Virtual Ethnography*, London: Sage, 2000.

11 Some examples of blog titles/urls that explicitly identify the gender of the writer through choosing descriptive terms or women's names are as follows: *I am an Iranian Doughter* (sic), http://iraniandoughter.blogspot.com (English, Inside Iran); *Khorsheed Khanoom, www.khorshidkhanoom.com/* (Lady Sun) (Persian, originally written inside Iran, and the writer continued to blog after leaving the country); *Een Yek Zan Azt* (This is a Woman), http://dokhijoon.persianblog.ir/ (Persian, Inside Iran).

12 *Bonyads* are charitable trust funds that originated under the rule of the Pahlavis. In post-revolutionary Iran, they were designated for distributing money from Iran's oil wealth and providing social services to the disenfranchised and/or the families of war martyrs.

13 Golnar Merhan, "The Paradox of Tradition and Modernity in Female Education in the Islamic Republic of Iran," *Comparative Education Review*, 47 (2003), pp. 269–286; and Mitra Shavarini, "The Feminization of Iranian Higher Education," *Review of Education*, 51 (2005), pp. 329–347.

14 Haleh Esfandiari, "The Politics of the Woman Question in the Islamic Republic: 1979–1999," in J. Esposito and R.K. Ramazani (eds) *Iran at the Crossroads*, New York: Palgrave, 2001. pp. 75–92.

15 Valentine Moghadam, "The Reproduction of Gender Inequality in the Islamic Republic: A Case Study of Iran in the 1980s," *World Development*,. 19, 10 (1991), pp. 1335–1350.

16 Zib Mir-Hosseini, "The Conservative–Reformist Conflict Over Women's Rights in Iran," *International Journal of Politics, Culture, and Society*, 16, 1 (2002), pp. 37–53.

17 http://weblog.parastood.ir/archives/000348.php, my translation.

18 http://z8un.com/archives/2005_05.html#000534, my translation.

19 Her description of the day of elections, along with some pictures of polling areas, may be found in her archives at http://z8un.com/archives/2005_06.html#000549; her post here is also noteworthy for the ways in which she chastises the self-styled opposition satellite stations which malign and muffle the voices of any Iranians who attempt to make a case for the benefits of voting.

20 http://z8un.com/archives/2005_06.html#000551, my translation.

21 See e.g. www.cnn.com/2003/TECH/internet/06/16/iran.blogs.reut.

22 Such accounts have tended to privilege the experiences of middle-class, secular women and often overlook the specificities of class and religion as they impact upon expressions of and limitations on sexuality. In her study of temporary marriage in Iran, for example, Shahla Haeri found that these religiously accepted practices provide women from certain religious classes with avenues for sexual satisfaction, whereas middle-class, self-described "modern" women were constrained by notions of virginity and limits on sexual experiences. For more information, see Shahla Haeri, *Law of Desire: Temporary Marriage in Shi'i Iran*, Syracuse, NY: Syracuse University Press, 1989.

23 In challenging the application of the modern/tradition divide in understanding fundamentalism, Minoo Moallem has argued convincingly that "Islamic fundamentalism is a by-product of colonial modernity and the process of modernization and westernization." Minoo Moallem, *Between Warrior Brother and Veiled Sister: Islamic Fundamentalism and the Politics of Patriarchy in Iran*, Berkeley: University of California Press, 2005, p. 9.

24 Michael M.J. Fischer and Mehdi Abedi, *Debating Muslims: Cultural Dialogues in Postmodernity and Tradition*, Madison, WI: University of Wisconsin Press, 1990; and Anabelle Sreberny-Mohammadi and Ali Mohammadi, *Small Media, Big Revolution*, Minneapolis, MN: University of Minnesota Press, 1994.

25 www.webneveshteha.com/.

26 Other blogging figures associated with Reformists include Sayed Atollah Mohajerani (http://mohajerani.maktuob.net/) and his wife, the former Reformist parliamentarian Jamile Kadivar (http://kadivar.maktuob.net/).

27 Mahmoud Ahmadinejad's personal blog, "The Personal Notes of Mahmoud Ahmadinejad," may be found at www.ahmadinejad.ir/. Examples of blog posts available on his site at the time of writing include "Freedom," a post about his reactions to Amir Kabir University students publicly heckling him (available at www.ahmadinejad.ir/fa/freedom/) and "Fingerprinting Travelers: A Sign of Power or an Insult to Human Dignity," which addressed U.S. immigration procedures (available at www.ahmadinejad.ir/fa/taking-fingerprints-of-passengers/). Ahmadinejad's governmental page, dedicated to the office of the president, may be found at the following URL: www.president.ir/.

28 Human wave attacks were practiced during the Iran–Iraq war, when Iran faced a technologically superior army supported by virtually every country in the Arab world, many European countries, and, most importantly, the United States. To make up for this, the Iranians resorted to sending dense waves of soldiers on to the battlefield, suffering many casualties but clearing fields for advance or for the recovery of Iranian territories.

29 Despite the fact that the Pasdaran and Basiji forces since their creation have drawn much of their support and membership from the traditionally disenfranchised segments of Iranian society, this has not been exclusively the case. The author of the blog under examination, for example, identifies himself as belonging to a "middle to higher" class family. His full self-description in his inaugurating post was previously available at: www.persianblog.com/posts/?weblog=pasdaran.persianblog.com&postid=1215904. His economic standing, of course, raises the question of class and accessibility to the Internet. It is likely that the propensity for blogging among Iranians may be determined more by economic rather than by political factors. The original URL cited here is no longer available. After a crash of blog server provider Persianblog.com in late 2007, the blogs and archives of thousands of bloggers were lost. The provider has now switched to an .ir domain, and the blog of Pasdaran may now be found at http://pasdaran.persianblog.ir/.

30 www.webgozar.com/.

31 www.Persianblog.com is one of the oldest and most popular sites providing hosting for Persian-language bloggers. Since the crash of its servers in late 2007, resulting in the loss of material from countless blogs, the service has now switched to an .ir domain and may be found at www.persianblog.ir.

32 www.persianblog.com/posts/?weblog=pasdaran.persianblog.com&postid=6246469, my translation, original text taken from the comment section of above post. Due to the crash of Persianblog servers in late 2007, this link is no longer functional.

33 One such example was previously available at: http://pasdaran.persianblog.com/1383_7_pasdaran_archive.html#2583387. Due to the crash of Persianblog servers in late 2007, this link is no longer functional.

34 See e.g. Vinay Lal, "Terror and Its Networks: Disappearing Trails in Cyberspace," available online at www.nautilus.org/archives/virtual-diasporas/paper/Lal.html.

35 www.persianblog.com/posts/?weblog=pasdaran.persianblog.com&postid=5935045, Due to the crash of Persianblog servers in late 2007, this link is no longer functional.

36 www.persianblog.com/posts/?weblog=pasdaran.persianblog.com&postid=5704606, my translation. Due to the crash of Persianblog servers in late 2007, this link is no longer functional.

37 www.muslimbloggers.ir/,http://weblog.autbasij.org/,http://zohour.mihanblog.com/; http://hezbollah14.persianblog.com/. The latter provides gendered lists of blogs organized under the headings of "Followers of Ali" and "Followers of Fatemeh." Both Ali and Fatemeh are exalted figures in Shi'i Islam. The cousin of the Prophet Mohammad

and the husband of his daughter Fatemeh, Ali is revered as the first Shi'i Imam. Fatemeh is similarly important in her position as the daughter of the Prophet, the husband of Imam Ali, and the mother of Imams Hassan and Hosain. As the Prophet Mohmmad had no sons who survived into adulthood, Shi'is who claim to have descended from the house of the Prophet trace their lineage through the line of Fatemeh.

38 http://majnoonevelayat.persianblog.ir/.
39 www.laleyebasiji.persianblog.ir/.
40 www.poetry.ir/index.php.
41 www.louh.com/.
42 http://parinaz.persianblog.ir/post/128, my translation.
43 http://parinaz.persianblog.ir/post/146, my translation.
44 http://khalezahra.blogfa.com/post-20.aspx, my translation.
45 http://2nyaye3khahar.blogfa.com/8504.aspx, my translation.
46 Ibid.

6   Areas of Iranian women's voice and influence

Jaleh Taheri

Iran's presidential election in June 2009 revealed both internal cleavages and the impetus for action, both of which became visible through extensive coverage in the international media. While the global media seemed to focus on chaos, despair, and frustration, it is also true that these aspects are mixed inextricably with determination and a sense of hope for a better future. This latter feeling, not despair or frustration, was what motivated men and women of all ages and classes to take to the streets of Iranian cities to protest official election results that they believed to be fraudulent, despite threats of government-sanctioned violence. The presence of women in these demonstrations was especially prominent. Indeed, in the three decades since the 1979 Revolution, women, through their extensive involvement socially, economically, and politically, voiced their demands for change and effectively to encourage new policies toward women. Considering the increasingly visible role of women in Iranian society, one may say that many Iranian women feel empowered to make demands of their state and society.

Empowerment as defined by UNICEF is the "collective action by the oppressed and deprived to overcome the obstacles of struggle and inequality which have previously put them in a disadvantaged position."[1] As I will illustrate in this chapter, Iranian women are involved in varyious activities that enable them to voice their opinions and effectively to urge the Iranian government and society toward change. In no way should Iranian women be considered helpless in the way that some writers in the West, both academics and journalists, have tended to portray them. They are empowered in every sense of the UNICEF definition. Hence, it is important for academics and journalists alike to acknowledge Iranian women's collective efforts, drawing international attention to their positive achievements despite the numerous barriers that they face daily. Female role models in each country are the product of that country's particular culture, history, and political character. Taking all this into consideration, I offer below descriptions of several ways in which Iranian women have been expressing their voice both individually and collectively.

Education

Since the Islamic Revolution in 1979, the percentage of educated women in Iran has increased by more than 50 percent. The literacy rate of rural women was especially low, only 1.2 percent in 1956, but it rose to 62.4 percent in 1996, and it has continued to rise.[2] Literacy among urban women was higher and rose throughout the 1960s, but in 1970, 55 percent of all females in Iran were still illiterate. As a result of the post-revolutionary literacy drive, by 1999, the number of illiterate women had dropped to 8.7 percent.[3] In the first decade of the twenty-first century, women comprised the majority of adult learners and even entered such fields as physics, which in previous years had hardly any women at all. This incredible increase illustrated not only the government's commitment to female literacy, but also the willingness of women to participate actively in their education. The post-revolutionary governments of Prime Minister Mir-Hosain Musavi (1981–1989) addressed many of the obstacles to female education, such as the need for gender segregation and the proximity and availability of learning centers for lower income women. As noted by Golnar Mehran,

> Co-educational settings and male instructors, especially if they are not local residents and not known and trusted among the community members, have been found to be the major factors in hindering female access to education and a serious cause of early drop-out from educational programs.[4]

Education of the masses was a critical goal for Ayatollah Ruhollah Khomeini, the charismatic leader of the Revolution. One of his several nationwide campaigns, called *jihads*,[5] was the Literacy Movement Organization (LMO), dedicated solely to educating all Iranians. Khomeini proclaimed that getting an education was a religious duty for all Iranians including women. He recognized the benefits of having an active and educated female population and promoted their involvement in public at various times. One obstacle the LMO addressed was the distance that women had to travel to learning centers, especially after dark. The LMO took every measure to hold meetings close to residential homes, sometimes even sending instructors out into villages and to private residences. "The burden now rests on the shoulders of instructors, both male and female, to live and work close to the learners."[6] These efforts gave thousands of women from traditional families an opportunity to receive an education for the first time. The gender segregation of schools was also a huge factor that promoted female education. Religious and conservative families did not fear for the honor of their daughters as they left for high school or university. The number of female university students has surpassed that of men, as they now comprise 65 percent of incoming students. For example, in the applied physics department of Azad University, 70 percent of the graduates are women, a statistic that would make many Western universities proud.[7] By the early 2000s, Iran had a significant population of educated women who were even choosing a career over marriage. Women's success in universities prompted some professors to express increasing concern about their male students. Some conservatives even suggest that there should be positive discrimination for men in certain key subjects. Hence in educational matters a woman's situation has greatly improved since the Revolution and continues to do so every day.

Employment

Women's formal employment rates have increased greatly since the Islamic Revolution and have reached higher percentages than they ever did during the pro-Western monarchy. Sociologist Roksana Bahramitash argues that "Increased employment for women could not have happened without the Islamist regime."[8] Khomeini's call for women to be the "strength of the nation" after the Revolution brought many women into the workplace. Furthermore, after the war with Iraq ended (1988) and Ali Akbar Hashemi Rafsanjani was elected president (1989), liberalizing policies and the economic crunch further drew women into the work place. Many women who had occupied volunteer positions during the war now searched for and demanded paid employment to help support their families. Many women worked in the health and education sectors, where in 1997 they comprised 40 percent of employees in the Ministry of Education and 12.5 percent in the Ministry of Health.[9] The number of female managers in government jobs (civil service) reached 34.7 percent of the total.[10] Although the number of women in positions of authority in the workplace overall is relatively small, women have still reached higher positions under the Islamic Republic than under the Shah's regime.

In addition to the increase in urban employment, it is significant to note that female rural employment has also increased. An important initiative for employment generation and poverty alleviation has been the creation of women's cooperatives. The women's cooperatives are registered under the legal framework of the Ministry of Cooperatives. Their main goals include the mobilization of women's productive resources and their self-employment with a small amount of initial capital. "

> The Ministry of Cooperatives has provided support and training for women in these cooperatives. For example, in 1998, about 43,000 women attended the training programs that were organized by the cooperatives' education centers across the country. Training has covered both the administration of the cooperatives and the development of technical skills.[11]

There is also the Imam Khomeini Relief Committee, a national charitable foundation that supports families without male heads of households. This foundation provides interest-free micro-credit loans for women to become engaged in income-generating work. Each year, training centers affiliated with the Imam Khomeini Relief Committee provide technical and training workshops to approximately 8,000 women.[12] Those women who graduate from these workshops may apply for loans after they finish their courses. These loans have given many underprivileged women access to income and financial independence which they had never experienced before under the Shah's regime.

Moreover, Iranian women experience more legal protection in the workplace under the current laws than do many women in other developing or developed nations. Under Iran's employment laws, women experience a significant amount of protection and even benefit during times of pregnancy, childbirth, and nursing. The current labor laws date from the early 1990s. These laws prohibit difference in wages according to gender, religion, political orientation, or race. Section 4, chapter 5, articles 75–78 prohibit women from working in hazardous occupations and jobs that require workers to carry weights above a certain limit without mechanical means.[13] Under the law, women are also entitled to 13 to 15 weeks' maternity leave, paid by the Social Welfare Organization. This is more generous than in many Western countries, including the United States. They are also entitled to keep their previous positions when they return to work. The law provides for nursing rights as well as for the establishment of childcare facilities at workplaces. The number of nurseries in the workplace has increased significantly since the Islamic Revolution. Islamic law, although viewed as patriarchal and oppressive from a Western standpoint, takes a more holistic approach to women who participate in the workforce. The current laws recognize the importance and significance of the birth and care of children by women. By way of contrast, in Western countries, it seems that governments and employers forget and/or ignore the fact that women biologically are the ones who give birth to children. Even in those Western societies that claim to be sensitive to feminists, the responsibilities of raising children almost always fall solely on the shoulders of women. This is definitely true in the United States where women are expected to raise their children and simultaneously have successful career without much state or family support.

Politics

After the global media coverage of those protesting as part of the 2009 to 2010 Green Movement, it is hard to ignore the prominent presence of women as political actors in Iran. The tragic death of the youthful Neda Soltani, documented and circulated by YouTube, shocked the world. During the months following the election, roof-top chants, many of them led by female voices, screamed, "Neda is not dead, our voice is not dead." The second line of the chant could not be more true. Women's voices in all aspects of Iranian life have gained in strength and confidence. The increase in female education has meant that women are more conscious of their rights (or what their rights ought to be). Just as women protested during the Islamic Revolution and in many other civil protests over the past 30 years they have again participated since June 2009 both in support of and against the regime of President Mahmud Ahmadinejad.

Iranian women comprise 50 percent of the voting population and hold significant power not only in their abilities to elect public officials but in their potential to hold political positions themselves. For example, Mohammad Khatami's victories in the 1997 and 2001 presidential elections were due mostly to his overwhelming support from Iranian women.[14] In addition, women comprised nearly 11 percent of all the local council representatives elected in 2003. Interestingly, there are more rural female representatives than urban ones.[15] Iranian women also head a few governmental organizations as well as hold seats in the

Parliament. The number of women parliamentary candidates has increased from 3 percent in the First *Majles* (1980–1984) to almost 10 percent in the Seventh *Majles* (2004–2008).[16] Furthermore, in 1996, the Ministry of Justice appointed 200 women judicial counselors to promote women's rights in the courts. Women activists like Shirin Ebadi have also worked tirelessly for women's rights under the Islamic Republic. Family law in Iran has been a particular focus of women activists in government because it regulates marriage, divorce, child custody, and women's right to work. Their efforts have not been without success. For example, divorce laws were reformed to ensure that divorced woman would receive adequate financial compensation for all of the years that they provided housework and childcare for their husbands (*nafaqeh*). This type of compensation for divorced women does not even exist in the United States because domestic work is not counted as real labor, since it is not paid.

Women were encouraged to participate in politics from the very beginning of the Islamic Republic. Ayatollah Ruhollah Khomeini considered the participation of women crucial to Iran's development and even to his own political success. Several times Khomeini praised women for their efforts and participation. He called them the "lion-hearted ones whose great efforts saved Islam from the foreigners (and) who alongside men secured victory for Islam."[17] In addition, due to the religious nature of the social movements promoted by Khomeini after the Revolution, a number of women who under normal circumstances would not have been involved became mobilized. Women entered the political sphere more than ever before and took the lead in several protests and in a number of new social organizations, such as the national literacy and family planning programs. Their new involvement in the Islamic state gave them opportunities to encourage change from within. "As the state called on women's voluntary efforts to deal with services that it could not provide, women's groups could put pressure on the state for more equality and political power as was the case for many health workers."[18] The more women were encouraged to become involved, the more they realized the worth of their efforts and the possibilities to effect change.

Khomeini's various social justice *jihads* drew in women from various backgrounds to help rebuild the nation. The *Jihad-e sazandegi* [Reconstruction struggle], for example, mobilized many devoted Muslim women to help rebuild the rural economy as part of their religious duty to build an Islamic nation. Similarly the *Basij-e Khaharan* [Sisters' Mobilization] brought many women together in an effort to make food and clothing for soldiers during the war with Iraq.[19] Many of these women were trained in basic first aid and worked in hospitals due to staff shortages. Brave Iranian women filled personnel vacancies where shortages occurred in other areas and at times even took up arms alongside men on the front line. Women were actually part of trained units and were given firearms to join men in the field. Women who were part of the *Basij* were well trained and an important part of Iran's defense forces. Women in Iran since the Revolution have contributed incredible amounts of time and resources to their country. At times it was their voluntary efforts that held the nation together. Furthermore, in recent years there has been a considerable increase in the amount of volunteer community work done by women. Women picked up the slack, and, as a result, there emerged new neighborhood organizations run by women to deal with issues such as protecting the environment through recycling programs.[20] Without its women volunteers and activists Iran's local environment would be in a worse state as these women bind together the fabric of the Nation.

New gender-specific governmental organizations were also created for the first time following the Islamic Revolution. The government established a number of institutions or organizations linked to the three branches of government. They include the Special Commission for Women and Youth, affiliated with the Expediency Council, and the Women's Social and Cultural Council, affiliated with the High Council of the Revolution. The most important organization is the Center for Women's Participation, which makes recommendations to both the executive and legislative branches. The head of this organization reports to the office of the president.[21] The Iranian Parliament also has a Special Commission for Family, Women, and Youth. Women's issues are consistently the topic of political discussions and campaigns. During his two terms as president, many of Khatami's speeches were addressed specifically to women. For example, he said, "We want a woman who is the pivot of the home to be manager and master of the house. At the same time, there should be absolutely no reduction in her social responsibilities and active presence in society."[22] Iranian women's political activism is a source of inspiration for women in the rest of the region.

Publishing

Since 2005, under Ahmadinejad's presidency, there has been a significant clampdown on newspapers, websites, and magazines, and this trend has impacted upon publications run by women and aimed at women. The closing of one of the most important women's journals, *Zanan*, in 2008, for example, was a great loss because *Zanan* had been a voice for gender equality for over a decade.[23] Women's magazines have contributed to establishing and setting the foundation for a forum of social and political protest in Iran. Many editors and journalists still continue to challenge social norms and governmental policies to keep the spirit of resistance alive. Since the early 1990s, women's magazines have provided alternative spaces of expression and played a crucial role in publicizing and disseminating intellectual debates on the condition of women. Magazines like *Zanan, Farzaneh, Payam-e Hajar, Zan-e Ruz, Huquq-e Zanan, Zan,* and *Zan-e Emruz* have exposed women publishers increasingly in such a way that has led to an increased focus domestically and internationally on women. According to Azadeh Kian, "Women's magazines play a crucial role in developing civic practices by creating contexts for political interaction between women and the ruling elite."[24] Indeed, these magazines highlight contributions from reformist clerics, who are increasingly attentive to the situation of women under Islamic law. These clerics contend that the current laws need to be adapted to the realities of contemporary Iranian society, in which women fully participate in social, economic, and cultural activities.

Political and religious authorities are aware of the significant social impact of these magazines and often respond to critical articles that they publish. The office of the Head of the Judiciary, for example, responded on several occasions to articles published in women's magazines.[25] These magazines publish highly intellectual debates and even popular articles about taboo topics. For example, *Zanan* published stories on violence against women, single-mother households, the spread of AIDs, and the plight of many runaway girls.[26] By constantly tackling taboo subjects, the magazine pushes the limit of what is acceptable to discuss. The articles increase awareness and open up opportunities for women to have further public involvement. Shala Sherkat, founding and chief editor of *Zanan*, 1992 to 2008, wrote in the first editorial of the magazine:

> We believe that the solution to women's problems lies in four areas: religion, culture, law, and education. In the name of religion, they (traditionalists) have wanted to hide women away in the home, to make them believe that they are instruments of biological reproduction ... that they do not need science, awareness, and social participation.... In our culture, women are regarded as the second sex and a secondary subject who have no personality without their husbands and gain respect only because of their children.... A part of the law is derived from religious interpretations that do not account for the factors of time and space.... Education is one of the foundations of individual awareness and enables women to rediscover themselves.[27]

Sherkat has pointed out that it is through these magazines that women are able both to educate and empower themselves. Sherkat herself has become somewhat of a heroine to young Iranian women with her dedication and bold criticisms. Throughout the magazine's 15 years in print, it has suffered from budgetary constraints and threats of closure (which became a reality in 2008). The writers for *Zanan* set the foundation and provided a platform where discussions about women's issues were catalyzed and encouraged, leaving a legacy that will remain for years to come.

Zanan owed much of its success and popularity to the fact that it advocated a brand of feminism that derived its legitimacy from Islam but still drew upon Western feminist sources. It spoke directly to the beliefs of a majority of Iranian women. This "middle of the road" position particularly resonated with the growing population of youth who remained connected to religion but were eager for change, especially political and social evolution. *Zanan*, despite its religious undertones, at times even collaborated with secular Iranian feminists. "*Zanan* is a voice of dissent ... [of people called] *now-andisheh-e dini* (new religious thought).... [They] show a refreshingly pragmatic vigor and willingness to engage with non-religious perspectives and seek dialogue with secular intellectuals."[28] Ideas are not rejected simply because they are Western, and nor is Islam seen "as a blueprint with a built-in and fixed program for social action."[29] The writers and editors of *Zanan* believed that Islam was flexible and its tenets could be interpreted to encourage pluralism and democracy; in effect, Islam should allow for change across time and space.

The editors of *Farzaneh* held very similar ideas to those espoused in *Zanan*. Its co-editors are Mahbubeh Ommi and Ma'sumeh Ebtekar (whom Khatami appointed as Iran's first woman vice president, 1997 to 2005; earlier, in 1979 to 1981, Ebtekar had been spokeswoman for the students holding the American hostages in Tehran). They stated,

> We are for the equality of rights between men and women and believe that, according to the Qur'an, men and women are equal. We should make a distinction between Islam and patriarchal traditions. Our laws largely are founded on some unreliable *hadith*, narrated by religious authorities. Several articles of the Civil Code, including those concerning the right to divorce and those prohibiting women's access to the judiciary are among them. It is necessary that religious reformists examine the authenticity of those laws and purify the Civil Code of spurious articles.[30]

Since *Farzaneh* began in 1993, just one year after *Zanan*, the magazine has printed several articles using esteemed religious figures to promote women's rights. The Prophet Mohammad is repeatedly cited owing to his esteem for women as reflected in the Qur'an.[31] They also highlight the Prophet's wife, Khadejah, his daughter, Fatemah, and his granddaughter, Zainab, for their political and religious leadership roles. Discussing women's legal rights from a religious perspective makes many of the demands in women's magazines more effective in influencing change than those of their secular counterparts. The use of Islam as a common language has been the key to their success. For example, the magazine *Payam-e Hajar*, which is edited by Azam Taleghani, provides a dynamic reinterpretation of Qur'anic verses.[32] In an article titled "The Necessity for the Reform of Laws Concerning Divorce, Polygyny, and Child Custody," published in 1992, the author refuted the legalization of polygyny and proposed a new interpretation of the verse (4:3) used to legitimize it. The author maintained, "God has recommended polygyny only in the case of social need, and only if men can preserve equity between their wives."[33] Furthermore, the magazine *Huquq-e Zanan* prints articles that reject men's unilateral right to divorce and challenge the established views on the subject.[34]

The use of magazines, therefore, has been one of the most powerful tools for expression and education that women in Iran have had at their disposal. "Women can now develop meaning making powers together, transform their grievances from private issues into public and political stakes, and ultimately challenge institutions."[35] The more that women are published and can expose gender inequalities as contrary to Islam, the more protection and rights they can obtain. This is a tactic used by women across the globe in order to give them some immunity as they fight for their rights. Shirin Ebadi mentions in her memoir that once she had reached a certain level of international recognition the Iranian government could no longer touch her without risking an international upheaval and protest.

Publishing stories about Iran's first women pilot or the country's first woman racing car ace is also important to advance the status of women in Iran as a whole.[36] The editor of *Zanan*, Shahla Sherkat, says, "I am always hopeful. In journalism, nothing is impossible."[37] Sherkat carries the dreams and determination of all Iranian women in that statement. The unprecedented unity that exists between Iranian women despite their divergent views makes them a powerful force to be reckoned with, as was evident in the aftermath of the June 2009 elections.

Cinema

Due to the nature of the censorship laws under the Islamic Republic, Iranian men and women have become extremely creative and resourceful in disguising their political opinions through different styles and mediums. This is especially notable in the making of films. According to Norma Moruzzi, "Government prohibitions on filmed violence, on any physical contact between (non-related) female and male actors, and restrictions on the import of mainstream commercial foreign films has paradoxically led to an extremely innovative film industry."[38] Especially after Iran's war with Iraq, women directors have produced films that challenge the depiction of women as docile social beings with no real decision-making capabilities. The film industry in Iran is extremely successful and has earned an international reputation. Iranian filmmakers tend to produce films with strong social commentary illustrated by complicated symbols and creative dialogues. Women have also established themselves as highly respected filmmakers with a popularity that often exceeds that of their male colleagues. In recent films women characters contradict the previous roles with strong and assertive personalities. Women now have roles as strong and authoritative characters. For example, in the 2001 film *Secret Ballot* directed by Babak Payami, the main character is a woman who is sent to a remote island to collect ballots for an upcoming election. This woman ballot collector holds the highest rank of the characters in the film. She is a very strong, independent, empowered, and determined character and, although she is wearing very conservative *hejab*, she marches all over the island (violating some traditional codes of female behavior) to collect ballots. This determined woman is the only person in the film trying to work toward change, and she is a heroine. This is just one of many films directed by a male that challenge the traditional roles of women. Other male filmmakers even praise the role of women and criticize the negative impact of traditional views, which hinder women's progress.

Women film directors are extremely popular and have a significant influence on public opinion through their films. Tahmineh Milani is sometimes considered to be the most popular woman in Iran. She is best known for her strong feminist and political convictions. She has directed several films including *Two Women*, *The Hidden Half*, *The Legend of a Sigh*, and *The Children of Divorce*. Her 2001 film, *The Hidden Half*, led to her arrest because it showed the brutal suppression of left-wing student groups by Islamic groups during the two years following the Revolution.[39] When she was arrested, protests erupted and women came out into the streets to support her. She was released after two weeks, although the charges against her of supporting counter-revolutionaries have never been dropped. Another important female director is Rakhshan Bani-Etemad who has been making films since 1978. Bani-Etemad ranks with Milani as one of the leading female directors in Iran. She pushes censorship codes to the very edge with her social realism films. In *Under the Skin of the City, Narges, The May Lady, The Blue Veiled*, and *Our Times*, she addresses poverty, criminality, divorce, polygny, social norms, women's oppression, and Iranian culture.[40] Samira Makhmalbaf is noteworthy, as she was the youngest film director in Iran, and perhaps the world, when, at the age of 17, she made her first film, *The Apple*, in 1998. She left public school at 14 to enroll in the special film school established by her father, the internationally acclaimed film director Mohsen Makhmalbaf. She has produced several more films in the past decade, including *Blackboards*, and *At Five in the Afternoon*. Her mother, Marziyeh Meshkini, is another director who focuses on how Iranian culture and tradition affect women. In her debut film, *The Day I Became a Woman*, Meskini advocates for women's rights by using subtlety, symbolism, and honesty.[41] Maryam Shahriar also produced an interesting film entitled *Daughters of the Sun*. The lead role in this film is a woman who plays the character of a girl who must dress up as a boy and leave her village to find work. She tackles controversial issues in this film especially since the lead character has her head uncovered and shaved. All of these women directors are very effective in producing films that use artistic expression to address particular political concerns.

The commentary in Iranian films is definitely impressive but can be confusing sometimes to the uninformed viewer. Films regarding the situation of women often use the personal story of one woman as a prism of national experience. According to Norma Moruzzi, "Everything is more complicated than an outsider would first expect, and the codes seem impossible to comprehend. It's easy to make mistakes; it's easy to misread the signs."[42] Probably one of the most important effects of films directed by women is that they give women a chance to share their opinions about life as women in the Islamic Republic. The social and political changes that have occurred over the past 30 years have had tremendous impacts upon the lives of women, and films are one way to digest these changes collectively. In her discussion of films directed by women, Moruzzi argues that the most important aspect is the "effort at understanding itself."[43] It is the actual engagement and dialogue about each woman's own life and the lives of others that is so essential. This dialogue is critical to the women's movement in Iran. It has promoted unprecedented solidarity among women from differing backgrounds and ideologies due to their shared experiences.

> The present openings of political and cultural reform were not only about regaining a separation of the public and the private (about getting the government out of decisions about who could watch satellite television and who would wear a head scarf) but were also about recognizing the intersection between personal and political life.[44]

Women in their own lives and as a collective negotiate this fine line between the personal and political every day. Feminists in Iran hope to define this line more clearly in such a way that all women will be free to have sovereignty over their participation and actions.

Sports

Sports and the stadium, in the Islamic Republic, became both a place of state propaganda and popular resistance and protest. Politics played itself out on the field and in the stands. Sports in many ways were the only outlet for many Iranian males, but women were also determined to get their fair share of the excitement. During the first years of the Islamic Republic, women's sporting activities were virtually non-existent, while before the Revolution they were only available to a minority of women who did not mind playing side by side with men. Due to the lack of public facilities, however, women began to move their private athletic activities into public spaces. Kian recounts a specific example of this movement when women began to jog in the streets and public parks, which enraged the Revolutionary Guards and municipal authorities.[45] The latter (males) declared that women were prohibited from engaging in sports in public and that women's athletics were provocative. Despite the anger of the authorities, women continued to jog in public, and this led to daily clashes between determined women and those who wished to enforce the law. These clashes, however, only inspired more women to take to the streets, and more women began to run in public parks. This movement had begun in upper-class areas, but it gradually spread to lower-class areas. Women's determination and numbers eventually brought them victory, and the authorities (reluctantly) approved of their outdoor sporting activities by designating several parks – Chitgar, Ayatollah Taligani, Sorkh-e Hesar, and Lavisan in Tehran – for women's sporting activities.[46]

Furthermore, since the 1990s, women's sporting clubs have grown and flourished in the wealthy neighborhoods of Tehran and other large cities. Eventually these facilities spread to less wealthy neighborhoods and even to very poor areas. Gholamhosain Karbaschi, Tehran's mayor in the early 1990s, created the Bahman Cultural and Sports Center in southwest Tehran (a relatively low-income area). Because of Karbaschi's efforts, poorer women gained the opportunity to participate in swimming, gymnastics, computer lessons, and drawing, all of which were all offered at this center.[47] Bahman significantly changed and impacted upon the lives of the many women who used its facilities. Many of the women came from conservative families, and this was their first opportunity to learn to swim or even to draw.

Another significant achievement was the formation of the Muslim Women's Olympic Games, which allowed female athletes from various Muslim countries to compete with each other for the first time in 1993 in Tehran. Furthermore, the daughter of former president Rafsanjani, Faezeh Hashemi, has been a prominent advocate for women's sport in Iran. Even though she is a devout Muslim who respects the segregation of the sexes, she does not accept restrictions by clerics on women athletes: "Now that sports facilities are segregated, more women can freely practice their favorite sports."[48] Her main concern is reconciling Islamic laws with the guidelines for international competition. She is extremely active in promoting flexibility in order to facilitate the inclusion of women athletes in international competitions.

Contrary to Western stereotypes, religious and conservative women like Hashemi have been some of the strongest advocates for women's sports. During the 1990s, Hashemi, herself, was a member of the leadership council of Fifth *Majles*, vice-president of the National Olympic Committee, and a member of the Islamic Republic's High Council for Women's Sports. She defended women's outdoor cycling (which had been banned along with soccer) by saying,

> Women's outdoor cycling is neither illegal nor illicit…. It has become a political issue because it was proposed during legislative elections and those who opposed it bestowed a political dimension on it. After all, their opposition was beneficial to outdoor cycling, for now there is a significant demand for it.[49]

Every activity that the government banned seems only to have made it more popular. For example, women were banned from going to soccer games, but when the Iranian team qualified for the World Cup thousands of women stormed Azadi Stadium. According to Marcus Gerhardt, the way women boldly defied the government demonstrates that this was no small thing in terms of resistance or dismissal of state policies:

> Official rules, however, failed to deter female spectators from literally invading stadiums in the late 1990s. For example, conservatives were powerless to stop spontaneous outpouring of women supporters who joined the mass celebrations at Azadi Stadium in 2 December 1997 to welcome the national team home from Australia following the qualification there to participate in the Soccer World Cup. Similarly, some one thousand women stormed the sports hall hosting the Asian Volleyball Championship and occupied – without permission – nearly a fifth of the spectator seats. As if there had not been a clear enough disregard for state policy, the women both young and old, entered into an intricate dialogue of singing and chanting with the male spectators. Beginning with a particular song or slogan, one side would cajole and tempt the other side to sing even louder, as the songs were chanted back and forth, the volume and rhythm rose to end in a deafening and euphoric crescendo of general celebration. However, the women spectators' enthusiasm had not yet reached its high point; as the Iranian volleyball team entered, led by star player Behnam Mahmoodi – undoubtedly one of the main reasons for such a large female contingency – the stadium was struck by a high-pitched screeching. As Mahmoodi and his fellow players warmed up, the female spectators began to chant, "Mahmoodi

dustarim, Iran dustarim" (We love Mahmoodi, we love Iran). Although their enthusiasm was largely an expression of the desire for entertainment, joy and fun, it was at the same time a protest against conservatives' obsession with discipline and moral order.[50]

Sports have been and are likely to continue to be an important place for women to use their voice both on and off the field. Iranian women have demonstrated their resolve and some have become phenomenal athletes. Their strength does not necessarily come from their physique. Rather, it comes from their hearts and souls. Iranian women are determined to struggle for equality with men in sports facilities and opportunities.

Clothing

Clothing is a tool that has been manipulated consistently by *all* Iranian governments since the 1930s. The regime of Reza Shah Pahlavi (r. 1925–1941) forced Western clothing on Iranians and instituted mandatory deveiling of women in public. The Islamic regime, in contrast, has made the veil mandatory in public and has promoted non-Western clothing. The result of using attire for political purposes is that now every private act or gesture in defiance of official rules becomes a political statement. The way one wears a scarf, the color of one's shirt, the length of one's *manteau*, or the amount of make-up one wears, all are political acts in Iran. Journalist Azadeh Moaveni titled her book *Lipstick Jihad* in reference to the politics of appearance in Iran.[51] If a woman is "religious," then she tends to wear the black *chador*. If a woman is not strictly religious, then she is apt to wear a *manteau* and headscarf in dull colors. Secular women, however, prefer, especially if they are young, to wear bright scarves that may be half-way off their heads, apply overemphasized make-up, and don overcoats that barely reach the knees and have shorter sleeves. Marjane Satrapi pokes fun at this phenomenon in her graphic "memoir," *Persepolis*. After the Revolution, the way people dressed became an ideological sign, as the character drawn to represent her says in one frame: "You would show your opposition to the regime by showing a few strands of your hair."[52] Although she illustrates the difference between a "fundamentalist" man or woman and a "modern" man or woman in a comical way, her book underlines the political importance of an individual's appearance in Iran. Indeed, since June 2009 there has been the new and unofficial addition of the color green – ironically the color of Islam – to the dress code, as it was the campaign color of presidential candidate Mir-Hosain Mousavi, and subsequently of the Green protest movement. Since that controversial election, those who wear green boldly display their disappointment and disagreement with the current regime. In the protests throughout the summer and fall of 2009, and even into 2010, both women in traditional *chadors* and skimpy *manteuxs* could be seen wearing green in solidarity with the Green Movement.

The most debated visible piece of clothing that now defines Muslim politics around the globe is the veil. Since the nineteenth century, the veil to Western political elites has symbolized the inferiority and backwardness of Muslim culture, and it continues to be an extremely powerful symbol. Indeed, the veil, as a symbol of the oppression of women, has been used to galvanize support for military intervention in the Middle East. In 2001 to 2003, U.S. President George W. Bush used the veil, or *hejab*, to justify American military attacks on Afghanistan and Iraq.[53] *Hejab* is being debated fiercely in Europe, and in countries like France the government has even gone to the extreme of banning Muslim girls from wearing any kind of head covering in public schools. The Western perceptions of *hijab* are clouded by racism and orientalist ideas. There is no understanding that a scarf covers a woman's head and not her brain or ability to speak for herself. The Swiss recently upheld their decision to ban headscarves at least on the basketball court and some schools in Belgium have also joined the ranks.

While the meaning of the veil in Western culture has remained static and unchanging, its function and social significance has changed tremendously for Muslims in the Middle East and in the West. "Veiling is a lived experience full of contradictions and multiple meanings."[54] Women all over the globe veil for different reasons: political, religious, or simply as a fashion statement. Yet, in the West the veil has never been portrayed as anything more than a tool for the oppression of women. Ironically, the veil has been used to liberate many women from the confines of their homes and to facilitate their presence in the public space, which was not accessible to them as long as they wore *hejab*. According to Shahrzad Mojab, "while it [hejab] clearly has been a mechanism in the service of patriarchy, a means of regulating and controlling women's lives, women have used the same social institution to free themselves from the bonds of patriarchy."[55] Women in Iran are using their clothing to express their ideas as well as using it as a ticket into previously male-dominated spaces. Observing *hejab* has been very helpful to women by protecting them from harassment and treatment solely as a sex-object. "It makes you safer in society," says a Tehran University student named Farnaz. "Of course it would be better if it were not obligatory. But it is very bad the way that men look at women without *hejab*."[56] The *hejab* has become useful like any other sort of tool that may be used both to help and to hurt. The largest concern about clothing for women in Iran is not so much the *hejab* as the lack of personal choice in what they wear. Every day, women exert bold gestures in their clothing choices to challenge the control of the government in their lives.

Conclusion

Due to their extensive involvement, the nature of women's demands has changed from "I want" to "I deserve" or "I am entitled to."[57] Women's presence in education, politics, publishing, sports, and film gives many women activists the justification to challenge the government for their demands of equal pay and equal opportunity. Empowerment has been defined as the "process by which people take control and action to overcome obstacles.[58] Women in Iran, according to this definition, are definitely empowered and will continue to become more so in the future. The overwhelming participation of women in the current Green Movement illustrates the presence of a population of women who are aware, active, and determined to stand up for what they believe. The government cannot ignore this involved and educated portion of the population, a fact that those who are pro-regime acknowledge.[59] Despite criticisms, the fact that Ahmadinejad selected women for his cabinet shows that there is a consciousness about the importance of women in politics whether political and religious beliefs are conservative or reformist. Iranian women understand that the government needs them and their work, and this awareness is a powerful bargaining chip. Women have been a main force of change in Iran and the change they seek is fundamental.

Notes

1 Golnar Mehran, "Lifelong Learning: New Opportunities for Women in a Muslim Country (Iran)," *Comparative Education*, 35 (1999), p. 203.
2 Ibid., p. 204.
3 R. Bahramitash, "Market Fundamentalism versus Religious Fundamentalism: Women's Employment in Iran," *Critique*, 13, 1 (spring 2004), p. 37.
4 Mehran, "Lifelong Learning," p. 205.
5 Khomeini's *jihads* may be compared to such U.S. programs as the War on Poverty and the Head Start Program.
6 Mehran, "Lifelong Learning," p. 205.
7 F. Harrison, "Women Graduates Challenge Iran," *BBC Online*, September 16, 2006.
8 Bahramitash, "Market Fundamentalism," p. 44.
9 Pooya Alaedini and Mohammad Reza Razavi, "Women's Participation and Employment in Iran: A Critical Examination," *Critique*, 14, 1 (spring 2005), p. 67.
10 Ibid.
11 Ibid., p. 70.
12 Ibid., p. 69.
13 Ibid., p. 68.
14 See further Azadeh Kian-Thiébaut, "Women and the Making of Civil Society in Post-Islamist Iran," in Eric Hooglund (ed.) *Twenty Years of Islamic Revolution: Political and Social Change in Iran since 1979*, New York: Syracuse University Press, 2002, pp. 56–59.
15 Heshmat Moinfar, "Women in Politics: Whispers of Power in Iran," (unpublished paper) Center for Women's Studies, University of Tehran, 2006.
16 Ibid.
17 Ibid.
18 Bahramitash, "Market Fundamentalism," p. 44.
19 Roksana Bahramitash, "Islamic Fundamentalism and Women's Economic Role: The Case of Iran," *International Journal of Politics, Culture and Society*, 16 (2003), p. 39.
20 Ibid., p. 43.
21 Alaedini and Razavi, "Women's Participation," p. 69.
22 Mehran, "Lifelong Learning," p. 202.
23 On the role of *Zanan*, see further Kian-Thiébaut, "Women and the Making of Civil Society," pp. 65, 66–67.
24 Ibid., p. 66.
25 Azadeh Kian-Thiébaut, "Political and Social Transformation in Post-Islamist Iran," *Middle East Report*, 1999, p. 15.
26 Haleh Esfandiari, "Iranian Women, Please Stand Up," *Foreign Policy*, November 9, 2005.

27 Quoted in Kian-Thiébaut, "Women and the Making of Civil Society," p. 65.
28 Ziba Mir-Hosseini, "Religious Modernists and the 'Woman Question,'" in Eric Hooglund (ed.) *Twenty Years of Islamic Revolution: Political and Social Change in Iran since 1979*, Syracuse University Press, 2002, p.76.
29 Ibid.
30 Quoted in Kian-Thiébaut, "Women and the Making of Civil Society," p. 67.
31 Ibid.
32 Ibid., pp. 67–68. Azam Taleghani is a very influential activist and has been extremely effective in reforming rape laws to protect women's rights. She is a conservative that few dare to challenge. The fact that she was raped in front of her father, Ayatollah Mahmud Taleghani, while imprisoned with him under the Shah in the 1970s, has given her unique power and influence.
33 Ibid., p. 68.
34 Ibid., p. 67.
35 Ibid., p. 66.
36 Shirin Ebadi, *Iran Awakening*, New York: Random House, 2006.
37 Esfandiari, "Iranian Women, Please Stand Up."
38 Norma Claire Moruzzi, "Women in Iran: Notes on Film and from the Field," *Feminist Studies* (spring 2001), p. 91.
39 Sherri Whatley, "Iran Women Film Directors: A Clever Activism," *off our backs* (2003), p. 32.
40 Ibid., p. 31.
41 Ibid., pp. 30–34.
42 Moruzzi, "Women in Iran," pp. 99–100.
43 Ibid., p. 94.
44 Ibid., p. 98.
45 Kian-Thiébaut, "Women and the Making of Civil Society," pp. 70–71.
46 Ibid., p. 71.
47 Ibid.
48 Quoted in Lamis Andoni, "Iran's New Activist Seeks Life for Women beyond the Veil," *Christian Science Monitor*, March 28, 1995.
49 Quoted in Kian-Thiébaut, "Women and the Making of Civil Society," p. 71.
50 M.Gerhardt, "Sports and Civil Society in Iran," in Eric Hooglund (ed.) *Twenty Years of Islamic Revolution: Political and Social Change in Iran since 1979*, New York: Syracuse University Press, 2002, p. 50.
51 Azadeh Moaveni, *Lipstick Jihad*, New York: Public Affairs, 2005.
52 Marjane Satrapi, *Perspolis*, Paris: L'Association, 2003, p. 75.
53 On the political use of the veil, see further Roksana Bahramitash, "The War on Terror, Feminist Orientalism and Orientlalist Feminism: Case Studies of Two North American Best Sellers," *Critique*, 14, 2 (summer 2005), pp. 221–236.
54 Shahrzad Mojab, "The Politics of Theorizing "Islamic Feminism": Implications for International Feminist Movements," *WLUML Dossier*, 23–24 (2001), p. 4.
55 Ibid., p. 5.
56 Burton Bollag, "For Iranian Women, Conservative Dress Fosters Liberal Views on Campus," *Chronicle of Higher Education*, 46 (2000), p. 64.
57 Kian-Thiébaut, "Women and the Making of Civil Society," p. 64.
58 Mehran, "Lifelong Learning," p. 203.
59 Author interviews, Tehran, July 2009 and February 2010.

7 Post-revolutionary Iranian youth

The case of Qom and the new culture of ambivalence

Farhad Khosrokhavar

In the West, two major models of secularization have been paramount: the French model based on *laïcité* [laicism) and the Protestant model that operates within the framework of religion, cutting ties with the Catholic model and infusing democratic ideals and individual subjectivity within the religious mindset. In the Islamic world, and particularly in Iran, the two models co-exist side by side. There is no clear-cut choice of one or the other, although the Protestant model seems to be the most pertinent. One major feature of this new type of secularization within the framework of Islam is ambivalence. This has been accentuated by the role of the State,[1] which is a theocracy in Iran and which pushes for positioning individuals and institutions toward Islam in general, and the specific interpretation of Islam based on the concept of *velayat-e faqih* (the political domination of Islamic jurists) in particular.

The youth in Iran is not a monolithic social group, as is often the case in other complex societies. One major rift within Iranian youth is that between those living in small towns or traditional cities and those living in the large cities. Qom is a traditionalist city, home of the major ayatollahs [senior Shi'i Islamic clergy and scholars] and their seminaries [*howzeh*]. Here, a new youth has emerged, one that shares some of the features of its elders but also has many new characteristics that give it its peculiarity. As will be demonstrated in this chapter, ambivalence toward many significant social and cultural issues is one of the major characteristics of this youth. Contrary to the dominant trend within the Iranian intelligentsia that interprets ambivalence in a negative sense (see below), I propose here a dynamic view of ambivalence with regard to the behavior patterns of the young girls and boys in Qom. The changes within the family, the affective relations, marriage, politics, the clergy, and the world at large are at the core of this ambivalence.

Changes within the family

The empirical research on which this study relies amply underscores changes within the family:[2] the interviews show that the image of the father has changed, even in a traditional city like Qom.[3] At the dawn of the Islamic Revolution of 1979, with the exception of a minority of modernized middle-class people in the larger cities, the overwhelming majority of Iranians lived within a patriarchal family structure, where the figure of the father was not unlike that of the Godhead. Symbolically, the revolutionary leader, Ayatollah Ruhollah Khomeini, was the magnified figure of the father or even the grandfather, combining the symbolic dimensions of patriarchy and political Islam. Nevertheless, one major fact was prominent in the Islamic Revolution: Despite the fact that the symbolic meaning of Islam was different among the traditional people, the modernized youth, and the different strata of the population, the Revolution intended, among other aims, to restore the broken social bonds, in particular for the "oppressed" *[mostaz'afin]*, who were perceived as the downtrodden and repressed of the Shah's program of modernization from above; many people believed that this would be done by re-establishing the social justice ideals and moral codes that were embedded in patriarchal interpretations of Shi'i Islam.

However, by the early 2000s, a major change had occurred: The majority of the Iranian population live in urban areas; the rate of literacy is significantly higher than before the Revolution; more than 2.5 million students attend universities; and modernization has reached out to many people of different social classes. In a city like Qom, where political and cultural domination by traditionalist groups (the clergy, bazaar, and small shopkeepers catering to the pilgrimage trade) is still very significant, the interviews reveal a new type of attitude toward authority and, more specifically, toward the authority of fathers and mothers. Its structure has altered dramatically in its symbolic dimensions and the figurehead of the father in the early 2000s would be closer to that of Mohammad Khatami, the former president (1997–2205), who did not rule according to patriarchal legitimacy but rather in a semi-fraternal manner, as compared with Khomeini, the founder of the Islamic Republic who embodied the figurehead of the patriarch. Even President Mahmud Ahmadinejad's populist figure is not that of an inflexible father, comparable with Khomeini but closer to that of a crony, a blood relative who helps his buddies and extended family in a non-hierarchic way.

One significant change has been for the father to get affectively closer to his children and in particular, to his daughters. Since girls are better educated than women of their mothers (the proportion of girls attending university is over 50 percent of all students and since 2005 the proportion of their success in the entry examinations for universities has been superior to men), they increasingly share men's universe, and their fathers treat them more and more, according to what young women report, like the boys, at least in matters that do not call into question female modesty and the issue of virginity.

Whereas in the past gender relations were mostly authority oriented, they are, within the family, much more "discussion oriented." Girls do reason and put forward arguments that are of the same nature as those used by their male counterparts. This is true in relation to their brothers and other members of the family. The girls' better education and their access to high school and university makes the cultural universe of the girls more and more akin to that of the boys, and in this respect they are closer to men's culture than ever before.

Family relations have changed in two different ways: children and parents are effectively closer to each other as the patriarchal image is increasingly questioned; girls and boys share more of the same culture, and, in this respect, an implicit equality is set in motion, with the notable exception of sexuality, especially in Qom (but less so in Tehran). Many older girls complain that parents in Qom do not see them as capable of working and living independently, unlike in Tehran. These views persist even though older girls have their high school diplomas and have demonstrated their capacity to handle the same problems as young men. The girls denounce the patriarchal culture of the religious city and ask for more equality, in particular with respect to gender relations and employment. However, the only place where the Qomi culture tolerates women working is in the educational field, because girls and boys study in gender-segregated schools. Thus, it is acceptable for women to become teachers in girls' schools or to be members of their administrative staff. Here, the major stumbling block is not only the patriarchal interpretation of religion but the city's dominant culture based on rumor-mongering and hearsay. There is an obsession about what others might say "behind one's back," as gossip can ruin one's reputation in the eyes of others. The traditional culture of mutual surveillance has become the obsession of many boys and girls. Many young men said that they would be disturbed if their future wives worked in the private sector, because neighbors would spread rumors about their inability to supervise their wife's modesty. They would lose their "sexual honor" and their wives would be treated as frivolous, even "immodest." The combination of patriarchal Islam and a culture of mutual surveillance and redoubtable rumor-mongering is at the heart of men's suspicion toward women's job aspirations in Qom. Some young women share this preoccupation, although they treat it as a prejudice against them and one to be fought against. What they fear is not so much Islam, but the fact that working outside one's home would entail suspicion toward them and the denial to them of Islamic modesty. In this respect, even the young girl preserves the major ingredients of the "culture of modesty," unlike in Tehran where it is being eroded by the inroads of secular modernization. Ambivalence is at the heart of it: The need to free oneself from the constraints of tradition and a culture based on mutual surveillance (the eye of the neighbor who follows young girls step by step in their neighborhood) and, at the same time, the anguish toward a modernity that breaks down social protection and leaves the individual alone in the large cities. In this respect, the "transformed culture of modesty" is an ambivalent means to deal with the contradictory aspects of modernization by selecting one's own preferences within the new framework, transforming the old one but withholding some of its major features.

The role of the family has changed in particular with regard to marriage. As recently as the early 1980s, the institution of marriage in Qom, as in most parts of Iran, was based on an alliance of two families. The role of the bride and the groom was at best marginal. By the early 2000s, even in Qom this role of marriage had been transformed. Still, the parents' role is still decisive. Mojtaba, a young man, stressed the role of his parents before introducing the "rationality" of their potential opposition:

Q: How do you intend to get married? According to your parents' choice or you own?

MOJTABA: She should please me, first of all, I would want to know her opinion about (of me), and then we should visit her parents to ask for her hand, but all of it should be done by respecting the traditions.

Q: If your parents reject the girl?

MOJTABA: She probably has some shortcomings. Still, I'll ask them if there is a reasonable problem (that makes them reject the girl)...

Q: And if [their opposition] isn't reasonable?

MOJTABA: If it is not reasonable, I'll talk to them some more, and we'll sort it out in the end.

Q: And if you cannot settle the problem with them?

MOJTABA: There isn't this single girl in the world. There are so many!.

Q: Isn't it important for you to marry the girl that you love? Are all the girls are the same?

MOJTABA: Up to now I haven't fallen in love with any girl. I might love one a little bit but not too much! I don't think so.[4]

This is a new culture of discussion and compromise with parents, one in which children have their say even though, in traditional families, the parents still have the final word. This is not only the case for the young men. Girls too ask to be heard, and even more to be listened to, in spite of the crushing influence of their parents. Inter-generational exchange and communication is still unsure and shy in Qom, especially in comparison with Tehran, where the new culture is much more outspoken and self-conscious.

The cultural and political influence of the clergy

In Qom, the major change is in the minds of the young female generation that aspire to work and to assert their ability outside the closed circle of the family. However, the other dimensions of the religious culture have not lost their grip on the youth generation. The reasons are religious as well as social and political. The clergy is very powerful here, and the grand ayatollahs dominate, each in his one way, the cultural and political life of the city. The central government is weak because the governor [*ostandar*] cannot impose the rules prevailing in other parts of Iran in cultural terms. For example, music (except for the songs of women) is acceptable in Iran except in Qom, where its use is much more restricted than elsewhere. Similarly, cinema, theater, concerts, and the teaching of music and the dramatic arts are widespread throughout Iran, albeit with restrictions barring any physical contact between men and women and the requirement that women wear *hejab*. In Qom, however, the overwhelming majority of clergy frown on all these activities with a tacit (and sometimes explicit) disapproval.

The public parks in large Iranian cities are places where young people of both sexes can gather, have their meetings, and sometimes talk, walk, and flirt discreetly under the shade of the trees, in particular during dusk when visibility is waning. In Qom, the only public park where youth can gather is patrolled regularly by the morals brigades, under the aegis of the Basij miliita, which in turn is under pressure from influential clergymen who denounce transgressions of Islamic laws, the immodesty of girls, the contagious influence of Tehran's mores, and the alleged laxity of the authorities.

In every notable middle-sized town in Iran, the semi-private Azad University has opened, leading to a cultural revolution whereby the local youth – both young men and women – mix socially despite sometimes attending gender-separate classes. While the quality of the teaching may leave much to be desired, the cultural and social modernization of the young generation within Azad's precincts is undeniable. In Qom, many ayatollahs deplore the "immoral" and "immodest" modernization initiated by the universities, in particular through the Azad University system, where young women learn to become autonomous, are taught modern sciences, and become alienated from the gender-segregated traditional culture with its taboos and restrictions. Nevertheless, the influence of the higher clergy is palpable in Qom, exercised through their persuasive power – they can declare an act "impure" and make it difficult for the people to ignore their religiously-motivated opinions; or their indirect economic clout – the bazaar merchants follow their rulings and all those jobs related to the bazaar are conditional upon respect for the clergy's religious declarations.

The Qom bazaar community itself is very conservative in its gender attitudes and adherence to traditional religious rituals. Many bazaaris are politically "quietist" and religiously pious; during public religious rituals (mainly the Moharram ceremonies and mourning of the martyrdom of the Prophet's family), they strengthen their corporatist bonds through self-flagellation and sharing collective meals. An important part of the city's economy is dependent upon the bazaar. Another part of the economy is tied to the religious tourism of thousands of pilgrims who come to Qom to visit the shrine to and tomb of Holy Fatimeh Ma'sumeh [Saint Fatimeh the Pure],[5] and for these pilgrims, respect for traditions, at least during their stay in Qom, is part of their religious duty. In all these cases, traditionalism is strengthened by the economic and cultural stakes as well as the presence of the two major conservative actors, the clergy and the bazaar merchants who impose their hegemonic view on the town. Another factor is the "culture of gossip." Even those people who are not religiously inclined or not tradition-bound fear the consequences of gossip. If a rumor circulates about the supposed "immodesty" of someone's daughter or the non-Islamic behavior of someone's son, then these youth will experience difficulties in their social relations. Many people will avoid their company; especially for girls accused of "frivolity," other girls will refuse to talk to them, and the culture of gossip isolates and stigmatizes them. It is as much this culture of gossip as the ascendancy of the clergy and the bazaar that contribute to the hegemony of traditionalist attitudes in Qom. The youth generations cannot contest this culturehead-on. They tend to soften some of its harsher attitudes, but not question it altogether.

Sexuality and its ambivalence

Whereas in many respects egalitarianism in the cultural field is making headway, even in a religious city like Qom, in particular between men and women, one major field escapes this tendency, and this is the field of sexuality. In Qom, sexuality still operates as a taboo. Girls and boys cannot socialize unless the final aim is explicitly marriage. Unlike Tehran where a de facto liberalization has occurred between the two sexes, in Qom and in many traditionalist desert towns in Iran, any premarital relations between men and women are strictly limited, and any transgression ends up with the durable dishonor of the girls. Here, inequality is obvious: Suspected of being in a non-authorized relationship, the girl loses her reputation and may no longer have access to the matrimonial market or aspire to a decent marriage. The reputation of a girl is of the utmost importance, and any behavior that calls it into question is to be avoided. Rumor-mongering and "behind-the-back" gossip about a girl operate in a perverse way in a city where traditionalism is the dominant value, the more so as the clergy dominate the cultural and political life of the city. Few dare to transgress its norms.

Gender relations outside of marriage are still very tenuous, but the new technologies, mainly the cell phone, have made the connections between young men and women easier. Before that, landline telephones could be controlled more easily by the parents, and a young man would not dare to call a girl. With the spread of cell phones, young men do call girls, but still, in the overwhelming majority of cases – and unlike in Tehran – the relationship is limited and rarely goes beyond brief exchanges of words, except among university students, who find occasions to exchange their ideas and feelings in a more relaxed way.

In one major respect, there is a change in gender relations. Up until the late 1980s, parents decided on the marriage of their children, in particular of their daughters. Although the interviews show that girls would decline to marry someone of whom their parents disapproved, the novelty is that they say they would refuse someone whom their parents would like to impose on them without their consent. The traditional "prearranged" marriage contract has been transformed into a "negotiated" marriage contract. The parents' say is still very important, but the younger generation refuses to submit entirely to the parents' verdict, and a new type of marriage is becoming dominant in which parents and their offspring discuss and negotiate the issue, bringing in their own views as part of the bargain. As many young women said, if the parents oppose their marriage with someone they loved, they would accept their verdict and renounce it, but if those very same parents intended to impose upon them someone whom they disliked, they would not accept their choice. The process of discussion and exchange of arguments has become part and parcel of the new youth subculture, and the parents are no longer able to impose on their children their own choice of a husband or wife.

Marriage is still a matter between two families, and the approval of the parents is one major part of it, but the future bride's view has become decisive and a tenuous individualism has made its way into the patriarchal structure. The fact that girls and boys are better educated than before, and in many cases cannot move simply into the footsteps of their parents has contributed to this change. For the first time, some girls and boys unhesitatingly pronounce the word "love" as a major component of their future marriage. This is proffered timidly, but it makes sense and denotes an individual dimension of marriage that cannot be summarized in the alliance of two families or the perpetuation of the family's name, but rather takes on an affective dimension that was previously largely absent. The place of love is still limited and many other considerations enter into play, such as the parents' approval, the "suitability" of the bride's parents, social class, and sharing the same culture (i.e., a man who is of a totally secular milieu from Tehran would have difficulties marrying a traditionalist girl whose parents believe that religion must shape their children's lives).

Gender relations: from a culture of segregation to a culture of partial participation

There is a universal sense of social and gender injustice among the young women who denounce gender inequality in the juridical and cultural spheres. This deep sense of injustice is itself quite new. Prior to the Islamic Revolution, it was shared only by intellectuals and a tiny minority of Westernized middle class men and women. By the early 2000s, even in a traditionalist city like Qom, this sentiment was very widely shared by women of almost every social class, even among clerical or bazaari young women.[6]

This sentiment of injustice is mainly the result of the modernization from below in Iran since 1979. The Islamic regime opened up vistas to young traditionalist girls by providing them access to school. Under the Shah, for many traditionalist groups the school was the site of moral depravation and therefore, in orthodox cities like Qom or even in other cities, including Tehran among many families attached to the patriarchal system, the trend was to avoid sending daughters to school and to find husbands for them at an early age. Although this traditional practice has not died out it has certainly been weakened, even among the staunchest patriarchal groups. The age of marriage has risen steadily in Iran, and even young brides get married at a much older age than was typical in the 1960s and 1970s; furthermore, the birth rate had fallen from 6.4 children per woman to 1.9 children by 2007.[7] This is a result of the acceptance by traditional families of the school system under the Islamic Republic. The access to schools and the university (girls constitute more than half of the successful candidates in the universities' entrance exams) has had a dramatic result: the gradual homogenization of the male and female subcultures. Before this modernization, women were restricted to the private sphere, even in urban areas, and among the lower and traditional classes they occupied a gender-segregated culture that was dominated by males in a patriarchal system. Women did not share men's culture but had their own subculture, with its rules and taboos. Among them, self-restriction in order to respect segregation played a major role. Even in those areas where women had to share men's work (in the tribal areas and in some rural areas where women worked outdoors, as in the rice fields in northern Iran), gender segregation was preserved, without being accompanied by exclusive indoor relations. Being restricted mainly to the private sphere and indoor ties, women were only mothers, sisters, daughters, and spouses. Even at the height of the Islamic Revolution in Iran in 1979, when large female crowds joined men to protest against the monarchist regime, except for a tiny minority of Westernized middle-class women, the overwhelming majority did so by assuming the role imparted to them by the patriarchal system. They protested against the "unjust" regime of the Shah that called into question the patriarchal system in an autocratic way.[8]

After three decades, the "Islamization" of the schools and higher education has had paradoxical results. It has contributed to the homogenization of the male and female subcultures to a degree that had been unheard of in the past. In the interviews, young men and women reason similarly, share arguments, discuss social issues, and in many ways take up positions in terms of "shared intersubjectivity," particularly in the political and social fields. In the cultural sphere, one major result of this partial homogenization has been the sentiment of injustice, which most of the young women resent deeply. Many young men do not share this feeling, because their access to the girls' universe is still restricted in Qom, and their parents believe and act in accordance with this dominant culture. Young women, however, despite their immersion in this culture where they are dominated by the patriarchal system in the name of Islam, have second thoughts and often express their malaise and their frustration with it. Initially, at the beginning of the interviews, they express their views in a language that is hesitant and shy, but they become more and more explicit after the dialogue with the interviewers, who include two young women. They are still under the aegis of a patriarchal culture, but they are already beyond it in the social and political sphere, the cultural domain being a much more disputed area among them. Some young women clearly denounce the injustice toward women, but most of them express their despair or their feeling of powerlessness toward a culture that does not recognize them as equals with men, although they have an educational level that matches, and sometimes even surpasses that of men. The accession to education has widened their horizons and given them a capacity to criticize and "distance" themselves from the dominant social relations. They think about this injustice but without imagining a new social framework within which they could shape their action with other women (unlike in Tehran). For some, the prestige and influence of the patriarchal version of Islam is paramount. Other women denounce the inequality in terms of job access, social and juridical recognition, and, in particular, marriage. The new female generation overwhelmingly rejects polygyny and claims the right to work, even though their husband might oppose it. When it comes to Islamic inheritance laws, however, and the practice of sons inheriting from their fathers twice as much as do daughters, many women accepted this tradition, justifying it because men carry the burden of the family subsistence, not women.

Thus, in many respects, gender inequality is more or less called into question but the contestation is far from confrontational. It is, at best, reactive and not pro-active in Qom, contrary to the situation in Tehran and other large cities where young women actively contest the patriarchal system. What is really new is the awareness of gender injustice in many other fields and the willingness to seek out solutions at the individual level, such as including in the marriage contract mention of the right to work or the denial of the right of polygyny to the husband, making any second marriage conditional upon the consent of the first spouse. If there is a social movement for the defense of women, these women would see it favorably, but they would not take the initiative in any feminist movement within their city.

Dominant culture of Qom

There is a minority of the youth generation that shares the secularized perception of religion and the more modern conception of social relations. However, such youth in Qom are, at best, a tiny minority, and the dominant culture is overwhelmingly one that imposes many restrictions in daily life in the name of the patriarchal version of Islam embodied in the clerical and bazaari domination of the city. This culture is maintained by the influential ayatollahs, and is supported as well by the bazaar and the traditionalist groups related to the bazaar. It still pervades daily life in the city, and this culture distinguishes Qom from Tehranin particular, but also from other Iranian cities.

For the youth generation, Tehran, which is only 90 minutes away by road, represents an escape from the restrictions of Qom. In Tehran, many Qom youth can experience autonomy, far from the close inspection of the family and the surrounding community. But Tehran is, at the same time, the symbol of unbridled freedom and sexual depravity that frightens many young people in Qom. They regard Tehran similar to the way in which many youth in Tehran regard Paris or New York. But Iran's capital also has the image of a Sodom and Gomora to many youth of Qom. These conflicting images demonstrate how paramount the influence of the capital is, particularly among those who have a family member living in Tehran or who went there to study at university.

With respect to clothing, especially for women, the dominant culture is very suspicious of the official *hejab* (a headscarf and a shapeless manteau for women), and even characterizes it as a form of 'nakedness'. The only *hejab* that the dominant culture of Qom considers as legitimate is the traditional *chador*, which covers the entire body of a woman. Nevertheless, the *chador* is progressively being questioned by the younger generation that expresses an intention to wear the strict scarf and wimple that entirely covers the body rather than the *chador*. However, up until the mid-2000s, only a tiny minority of the youngest girls in the Qomi young generation actually wore this scarf, although the tendency to do so is on the rise. Nonetheless, the culture of mutual supervision and gossip is still very prevalent in the major neighborhoods of the city, and this culture is even more important than the strictly religious one in terms of preventing the spread of the Tehran model of *hejab* to Qom.

When it comes to music, there is a similar problem of the dominant culture being suspicious of the official Islamic culture authorized, even spread by the Islamic regime. For example, on radio and television – the Voice and Vision of the Islamic Republic of Iran – music is authorized, the only restriction being the singing of women. In Qom, traditional ayatollahs are against music, which they perceive as impure (*haram*), and their followers see it in the same way. However, the majority of young believers do not agree with them on this issue, although they have chosen the ayatollahs as their spiritual leaders (*marja'*). In this respect, individualization has set in and many young people refuse to abide by the rule of their traditionalist religious leaders. Here, the role of the central government is rather "progressive," unlike in other large cities where it is repressive and against the major trend of social and cultural change.

Uneven secularization: toward a culture of ambivalence

Predominantly, cultural change occurs in Qom in an ambivalent manner. The impact of patriarchal Islam is still paramount but in many cases change occurs without frontally calling into question the dominant culture. The result is guilt feeling as a result of the transgression of the taboos. But the transgressions in some respects seem to be occurring more frequently, and the feeling of guilt is being suffused with a new culture of ambivalence that appears to renounce coherence in the name of the newly acquired liberty. The progressive change is still the more remarkable as the tight noose of the clergy and its political domination remains unshaken in the city.

Generally, secularization is seen as an irreversible process where individualization, democratization, the separation of the public and private sectors, and the confinement of religion to the private sector go hand in hand. This idea, in its main outlines, was paramount up until the 1970s in the Western world. Since then, even in the West its hegemony has been increasingly questioned. In Qom, secularization occurs in a fashion that wields its own peculiar features. Among young women, the desire for higher education is almost universal. Hand in hand with this desire goes the aspiration for some financial autonomy vis-à-vis future husbands. However, the culture of traditional marriage is preserved in its major outlines, and no young man or woman imagines their life outside the bonds of marriage. It is within this framework that some form of emancipation is imagined by girls who reject in large majorities polygyny and the denial by their future husbands of their freedom to work in the name of Islamic gender segregation.

Still, in many respects the questioning of the traditional culture is marginal. Consider, for example, the area of judicial inequality between men and women with respect to inheritance, court testimonies (a woman's testimony legally is valued as only half that of a man's testimony), divorce, and travel (the legal authorization of the husband or male guardian is necessary for a woman to go on a foreign trip). Girls are usually very conscious of the injustice in these areas, but their sentiments are ambivalent since these inequalities are founded on the patriarchal version of Islam that is still awe-inspiring in their eyes. Secularization (in the case of religiously based laws) occurs not so much in terms of the separation of the public and private spheres, but within each sphere as a result of attitudinal changes that do not fundamentally transform the traditional culture among the young in Qom. Polygyny, for instance, is rejected almost universally by young women and even by some young men; and women's assertion of the right to have a job is a new and salient change. This secularization impacts upon the religious sphere in an uneven manner. The clergy is usually rejected as a corporatist body, but its individual members (notably the "sources of emulation" [*marja' taqlid*] still preserve their prestige. The anti-clerical attitude of the younger generation is more of a reaction against the clerical political and economic hegemony than a result of the secularization of religion. The latter occurs in the way people define their own sphere of competence, notably in leisure activities, particularly music, as many traditional young people deny the right of the clergy to prohibit music in the name of Islam. In effect, the young assert their own right to define what is religiously licit and illicit in many spheres. Again, religion is not denied the right to define within the overall public sphere what is permitted and what is forbidden, but within each sphere there is an undeniable, albeit unsettled individualization. The structure and the nature of the two spheres are not questioned, but rather some attributes within them are claimed to belong to the personal sphere. With respect to women's emancipation, while there is a deep sense of injustice, this sentiment does not entail the desecration of the causes of injustice. Criticisms about the causes (traditional misogynist interpretations of religious principles) are at best restricted in their spheres by the pervasive tendency of obedience to authority. Nevertheless, in some respects the old submissive culture is being denounced as patriarchal and unjust.

The ambivalence described above is one major feature of this type of secularization. The dominant picture is not that of a new model or of a new concept replacing the old one. The prevailing situation is the concomitance of the old and new, a strong guilt feeling among the young people when they transgress this culture, but despite this feeling, their constant transgression of the traditions in some respects, namely gender segregation and the exclusion of women from the public sphere. This ambivalent culture maintains its hold upon the minds of the youth generation and manifests itself in their contradictory attitudes during the interviews. In many cases, young men and women assert that an attitude is "immoral," and then during the interview they recognize having acted against the taboos that still keep their hold on them. This culture of ambivalence and guilt feelings is not a mark of the hegemonic hold of the traditional culture, but rather a sign of its "lateral questioning" by those youth who dare to violate its taboos without calling into question its moral hegemony or its political clout.

Duality is at the heart of the new youth culture in Qom and, beyond that, at the heart of the intellectual life in Iran,[9] and more generally in the Islamic world. In Iran, it sometimes has been interpreted as a sign of cultural schizophrenia or as the icon of repressed traditionalism that is covered with a veneer of modernity, remaining at the bottom "religious" and unable to modernize.[10] It is schizophrenic in one sense, but at the same time the beginning of a gradual freeing from the hold of patriarchal culture. The new culture of ambivalence allows young people to connect to the world of their parents and to "keep in touch" with the dominant culture in Qom although emancipating progressively from its ascendancy, without frontally rejecting it. It marks a transition that can last a long time, with the two segments, the old and the new, entertaining complex relations with each other without one breaking off ties with the other. Dariush Shayegan criticizes a view of religion that does not take into account the major trends of the modern world where cultural homogeneity and religious absolutism are called into question. The quest for a holistic identity based on a monolithic view of Islam is alien to the evolution of the post-modern world and results in the isolation and regression of (Iranian) society.

Other well-known intellectuals, such as Javad Tabatabai and Aramesh Dustdar who are influential even in religious circles, hold views that point to the inability of Iranian culture to integrate modernity into its framework. Aramesh Dustdar[11] and Javad Tabatabai,[12] each in his own way, deplore the deep roots of religion in Iranian culture. For Dustdar, Iranian culture originates in an unconscious religious attitude that prohibits the understanding of the modern world based on secularization and rationalism.[13] Even when Iranian intellectuals deem to think in a non-religious way, religious thought continues to subjugate them. For Tabatabai, the decline of Iranian political thought goes back to the repression of Islamic philosophers' thought in the eleventh and twelfth centuries, and since then it has been impossible for Iranian-Islamic culture to understand modernity adequately.[14]

The perception of the young in Qom contradicts in many ways these holistic views of cultural schizophrenia or the inability to modernize adequately. First of all, the disjunctive pattern of feeling and thought is not uncommon in the West. Even if one were to suppose that the chasm is deeper in the Muslim world in general and in Iran in particular, the result is not "cultural schizophrenia" but a pattern of action that is far more dynamic than what is supposed by these thinkers. In most cases, the discrepancy between what one feels and what one does induces a change that is partially willing and yet is partially unwilling. This makes one act in such ways that would be deeply disruptive and guilt-ridden if one had to express or accept the action without ambivalence. The latter makes it easier for one to act in a way that transgresses social taboos without having to recognize the transgression explicitly, thereby irredeemably escaping culpability and a deep destructive sense of guilt or malaise. This disjunctive pattern of behavior among the young (the gap between what they feel and think and what they do) may be likened to "cognitive dissonance," although there are major differences between them. Ambivalence suffuses the psyche with 'mild guilt feelings', but it renders the 'sin' minor rather than 'mortal' and gives youth leeway to act without having to assume the consequences of their action entirely.

To make this discussion more palpable, we will examine attitudes toward leisure, in particular sport and music, to shed light upon the complexity of this ambivalence and the surprising way in which it opens up new vistas for the young. Let us take the case of a young man from the rural areas of Qom, as he provides a rather interesting picture of how the young make a choice between sport and religious ceremonies that in reality shows how soccer has become so important as a means to mobilize them, with religion assuming a secondary role:

QUESTION: What do you do [in your village] during the holy month of Moharram?

ANSWER: We participate in the [religious] ceremonies, of course!

Q: What is more important, the soccer matches or the religious mourning cere-monies in this month?

A: The young people go at the "appropriate" time to the religious ceremonies of *Ashura* and *Tasu'a*[15] and then do sport; they have nothing else to do, and they do these things.

Q: Do you mean soccer?

A: Yes.

Q: Between the mosque and soccer, which do they choose?

A: If it is between the mosque and soccer among the youth of our district, believe me, they will choose soccer in the morning, but then at night they go to the religious ceremonies.[16]

An issue in which a new type of personal preference is preponderant in an ambivalent manner is the religious rulings of the ayatollahs on music, its per-formance as well as listening to it. In traditional Islam, music, apart from the recitation of the Qur'an [*talawa'*], is deemed impure. This has been the domi-nant view among traditional religious authorities in Iran, even though the Islamic Republic has partially liberalized music. This process started with revolutionary Islamic music and then moved progressively to include Iranian classical music and, since the second half of the 1990s – especially after the 1997 election of the reformist Khatami as president – "pop music" sung by men (although marginal-ized since 2009). In this area, young, observant Muslims have questioned many of the precepts of the religious authorities by making their own ruling: the indi-vidual can have, in this respect, a say in his religious life, despite the banning of something by the *marja' taqlid* whom he follows in all other aspects of his life. In this respect, religious young people are aligned with non-religious people.

One way to avoid breaching religious norms openly is to refer to the diversity of *fatwas* by ayatollahs: Since different religious authorities have different and sometimes contradictory views on music (its licit or illicit status), the individual is free to have his own opinion on it. This explanation of listening to music even though it is forbidden by one's own *marja'* opens the way for personal initia-tives. The individual needs to justify his aspirations in religious terms even though he is partially conscious that he is "manipulating" religion. The ambiva-lence is the need to "justify" one's attitude; emancipation lies in playing off some religious authorities against others. Here too, ambivalence helps free the individual and contributes to his secularization and not to his "schizophrenia." Another way of questioning the impurity of music is by referring to one's own state of mind and subjectivity when listening to it: If one is not put into a state of such excitement that one might trample on religious norms, the music becomes religiously acceptable. Here, the individual sets the religious norms himself, despite the rulings of religious authorities, as, for example, does this young woman from Qom:

> In our religion there is no prohibition of music because the music that I listen to does not push me to call religious norms into question. Most of those (*marja'*) who forbade music did not feel the need for it mentally .... But in my view, there is no incompatibility between our religion and music.[17]

A young man from Qom also admits to ignoring the ban on music, although he is religiously minded and follows a *marja'*:

QUESTION: You go out sometimes with your friends to dance at night in their places?
ANSWER: Not at night (it is too obvious) but during the day, that happens to me sometimes.
Q: But to sing, to dance, and these things are a sin from the religious view, isn't it?
A: I don't think so.
Q: Do you have a source of emulation [*marja' taqlid*]?
A: Yes .... They all say that it is impure, but I don't listen...[18]

In this case we see the individual's own views taking precedence over the views of the religious authority. This may be compared with the attitude of many young Catholics who do not take heed of the Pope's prohibition on premarital sexual relations despite the fact that they are deeply religious. Individualization here means choosing one's own way of following (or not following) the religious authority who is supposed to have the final word on matters in which religion has a say, according to religious customs.

A young woman, who is otherwise very religious, follows a similar path:

Q: What about music?
A: I listen to whatever is beautiful (to my ears), authorized or not.
Q: Your mother doesn't object to that?
A: No!
Q: Isn't that against the (rulings of) religion?
A: I didn't say I don't do anything against religion. It is forbidden, but I do it. I couldn't accept that it is a bad thing.[19]

Here, the girl, who happens to be from a religious family in Qom and otherwise follows the religious commandments quite strictly, refuses to submit to the ban on music and asks for rational arguments as to why it should be banned. This individualization is the beginning of a deep secularization.

Ambivalent attitudes toward religion and its prescriptions are promoting secularization in unexpected ways.

Another young person shares the same attitude:

Q: Do you listen to music?
A: Yes.
Q: What kind of music?
A: Calm music, as well as "Los Angelesi" music (Iranian pop music made by the Iranian Diaspora in the United States and illegally reproduced in Iran).
Q: You are a pious Muslim, a *moteshari* (as you said), how come you listen to music, isn't it a sin?
A: No, my religious views (are not at stake), I have faith in my daily prayers but I also believe in these sorts of thing (like listening to music)
Q: Even though religious texts ban music, you keep on listening to it?
A: Yes.[20]

In some cases ambivalence leaves a deeper imprint on the people, and they experience guilt feelings. Despite this, they overcome their internal inhibition and act in a "sinful" way without entirely recognizing it:

Q: Do you listen to music?
A: I try to listen to music that is not too cheerful and not a song either.
Q: Why? Do you think it is a sin?
A: Even if it is not, it leaves its imprint on my mind. When I listen to songs at weddings or at home for one or two weeks, then I sing them in my head and that makes a negative influence on me.
Q: Do you listen to the songs of Hayedeh, Gougoush [women singers during the Shah's regime, and who were very famous in Iran] and the others?
A: I listen to them at weddings.
Q: Don't you think it is a sin?
A: I try not to listen to them, and at weddings, I try to sit far away (from the loudspeaker) in order not to hear them.[21]

Another woman answers the same question in an ambivalent manner, displaying an internal tension between the feeling of guilt and the wish to listen to music:

Q: You said you listened to Gougoush and Abi. You are a believer and you do your daily prayers (as you said before), isn't that right?
A: Yes, it is true.
Q: Isn't that a sin?
A: It is true that it is a sin. But I think that in certain circumstances, it is a lesser sin![22]

Another young person justifies listening to music by referring to self-control. If one maintains one's self-control, listening to music is not forbidden:

Q: What type of music do you listen to?
A: Any sort...
Q: Don't you think all of it is forbidden by religion?
A: No, because I know that we have a principle in Islam: If the music causes me
    to lose control over myself, the prohibition is OK (it is forbidden). But it is
    rare to be in that situation, and then there is no problem .... And beyond
    that, things have changed from the past....[23]

Of course, even in Qom there are groups of secular youth that do not follow religious rulings and ambivalence does not play a role in their attitudes, as in the case of this young woman:

Q: What instrument do you play?
A: I play *setar* [an Iranian instrument] and *dombak* [Iranian drum].
Q: Can one play them and wear the *chador* (as you do)?
A: ...I wear it because my parents like it ... I think that one can wear the *chador*
    and play music. At school [girls' school], I even sing.
Q: Don't you think the voice of a Muslim woman should not be heard by men
    (as tradition stipulates)?
A: I don't believe that either.
Q: What does music give you?
A: Music brings everything to human beings, it brings religion and the world
    together [alluding to the proverb *din ou dunia* (religion and authority)].
    Music opens up doors even if you feel all doors are closed. This one is open
    because you have chosen it yourself, your hands have chosen it (you play
    music). This is a world that is interesting to me.[24]

Political ambivalence

Ambivalence in politics is a major feature in the description of many young
people. They reject almost unanimously the clergy's political rule in the name of
Islam and attribute to it many ills, namely its immoderate love of material goods,
its political corruption, its aristocratic vision of itself, and its undisguised con-
tempt for ordinary people. At the same time, many still have a personal relationship toward their own "pole of imitation" (*marja' taqlid*), who is usually an
ayatollah who gives them guidance in case of doubt about what is allowed and
what is forbidden in religious matters. Many reject *velayat-e faqih* (the rule of
the Islamic Jurist, incorporated into the constitution as the political system in
Iran after the Islamic Revolution of 1979). Still, many traits of a democratic
system seem odd to them, sometimes even against their wishes, among them
equality between Muslims and non-Muslims, men and women, Shi'is and
Sunnis. They have an ambivalent attitude toward democracy, even though many
of their aspirations only can be fulfilled within a democratic framework.

This ambivalence can be illustrated by concrete cases. For example, Roya, a
young woman, is deeply aware of the discrepancy within her own mental landscape:

Concerning the contradition between theocracy and democracy.

QUESTION: In what kind of political power do you believe: religious or democratic?

ANSWER: My reason supports the democratic one but my faith tells me that there is a superior reason to my reason.... The Qur'an says things that I blindly accept because of my faith. If I refer to my faith, I say, the religious government, partially limited, it is true. But if I talk according to my reason, I choose the democratic government.

Q: Should all the Iranians – Shiite, Sunni, Armenian, Muslims and non-Muslims – have the same rights?

A: Yes, they should have the same rights.

Q: If there are two candidates for president of the Islamic Republic, one Iranian Armenian or Iranian Jew and the other Iranian Muslim, and if the first has a better program, for whom would you vote?

A: Certainly for the one who has a better program.

Q: And if their programs are the same?

A: I'd vote for the Muslim.

Q: For some people, religion and politics have been mingled and this is bad for religion; others think, on the contrary, that this has beefed up religion.

A: If we leave aside our religion, what we'll do won't be in keeping with our thought and we cannot do it.... Generally speaking, one should not separate religion and politics.[25]

The ambivalent situation of religion in Roya's mind allows her to vote for a Jew or an Armenian if their political agenda is superior to that of a Muslim. If they are co-equal she will choose the Muslim; otherwise the non-Muslim will prevail. This would have been impossible in a traditional Iranian mindset as recently as the early 1990s, as the Muslim in every case would have been preferred to the non-Muslim. Roya refuses to separate religion and politics, but she would still opt for a non-Muslim if he had a better political agenda than a Muslim.

Another young woman, who refused to talk to a male interviewer, simply refuses to settle on the issue:

Q: Between two candidates for president, one Christian and the other Muslim, if the Christian has a better agenda than the Muslim, for whom would you vote?

A: For none! One is a Muslim but not intelligent and his being a Muslim does not help us here. The Jew or the Christian has a good political agenda but I am afraid (to cast my vote for him) because religion has to be taken seriously.[26]

Here too, the refusal to choose is a departure from the traditional mindset, which would not have hesitated in choosing the Muslim over a Christian or Jew, despite being "people of the Book" (i.e., belonging to a Abrahamic religion like Muslims), because they are supposed to be religiously impure and not eligible for the office of the president. Here, she is sitting on the fence and does not know how to choose in a stalemate situation.

Another young woman, Fereshteh, is similarly in a deadlock:

Q: Do you prefer a government based on religion or on the popular vote?
A: Both! There are lots of things like this one that I am unable to decide on in my mind, do you understand? When I check through these questions, I see that on the (exclusive) basis of popular vote, there will be problems. And if it is on the (exclusive) basis of religion, other problems emerge. For this reason (I prefer) a mixed form of government, both should be present within the government, but one should not be too rigorous on religion or on the popular vote!
Q: What are the drawbacks of the people's vote?
A: For instance, they don't respect religious problems or our religion might die out and those things required by the Qur'an will subside.[27]

Here too, there is no clear-cut choice, and the interviewee lingers in choosing one way or the other. She is conscious of the ambivalence but cannot cut the Gordian knot:

A: There is a contradiction in my thought. I love democracy, but I know that if freedom is granted to the individual, he can exercise it anyhow and endanger religion. This is not only my problem, but also that of those who, for a hundred years are in a dilemma. They want freedom, but when it comes to religion, they say, "My God! What should I do?"[28]

She is not ready for a secular democracy, contrary to many people in large cities like Tehran, but she does not support a theocracy that would deny people their say in political matters. She would like a compromise between the two, and, insofar as she is in favor of some kind of religious freedom, that separation is difficult to define in a precise way. However, due to this ambivalence, a kind of "Islamic democracy" is within reach, contrary to traditional Muslims, who would not support any system based on popular vote.

Conclusion

Two major models are at work in the modernization of youth in Iran. In the larger cities like Tehran, complete secularization undermines the religious norms and breaks down Islamic prohibitions among social classes in the younger generation. But this type of change is only partial and many people, young and old, do not break off religious ties in a radical manner, nor do they separate in a clear-cut fashion the realms of religion and government. Their change occurs by reinterpreting religious norms and by adapting to new sets of ideas that are derived, in their viewpoint, from Islam. In many Iranian cities, and in particular Qom, this type of secularization is paramount. In this second pattern, ambivalence plays a major role, as already mentioned. The new culture of ambivalence has undeniably positive side effects. It lessens the guilt feelings caused by the transgression of religious taboos among youth who are predominantly attached to the Islamic frame of reference. It tears down the walls that were erected in the name of patriarchy within the Islamic religion. It gives new leeway to the individual who can accomplish his aspirations without feeling oppressed by the sense of calling into question God's prohibitions. It allows for the intermingling of girls and boys, listening to music, the practicing of outdoor sports for girls, premarital relations, and many other changes within the affective and social life of the young without cutting off the ties with the past and creating a vacuum in the minds of those who transgress the taboos without necessarily recognizing it mentally. They minimize the transgressive side of their conduct and reinterpret it within the framework of a new religious sentiment. This new culture of ambivalence, in part instrumental, in part sincerely adhered to, makes possible democratization without a visible rupture with Islam. Had it not been for this new culture of ambivalence, many young people who took part in the street demonstrations in Iran for the recognition of Mir-Hosain Mussavi as president following the contested presidential election of June 2009 would not have been active in the name of Islam (albeit many participants were secular).

The secularization of Islam in the 1970s induced a revolutionary movement under the influence of Ali Shari'ati, and other Islamic intellectuals and clerics like Ayatollah Khomeini. The movement was not democratic in its core values. However, the contemporary social movement wields a democratic content caused by the new type of secularization within the Islamic framework in Iran. The ambivalence of this worldview is contributing to its change in the direction of tolerance and opening, and is against the holistic view propounded by the Islamic Revolution of 1979. A new type of Islamic individual is emerging, one who pushes toward a more egalitarian and tolerant society. Even in a city like Qom, still under the aegis of the religious institutions, there have been changes. The new youth in it calls indirectly into question many Islamic taboos that were sacrosanct two decades ago. The ambivalence that impregnates the seminal cultural and political notions in the minds of many young people in traditional towns explains why an utterly democratic movement that has been developing in Iran following the June 2009 presidential election, and which is against President Ahmadinejad, has been less dynamic in medium-sized cities and stronger in the larger ones. In cities like Qom, the mindset is "in between": neither pure theocracy, nor pure democracy, but an ambivalent combination of both. This is related to the secularization process and its variable degrees of development. In Qom, the young generation do not share the "certainties" of their elders; rather they are looking for something new, even though they have not cut off their ties from religion and its framework. They are willing to open up to a new world that would not frontally reject their culture but would not sacrifice either their aspirations to have a say in the political process in the name of an ambivalent sovereignty of the people. In a shaky manner, a culture of discussion and "intersubjectivity" is opening up new vistas in their minds. The hierarchic paternalistic worldview yields to a new culture in which arguing and reasoning have their place. In Qom, this new culture blends in an ambiguous manner, with the old one in which the younger had to give way to the older, the son to the father. Patriarchy is no longer what it used to be. It is tempered by a new generation of young women and men, better educated, more cultured, less inclined toward utopias (be they radical Islamic), and more prone to become "actors of their own life."[29] Ambivalence crosses this new subjectivity from end to end.

Notes

1 For analyses of the diverse theories concerning the secularization and the role of the state, see the encyclopedic work of James Beckford, *Social Theory and Religion* (Cambridge: Cambridge University Press, 2003).

2 Methodological note: The empirical research was undertaken between 2002 and 2005 in the three cities of Tehran, Qom, and Qazvin. In Qom, a sample of 60 young people between the ages of 19 and 30 were selected, half girls and half boys, and taking into account social stratification and status backgrounds. The method chosen was long, semi-structural interviews, between two and three hours in length, with a questionnaire and an open-ended discussion at the end. The interviews were conducted either by Amir Nikpey or jointly by the author and Nikpey; two research assistants, Nahid Keshavarz and Faezeh Mohammadi, accompanied the interviewers. The interviews addressed the following issues: the affective life within the family and, in particular, relations with parents, love and marriage; religious attitudes and the clergy; politics and the legitimacy of religion in government; the problem of racism (toward the Afghans); and the image of the West, in particular the United States. A book dealing with all of these attitudes among the young in the three cities was published in French: Farhad Khosrokhavar and Amir Nikpey, *Avoir Vingt ans au pays des ayatollahs* [Being 20 years old in the country of the ayatollahs] (Paris: Robert-Laffont, 2009). This chapter is based on that research, including some material from the book.

3 The city of Qom is one of the most important Shi'i religious centers in the world (often considered second or even co-equal to Najaf in Iraq). Qom is located 150 kilometers south-west of Tehran and had a population of 959,116 in the 2006 national census, ranking it as the eighth largest city in the country.

4 Interview with Mojtaba, Qom, October 2004.

5 St. Fatimeh Ma'sumeh was the sister of Imam Ali al-Reza, the eighth of Shi'i Islam's 12 Imams. She fell ill and died in Qom, ca. 815, while traveling from Medina to Merv in Central Asia to visit her brother. Her tomb subsequently became a pilgrimage site for Shi'i Muslims; during the reign of Shah Ismail Safavi, the current shrine was erected (1519) around her tomb.

6 There are major changes in the mental landscape of women since the 1970s and 1980s; for views in that period, see, for example, Shahla Haeri, *Law of Desire: Temporary Marriage in Shi'i Iran* (New York: Syracuse University Press, 1989). The modernization of attitudes compared with the period covered in that book is manifest.

7 See further Marie Ladier-Fouladi, *Iran, un monde de paradoxes* (Paris: L'Atlante publishers, 2009).

8 See Farhad Khosrokhavar, *L'utopie sacrifiée, sociologie de la revolution iranienne* (Paris: Presses de la FNSP, 1993).

9 For discussions of intellectuals in Iran, see the doctoral dissertation by Mohsen Mottaghi, "L'émergence du nouvel intellectuel religieux en Iran post-révolutionnaire" (École des Hautes Études en Sciences Sociales, 2004); Mehrzad Boroujerdi, *Iranian Intellectuals and the West: The Tormented Triumph of Nativism* (New York: Syracuse University Press, 1996); and Ali Gheissari, *Iranian Intellectuals in the Twentieth Century* (University of Texas Press, 1997).

10 See Dariush Shayegan, *Cultural Schizophrenia: Islamic Societies Confronting the West* (New York: Syracuse University Press, 1997), in which he analyzes the mental and cultural predicament of youth caught between a pre-modern and a postmodern culture as "schizophrenic." For further development of this argument see Farhad Khosrokhavar, "The New Iranian Intellectuals in Iran," *Social Compass*, 51, 2 (2004), pp. 191–202.

11 See Aramesh Dustdar, *Molahezat e falsafi dar din, elm va fekr* [Philosophical considerations on religion, science and thought] (Tehrran, 1359/1980); and his book under the pseudonym of Babak Bamdadan, *Derakhsheshha-ye tireh* [Somber incandescences] (Paris, 1997).

12 See Javad Tabatabai, *Zaval-e andisheh-ye siasi dar Iran* [Decline of political thought in Iran] (Tehran, 1373/1994).

13 See *Dustdar, Molahezat e falsafi*; and Bamdadan, *Derakhsheshha-ye tireh*.

14 See Tabatabai, *Zaval-e andisheh-ye siasi. dar Iran* [Decline of political thought in Iran] (Tehran, 1373/1994).

15 *Ashura* and *Tasu'a*, the tenth and ninth of the lunar month of Muharram respectively, are the two holiest days of the year for Shi'i Muslims. *Tasu'a* commemorates the date in 680 that Imam Hosain, the grandson of the Prophet, was wounded in battle, and the following day, *Ashura*, commemorates his martyrdom; when he died, the soldiers of the caliph, Yazid, severed his head from his corpse to bring it back in triumph to Damascus.

16 Interviews, Qom, February 2005.

17 Author and Amir Nikpey joint interview, Qom, May 2005.

18 Ibid.

19 Ibid.

20 Interview, February 2003.

21 Interview, November 2004.

22 Interview, March 2004.

23 Interview, November 2003.

24 Interview, October 2004.

25 Interview, Qom, September 2003.

26 Interview, Qom, October 2003.

27 Interview, March 2004.

28 Ibid.

29 This idea is developed more fully in Khosrokhavar and Nikpey, *Avoir vingt ans au pays des ayatollahs*.

8 Changing attitudes among women in rural Iran

Eric Hooglund

Between 2001 and 2005, I undertook several trips to Iran in connection with a research project to study macro-economic and social changes in the rural areas of Fars province. The objective of this research was not to study the micro-attitudes of village women, but during the course of my field research, which involved participating in large communal gatherings such as weddings and extended family picnics, as well as attending intimate dinners in the homes of friends and colleagues, I had opportunities to interact with several young women who wanted to try out the English-language skills they had learned in high school. These occasions inevitably led to brief or lengthier conversations in Persian about various topics they seemed comfortable discussing. That I was a foreign guest, an *Amrikai*, and could speak their language were novel facts that prompted their interest in initiating such conversations. These conversations were random and spontaneous, but I was fascinated to hear the views of these young women, views which seemed to indicate that their attitudes toward various social issues differed from those of their own parents. I recorded the conversations each evening in fieldnote journals I keep while engaged in research.

The young women were all born after the 1978 to 1979 Revolution, and at the time of our initial conversations they ranged in age from 16 to 22 and were unmarried. Most were attending or had completed high school, and a few had passed entrance exams for and were enrolled in various higher educational institutions in different small towns of Fars province. I had an opportunity to talk with a few of the women on successive research trips; some of them had become engaged or got married since our initial conversations. Being able to converse with some young women as their ideas developed over a five-year period provided an unanticipated and more complicated view of their attitudes. The significance of the views of these young women is that they reflect the changing attitudes among women in at least one rural region of Iran.

The villages in which these conversations took place include Beyza, Dukuhak, Guyom, Kelestan, Qalat, and Qomsheh, all to the north-west of Shiraz, the administrative, commercial, and cultural center of Fars and one of Iran's largest cities; and also the village of Lapui, north of Shiraz. All of these villages are on or near major paved roads, and none are more than 75 minutes by car from Shiraz. This proximity has facilitated the process of urban culture penetrating these villages in diverse ways since the early 1980s. At the time of the 1978 to 1979 Revolution, these villages were major centers of agricultural production, all of them producing two or three times more crops than needed for local consumption (although the surplus was controlled by and sold to benefit absentee landlords).[1] In the subsequent 30 years, however, income from various non-agricultural sources has become important for some households; indeed, in villages such as Dukuhak, Guyom, and Qomsheh, less than 10 percent of households depended on farming for income by the early 2000s.[2]

The economic changes in these villages have been accompanied by the emergence of complex social stratification patterns. In villages such as Dukuhak, Guyom, and Qalat, there are households whose incomes, lifestyles, and values are similar to those of middle-class urban households in Shiraz. Young women in such families tend to express aspirations to obtain an education and earn an income, even after marriage. In contrast, young women raised in low-income households in these same villages tend to have more limited aspirations; few of them aspire to education beyond high school or paid employment but rather focus on finding a good husband. In villages such as Beyza and Lapui, where agriculture is still important for a majority of households, young women tend to value participation in income-producing, farm-related activities organized through the rural cooperative societies over higher education.

It is important to stress that the views recorded here are not the result of structured research. Rather, as mentioned above, they were gathered for the most part during informal conversations with young women at family social occasions. However, the curiosity of the women about me as an American and about my research in the villages obviously guided the conversations toward certain topics of mutual interest. Inevitably, several themes came up repeatedly in these conversations, and these will be the focus of this chapter. I have identified nine discreet themes, for each of which I gathered views from five or more young women. These themes are: family, education, work, marriage, religion, gender inequality, domestic politics, relations with the United States, and Iran's nuclear program.[3]

Family

Historically, the extended family was important as a source of emotional support, and virtually all socializing among women occurred within the extended family. In fact, at the time of the 1978 to 1979 Revolution, the typical village household tended to be a multi-generational compound comprising a senior male and his adult married sons with their children; the extended family included the siblings of this senior male and their own children and grandchildren, usually in adjacent or nearby compounds. However, as a result of social changes that have been documented in several other chapters in this book, all the young women in this chapter have been raised in what essentially may be termed nuclear family households, they are staying in school longer than did their mothers – finishing high school and even going to college – and they are marrying later. Closely intertwined with these changes have been altered personal relationships between parents and children. For example, whereas in the past (1990 and earlier), children hardly ever questioned the authority of the father, it is now more common for there to be some degree of give-and-take, and several young women even boast of their fathers favoring them over their brothers.[4]

I observed this give-and-take between parents and their teenage children when I was a guest in homes or at family gatherings in public parks. I immediately recognized how differently this youth generation related to their parents in comparison with family dynamics 30 years earlier, when I had done research in these same villages. Indeed, several of the fathers in the early 2000s were men whom I had known as teenagers in the late 1970s, and they would often make comments – usually jovially – to the effect: "You [meaning me] know I never dared to speak to my father the way my own kids now talk to me." However, I did not ask the young women any questions pertaining to their relations with their parents or other family members. Rather, their attitudes on intra-family relations emerged during conversations which we had about the differences between Iranian and Western cultures, questions prompted by scenes that they remembered from foreign movies, DVDs which are dubbed into Persian and rented or sold (both illegally) by vendors.[5] Maryam, for example, contrasted the way she and her friends treated their parents with characters in several American films:

> Are all American girls and boys really like that? I mean, in those movies they do not respect their parents at all. I am not saying that we don't have problems with our parents here in Iran. Our parents are very strict. I mean they never would allow us to go out on a date with a boy, like in those movies. I do think boys and girls should have opportunities to meet and talk about things, to get to know each other. Not a date like in those movies, but just get together, like in a café or restaurant, which, of course, is impossible, because if the morals police find [unrelated] boys and girls sitting together, they treat them even worse than any parents would do. Maybe kids my age can do that [date] more easily in Tehran, or even in parts of Shiraz, but not here. I understand why my parents are concerned. We talk about these matters [why not to talk with boys]. My parents, especially my dad, are old-fashioned. But they are good parents and I respect them. Yes, sometimes, I get mad at my mom or dad or both, but it's all right after a few hours, and we can joke. I would not talk to them [parents] like the girls in the movies do. But, is this just a movie, or is this how Americans really behave?

Here, Maryam's concern, which other young women shared, was that American and also European cultures seemed to value the individual as being more important than the family. For these Iranians the family was central in their lives, even though they also seemed to yearn for more personal freedom.[6] As Jaleh put it:

> I really don't see anything wrong with talking to boys, whether in a café or park or on the telephone. My family would be very upset [*narahat*] if they

knew how much I talked to boys! So, I don't tell them. But, I never would do anything disrespectful. I mean, I would not go on a date like in those foreign movies, just a boy and girl alone, and let a boy take advantage of me. My friends and I, we go on "Irani dates," that is a group of us girls meet a group of boys in the cafeteria, a pizza pace, internet café, or some other place, and we just talk and have a good time. It's all innocent. And we girls talk among ourselves, and we know which boys try to pressure girls [to be alone with them], so we know how to be careful. But my parents, it was different when they were young, so they don't understand. And at home, they watch the foreign movies with us, so they are scared that we might behave like those movie stars. And some girls here do go too far [go out alone with boys], but not in our group.[7] But I reassure my parents that I would not go out alone with a boy. And that's true. But I don't tell them that I sit in cafes and talk with boys, because they can't understand the difference.

These attitudes demonstrate that the young women are open to change and find ways to embrace change that avoid harming valued family relationships. They do not see this position as hypocritical but rather as pragmatic. Because family ties are an important value for them, they are perplexed that this does not seem to be the case in the foreign films they watch, ones that valorize boy–girl (sexual) relationships over family ones. Nevertheless, however much they seem critical of this aspect of foreign culture, this negative attitude does not dampen their curiosity about and even enjoyment of other aspects of these same cultures, especially their latest fashions and cosmetics, films, music, and sports. Indeed, it sometimes was embarrassing to discuss popular culture with them, as many of these young women had far more knowledge about American pop music stars and British soccer teams than I did.

Education

Prior to the Revolution, it was rare for a girl raised in these villages to attend high school, the common practice being for parents to withdraw their daughters from school after they had completed the five-year primary cycle. By the mid-1990s, however, education had become highly valued, and few village families wanted their sons or daughters to leave school before obtaining their high school diplomas. Of course, not all teenage girls enjoyed studying, and some, perhaps even a majority, preferred watching television over preparing algebra or physics homework. However, those girls who excelled in high school generally received family encouragement for their aspirations to attend college. Masumeh explains:

My parents are so proud of the grades I get in [high] school. My mom tells me not to worry about helping her fix dinner, to do my homework. My dad says that I should think about college. He has said several times that I ought to take those classes in Shiraz that prepare you to take the [college] entrance exams. He even says that if I don't pass [the entrance exam] in the spring, then I should just study every day at home [after graduation in June] for one year so that I'll pass them next year.

Going to college no longer means, as it did in the past, being accepted into the University of Shiraz, since there has been a major expansion in the number and variety of post-secondary educational opportunities available, not only in Shiraz but in the many medium-sized and even small towns of Fars province. None of these higher education facilities, however, are located in the villages. This means that if a girl is accepted by a college that is so far away as to make commuting to on a daily basis impossible, parents must face the prospect of a daughter moving away from home. Many parents are not willing to let an unmarried daughter live away from home, as Forough notes below:

I am lucky at home. My parents really listen to me. And my father, ever since I was in primary school, said I should try to go to college. After I passed the [entrance] exam for Azad [University], he helped me find a place to live. He is really supportive, and he won't let my mom talk to me about marriage. He says that I must finish college first. My two cousins are not so lucky; my uncles wanted them to get married as soon as they finished [high] school. My dad tried to persuade them to let their daughters come to college with me. They couldn't say that college ruins girls, as that would be an insult to my father, but they were nervous [*narahat*] about their daughters living far from home in a strange town. So they kept saying, 'their husbands can send them to college after they get married. We'll write that in the marriage contract.'

Work

A conversation with two young women, both recent high school graduates but unmarried, illustrates attitudes about work. Fatemeh A. and Zeinab were working in a small factory created by the local rural cooperative to process and package village crops for sale to urban grocery stores. They both expressed satisfaction with a job that was within walking distance of their homes, enabled them to earn money that they could save or spend, and involved them in work that they believed was benefiting their village community. For Fatemeh A., it was appropriate for a woman to work only if the job was appropriate, as she explained:

During Now Ruz [Iranian New Year, always on the vernal equinox and generally celebrated over a two-week period], I rode on a bus with my father and uncle to Tehran, where we attended the rural cooperatives' convention. We stopped in Kashan [a medium-sized city between Qom and Esfahan] to eat lunch at a family restaurant. I was shocked that girls my age were serving food to everybody. I didn't say anything, but I felt very bad. Women should not be doing this sort of work. It is not right.
ZEINAB: Why not? I have gone to the north [*shomal*, meaning here the

Caspian Sea coast, which has several summer resort/beach towns] with my family, and there women work in restaurants, sell food in the markets, operate restaurants and *villas* [private houses that rent rooms to tourists], even work in the rice paddies. Are you saying that work for women is a sin [*gonah*]? Even the Prophet, peace be upon him, his wife was a businesswoman.

FA: No, No. I am not saying that it is a sin for women to work. Some work is right [*dorost*] for women, but other work is not right [*nadorost*] for them, such as serving people, especially all kinds of men who are strangers to them. Here [in the village], we know everyone, and no man would bother a woman or girl. But in the cities, some men are rude, they may look at woman in a bad way, and they say bad things to them. Women should not work in places where there are a lot of men who don't care whether they mistreat women. Such jobs are not appropriate for women.

The interesting point about this exchange is that the young women are arguing not about whether woman should work but rather about what kind of work is appropriate for women. In general, the majority of young women with whom I spoke seemed to share Fatemeh A.'s ambivalence about jobs that involved women in selling to or serving the general public. The work for women that seemed to be most esteemed was in education (teachers of primary, middle, or high schools) and healthcare, jobs which required one or more years of post-secondary education. Such jobs are available through the Ministries of Education and Health, which, as other chapters in this book show, employ large numbers of women. Other government ministries and agencies also employ women, although their positions typically are very limited to non-existent in villages. In Shiraz, however, there are various private sector jobs that employ women, including art galleries, consulting agencies, internet cafés, manufacturing companies, publishing, tourism bureaus, and tutorial services. In the villages, but only in the largest ones, women entrepreneurs do operate beauty salons and tailoring services, usually from their own homes. Even though there are acceptable jobs available for the increasing numbers of women with high school and college degrees, there are not necessarily sufficient jobs to meet the demand for work. As discussed in other chapters, Iran's economy has not been dynamic enough since the mid-1990s to generate job growth commensurate with the numbers of young women and men annually entering the job market.

Marriage

All of these young women expected to get married, and several did become engaged or married by the end of 2005. However, each was adamant that she, not her family, would choose her husband, and they all had idealized concepts of marriage that included love as a primary quality. Farzaneh, whose engagement and wedding I attended, recounted her experience:

I knew Mehrdad since I was 10 or 12 because he is the younger brother of my *ameh* (father's sister)'s husband. When I was in high school, my mother suggested sometimes what a nice boy Mehrdad was and what a good husband he would be. But I always said that I didn't want to think about marrying until I finish high school. During my last year of high school, Mehrdad and his parents made a *khastegari* [marriage proposal] visit to my home. I was not happy. I told my parents that I wanted to finish high school and go to college. We really argued about this for many weeks. Finally, my dad gave in, saying that, if I agreed to consider marrying Mehrdad, then he would let me study for the college entrance exam for one year. If I passed, then I could go to college, but, if I did not pass, then I had to think about marriage. I insisted that neither I nor they [parents] really knew what kind of boy Mehrdad was, and before I could decide about him or anyone else, I had to get to know the person whom I would marry and live with. They agreed that Mehrdad could visit as often as he liked during the year I was studying for the *concor* [college entrance exam]; the family would stay in the background so that Mehrdad and I could talk together and get to know each other's ideas. During that year, I realized that Mehrdad thought about many issues the same way I did, and I really came to see him as a friend. When I did not pass the *concor*, he was as sad as I was, and really, he did not just say, "That's too bad" like everyone else, but he listened to me and shared my pain [*dard-e delem*]. He said that if I continued to study, I might pass next year, and he would wait for me. But I was tired of studying. I had worked hard. I had tried, but how could I do more than I already had done? And I was comfortable with Mehrdad. So, after a few weeks I said to him, "Let us together tell our parents that we are ready to get married."

Zahra B., in contrast, went to college in a small town about three hours away by car, and there she met a young man, Ali, with whom she fell in love. I learned the details from her when I was invited to their engagement dinner:

At first my parents were not happy. My mom kept saying, "We don't know his family, or what kind of person he his." My father, who was disappointed, would say, "We just want you to be happy, but this boy is a stranger, from another province. Of course, we trust you, but you're young, and if this is a mistake, how can we help you after you move away with a stranger?" In the end, Ali's parents came for khast-egari, even though he and I already had agreed to get married. Both sets of parents got along and became reconciled to our marriage.

It is not only the tradition of arranged marriages that is being challenged in these villages, but also the tradition of newlyweds living with the groom's family for a few years after the wedding. Nilufar expressed views on this issue with which several other young women nodded in agreement.

Ehsan's parents and my parents are friends, even relatives on our moms' side, but none of the parents had any idea that Ehsan and I were talking to each other, so when we announced we wanted to get married, all four were shocked. And Ehsan and I made all the plans, the *kastegari*, the *aqd* [marriage contract], everything, and the parents had to go along. They were unhappy and happy at the same time. But I told Ehsan from the beginning that I was not going to live with his parents. No way. I don't even want to live here. We both work in Shiraz, so that is where we ought to live. That is what I insisted on in the *aqd* agreement, that we have an apartment in Shiraz. Ehsan's parents were not happy at all, and assumed that they could talk us out of it, as his dad was always telling Ehsan how much rent he would have to pay in Shiraz, but we could live in the apartment in the family home here and save money. I always was polite during these conversations. But later, I would tell Ehsan, "We have to have our own lives. No interference from your parents or mine." And he understands.

The young women who have jobs want to continue working after marriage, and all say that they plan to wait for at least a year before having children. According to Najmeh, "The first years of marriage are an opportunity for couples to get to know each other and to save money so that their future children can have comfortable lives." Even though all of these women grew up with two or more siblings, they now consider two children per couple to be the "ideal" number. While "two" was the most common response to queries about the number of children they would like to have, both Zahra A. and Bahar said they would be content with one child to whom they could devote all their attention.

Religion

All of the young women have been raised as Shi'i Muslims. While all say that they try to be good Muslims, most admit that they do not pray regularly, even those who say that their own mothers do pray at least once per day. The religious traditions that they like are the festive observances at which large and special meals are served. Most of the young women say that many religious traditions are "old-fashioned" and no longer suitable. In particular, over half (19 of 28) have ambivalent or negative attitudes about the requirement that women and girls over nine years of age must wear *hejab* [modest covering of the hair and body] in public. Mina, for example, says,

My mother really thinks I dress too immodestly when I am in the city [Shiraz]. I admit it. I do. I really hate *hejab*. Why do these old men [the clergy] think they have a right to tell women how to dress? This is not Islam at all. It's just what men with bad ideas think. We [women] should be free to wear what we want to, just like in Europe. My Dad really is more liberal than my mother, and he never says anything if, when we are together outside, I fix my *rusari* [headscarf] so that most of my hair shows. My mother, she's just afraid of what people will say. Who cares? I'm not afraid of telling anyone, even my *amehs* [paternal aunts] and *khalehs* [maternal aunts] to mind their own business.

But Leila's attitudes seem more typical:

I believe that *hejab* is to protect women from men who are bad Muslims. Of course, it is more comfortable to wear a *rusari* and *manteau* (long, shapeless coat), but sometimes when I go to Shiraz, I wear my *chador*, which I have for religious occasions. I wear it in the city because some men there look at women in a really bad way, and the way they gawk makes me feel awful. And they even say very bad things. When I wear my *chador*, they don't bother me at all. It shouldn't be this way [that men harass women]; men should treat every girl like a sister, but the reality is that too many of them do not respect women. This is not the fault of Islam that men are so bad. They might say their prayers five times a day, but men who treat women badly are not good Muslims at all.

At this point, it is appropriate to point out that absent in this chapter are the attitudes of pious young women who practice religion and accept government interpretations of what constitutes an Islamic society as described in other chapters. No effort was made to exclude such women here; on the contrary, it would be interesting to hear their views on these same issues. However, I never had an opportunity to meet religious young women at those social gatherings I attended. Furthermore, I am unaware of any systematic study that tries to assess what percentage of women may fall into the category of the religiously devout. Even if they are a minority, it would be a sizable one, judging by the number of religious women (i.e., those who demonstrate their piety by wearing black *chadors*) that one sees in public spaces in large cities. These women obviously do not criticize *hejab* or Islam, but they may share similar attitudes about work as their less pious sisters, because they do have active roles in society, especially in terms of working for the security services (women's police and the *Basij-e Khaharan* [Mobilized Sisters], a morals patrol that makes sure women respect proper *hejab* in public) and the various Islamic charities. Perhaps their presence is more muted in villages, where social roles of extended families force both types of women to interact politely at various family functions.[8]

Gender inequality

Because these women seemed generally assertive and self-confident, I was surprised to hear an outburst of angry complaints about the government's inequitable treatment of women. This came from Parvin, as she was recounting preparations for her forthcoming trip to Sweden to visit her uncle and his family. According to Parvin,

Getting all the permissions to leave the country has been unbelieably frus-
trating. Even though I am 23, they [the government] say I cannot depart the
country without my father's permission. My father is paying for my trip, but
he can't go with me, as we are not wealthy by any means. Of course, he is
ready to sign whatever is needed, but everything has to done on special
forms and stamped in my passport, and that means going to so many [*sadha*]
different offices to get official signatures from bureaucrats who usually are
not at their desks, and so it is necessary to come back many times. It has
been such a waste of time, to go to Shiraz almost every day for two weeks.
And for what purpose is all this? Because I am a woman, and the government thinks I need a guardian? My brother Ali went to Sweden last year
when he was only 17. But boys over 16 are considered adults, and thus they
do not need any guardians and do not need to play all these games to prove
they have permission to leave the country. Does the government think
women are like children forever? What fools have written these dumb laws?

Parvin's complaints about the double standards in law prompted agreement
among the four other women present, and each, in turn, provided examples from
personal knowledge or experience about inequitable divorce and inheritance
laws.[9] In addition, *hejab* was raised as another issue of discrimination against
women. "Of course, we all believe in dressing modestly when we are out in the
city," said Fatemeh B., "but there is no need for laws about how women should
dress, and no one likes other women acting like cops and telling us that our
hejab is bad." Finally, Azadeh sighed, "Yes, we women give birth to boys and
raise them to be just men. But, too many men then think women – their mothers
– are children who do not know anything!"

Domestic politics

My trip in June 2005 coincided with a presidential election, and, consequently, I
expected to hear considerable talk about politics, as had been the case on prior
trips in 1997 and 2001, when everyone seem engaged with the presidential elections. The first round of voting featured eight candidates (although one withdrew
two days before the balloting), but general interest was comparatively restrained,
with most political discussions limited to assessing the relative merits or demer-
its of only four candidates, while the other three (including Mahmud Ahmadinejad) seemingly had not penetrated the thoughts of voters in Fars. The few young
women who were enrolled in college expressed a preference for Mostafa Moin,
who was running as the candidate for the party that supported the incumbent
president, Mohammad Khatami. Parvin, for example, insisted that Moin "understood" the problems of Iranian women, citing as evidence his appointment of a
prominent female politician to be his campaign spokesperson.

It did not surprise me that Parvin and a few other young women should prefer
a candidate who identified with Khatami's reform agenda, because these villages
had voted heavily for Khatami in both 1997 and 2001. Many people continued

to praise him and express regret that he could not run for a third term (prohibited by constitutional law). However, Parvin's views proved to be exceptional. The young woman who had not gone to college, for example, did not seem to know anything about Moin, and, in actuality, appeared to be apathetic about the election process. Several acknowledged, when pressed, that they were thinking of not voting because they could see no difference between the two candidates they heard about most in their homes: Ali Akbar Hashemi Rafsanjani, a former president; and Mehdi Karrubi, a Majles deputy. Nasrin summed up attitudes to which others nodded in assent: "They're old. They've been around since before I even was born; it's time for them to retire," said Nasrin. In contrast, the young men who were brothers or cousins of these young women tended to incline toward two conservative candidates, Mohammad Bagher Qalibaf, a former commander of the national police, or, prior to his late withdrawal from the campaign, Mohsen Reza'i. Typically, the local male youth made comments to the effect that these candidates "understood our generation better."

In these villages, 40 to 45 percent of eligible voters did not bother to vote in the first round, and most of these non-voters were women. This situation contrasted sharply with that of the two previous presidential elections, when turnout among women was very high; and it seemed to be an indication of the general ambivalence about all the candidates. Karrubi received more votes than any other candidates, but not more than 32 percent in any village, with Rafsanjani and Qalibaf ranking second and third respectively. This pattern was similar throughout Fars province, but differed significantly from the nationwide count: Rafsanjani emerged as the front-runner with 21 percent of the national vote, while Ahmadinejad came in at second place with 19 percent. Karrubi, who had obtained 30 percent of the vote in Fars, came in nationally at third place, with 17 percent of the vote. The result, which necessitated a second-round run-off election between the two highest vote-getters, was received with surprise in the villages. Ahmadinejad was virtually unknown, even though people had seen him on the live, televised candidates' debate during the week before the election.[10]

In reflecting on the election results, Roya seemed to express the general sentiment of most of the young women in the period between the first and second round of the presidential election:

I don't know who he [Ahmadinejad] is. Would he be better than Hashemi [Rafsanjani]? I don't know. Some people say anyone but Hashemi. But others say that this guy, Ahmad ... or whatever his name is, would be worse. How can he be worse? He at least is not a clergy. I don't remember when Hashemi was president, but my parents don't trust him. They say he doesn't care for people like us, that he is for the rich [*puldaran*]. I did not vote yesterday, and I don't know if I'll bother to vote next week. The last election [2001] was the first time I was old enough to vote. I was excited, and I was so happy to vote for Mr. Khatami. He is the best president that we have had. I don't think the people helped him enough. Not just poor people like us, but all those men who want to be president ... they didn't help him either.

And now they want to be president in his place? My father is right. He says all politics is dirty. I just don't care about any of these people [the candidates]. Mr. Khatami, he is different. I wish he could be president for longer. I would help him.

U.S.–Iran relations

I was in these villages on September 11, 2001, and learned of the events of that day by watching the scenes of the planes flying into the Twin Towers on television with a family that included five of the young women (sisters and cousins) in this chapter. The shock, disbelief really, among all the people in that room was palpable. The genuine expressions of sympathy I received over the next several days and a spontaneous candlelight remembrance ceremony held at a private research institute in Shiraz caused me to feel that, perhaps out of this terrible tragedy of senseless death and destruction, a new era could open in U.S.–Iran relations. Indeed, during the following weeks, after Al-Qaeda had taken responsibility for the terrorist attacks, Iran cooperated in discrete ways with U.S. plans to invade Afghanistan, where Al-Qaeda had established its base. Iran played a critical role, for example, in persuading the Northern Alliance, which Tehran recognized as the legitimate government of Afghanistan but Washington did not, to work with U.S. forces against the Taliban government.[11] Iran's "reward" for cooperation on Afghanistan came at the end of January 2002, when U.S. President George W. Bush denounced Iran, along with Iraq and North Korea, as members of an "axis of evil."[12] From that point, Iran, in the perception of U.S. policy and in the mainstream U.S. media, became a pariah, or 'rogue state.' Inevitably, questions about U.S.–Iran relations were raised in conversations during three subsequent research trips to Iran between 2003 and 2005, a period during which U.S. forces invaded, occupied, and became bogged down in an insurgency in Iraq, a country with which Iran shared a 700-mile border and a centuries-long history. In addition, Iran's eastern border was with Afghanistan. In effect, surrounded by a U.S. military presence, literally witnessing daily on television news the increasing civilian casualties in Afghanistan and Iraq, and reading the frequent calls by various U.S. officials for regime change in Iran, it was perhaps not unnatural that many Iranians might feel a sense of anxiety vis-à-vis U.S. intentions. This anxiety, even fear, was a sentiment that I encountered among the young women whenever conversations turned to U.S. policy.

In 2005, Yasmin, an articulate 20-year-old computer science major, startled me with her question: "Why does America hate Iran and want to attack us?" My efforts to explain the difference in the American system between political rhetoric and an actual decision to go to war were not persuasive. Yasmin continued,

America talked a lot before invading Afghanistan and then Iraq. For the past two years, they [Americans] always are saying that Iran is doing this and that. They want to attack us, bomb us, like they are doing in Iraq, Afghanistan. It is our homes they will bomb, just like we see them bomb all those houses, that whole city [Falujah] in Iraq. It is on the news. We can see it. It's true. It's not just the Iranian [government] TV. Look at the satellite channels, at the BBC ... al-Jezira ... CNN, and that one even is an American channel. I'm not saying, you, the people of America, want to do this. But the government of America does.

LEILA [interjecting]: That is right. Our leaders brag about how they don't fear America. But what do they know? They do not have anything to stop bombing raids. My uncle [an officer in the Revolutionary Guards] says that we don't have a real air force to defend against an American bomb attack. He says all we have are helicopters. How are they going to stop American bombers?

Nuclear program

Iran's nuclear energy program was not a topic of conversation in 2001, but in all subsequent trips it was a hot issue, primarily because of revelations in 2002 that Iran had developed facilities for processing and enriching uranium (before 2002) but had failed to disclose this information to the International Atomic Energy Agency (IAEA), which, as a member of that group, it was required to do. These revelations prompted the Bush administration to claim that Iran's nuclear energy program was a cover for a secret nuclear weapons development project. This charge is one that Iranian President Mohammad Khatami repeatedly denied, as did his successor, Ahmadinejad, after his election as president in 2005. The young women were aware of the nuclear controversy, but there was not a uniform view among them (or in the general population either). Based on our discussions, three general perspectives as to whether their government had a secret weapons program emerged among the women. Before looking at these perspectives, however, it is important to stress that all these women – as do the majority of Iranians in opinion polls – believe that Iran has the right to develop nuclear technology for peaceful purposes. Thus, for them, the issue is not about nuclear technology per se but rather about the kind of nuclear technology their government may be developing. Leila, for example, believes the government is truthful in its oft-repeated denials of having a secret nuclear weapons program (although she is critical of the government on other issues):

Even our Leader [Khamenehi] has said that it is un-Islamic to build a nuclear weapon. I believe the government, and someone as honest as [President] Khatami never would lie about anything, and certainly not about such a big issue as this. And how can [U.S. President] Bush keep saying that we have a bomb? Look, we allow international [IAEA] inspections all the time. Where is that place? Near Esfahan, I think. Natanz? Yes, that town is where they are enriching the uranium, and we see it all the time on TV, the international people [from the IAEA] inspecting the uranium and putting some kind of seal on it. I believe what they say on TV, that Bush makes these false charges to justify his hostile policy toward Iran, just like he did about

Iraq. It is scary. America might bomb us just like in Iraq. And they are going to bomb Natanz? Why? I have seen it on TV. It is just a little town in the desert. So, they are not going to waste their bombs there. Maybe they will bomb Shiraz, which is a big city, and here, we are just 15 kilometers from Shiraz. And it is we, the innocent, who will suffer ... like in Iraq ... and like in Palestine, also, as the Israelis do whatever they want there just like the Americans in Iraq.

Farzaneh, in contrast, was not convinced that the government was truthful when it denied having any program to develop a nuclear weapon. She opined that it was possible the government really did have a secret weapons program, but, since it was supposed to be secret, the government could not talk about it openly. Furthermore, she felt the government was justified in having a secret weapons program:

Our leaders should be developing nuclear weapons. It is their duty. Why?... Because of America! It has thousands of nuclear bombs, and it always is threatening Iran. Thus, if we have some, even one bomb, then America would treat us more respectfully. Why should America and Israel have all these weapons and say no other country can have them? We are not backward, primitive, we just want to be treated equally. I know nuclear weapons are bad, and one bomb can kill thousands of people. Really, no one should have them. But it is wrong for one or two countries to have them, then threaten others and say no other country can have them. That is my view: Either no country has them or all countries have them.

Farzaneh's position disturbed Forough, who insisted that all nuclear weapons were dangerous, and it would be wrong for Iran – or any other country – to develop them. In fact, she went further than anyone else by declaiming that if Iran was found to have a secretive nuclear weapons program, then she would support international sanctions against her own country. Despite her strong moral opposition to nuclear weapons, Forough did support Iran's right to develop nuclear technology, "to use in medicine and for electricity." A peaceful program, she said, should have no problem with international monitors inspecting its nuclear facilities, adding that this practice needed to be applied to all countries, "even America." She also agreed with Leila about the suspicious motives behind the U.S. charges against Iran, but she thought that her own government needed to engage more seriously in diplomatic negotiations to resolve the impasse and to demonstrate the peaceful nature of its nuclear program.

Conclusion

This chapter has provided a snapshot of views among some young women living in villages near Shiraz. These women may be considered to be part of the "raw data" that comprise the statistics presented by the authors of other chapters on the rising rates of female literacy, education, gainful employment, delayed marriage, etc. Because two-thirds of Iranian women live in cities, rural women no longer represent "typical" females, as may have been the case on the eve of the 1978 to 1979 Revolution, when the majority of women did live in villages. But can we assume that these young women are representative of their generation in all 70,000 Iranian villages? I suggest that such an assumption would be inaccurate. Rather they represent a particular class of young women living in villages located near Iran's largest cities. This particular class is a new rural middle class, one comprising nuclear families whose incomes may be derived entirely, partially, or not at all from farming. This new class is a post-revolutionary development, and may comprise half of all households in some villages but as few as 10 percent in others. Furthermore, this class is divided along religious lines: families that are very strict in their religious practices; and families that adopt a more lax attitude toward religious practices, although the latter are not secular. In political terms, the former tend to identify with various Conservative parties, the latter with Reformist parties.

What is significant about these religious orientations for this study is that all of the young women whose attitudes are described here are from families that are less strict in their religious practices. Thus, they represent a particular cultural orientation within the rural middle class, and cannot be assumed to represent the majority of rural young women in contemporary Iran. It is plausible that rural young women who live in religiously conservative middle-class families share attitudes similar to those that Farhad Khosrokhavar has documented in his chapter on youth in the religiously conservative city of Qom (Chapter 7). However, this is a topic that requires systematic research. Hopefully, this chapter – as well as all the others in this book – will stimulate aspiring scholars to investigate the manifold ways in which class and culture impact upon gender issues in both rural and urban Iran.

Notes

1 Socio-economic conditions in this region during the 1970s are examined in the last chapter of my book, *Land and Revolution in Iran, 1960–1980* (University of Texas Press, 1982), pp. 138–152.

2 For an overview of the economic changes in villages since the 1978 to 1979 Revolution, see Eric Hooglund, "Thirty Years of Islamic Revolution in Rural Iran," *Middle East Report*, 250 (spring 2009), pp. 34–39.

3 I want to extend a special thanks to the young women who shared their views with me: Azadeh, Bahar, Farzaneh, Fatemeh A., Fatemeh B., Fereshteh, Forough, Jaleh, Laleh, Leila, Maryam, Masumeh, Mina, Najmeh, Nasrin, Nilufar, Pari, Parvin, Roya, Sara, Setareh, Shirin, Simin, Soraya, Yasmin, Zahra A., Zahra B., and Zeinab. I am also grateful to colleagues who provided valuable comments on drafts of this chapter: Jabbar Bagheri, Roksana Bahramitash, Jaleh Taheri, and Carol Taylor.

4 I discussed some of these economic and social changes in Eric Hooglund, "Letter from an Iranian Village," *Journal of Palestine Studies*, 27, 1 (autumn 1997), pp. 76–84.

5 The most popular foreign films in the early 2000s seemed to be, in approximate order of numbers available, American, French, British, and Japanese (the latter being mostly the animation, known as "anime").

6 I am grateful to Jaleh Taheri for pointing out that the family in Iran provides not only affective support but protection from a "predatory state"; more generally, the family also provides protection from a society in which "bad things" can happen to individuals, especially women. For more on the role of the family as a source of protection (as well as of suppression) for women, see Fatemeh Sadeghi, "Double Agency: Women and Power in the Post-revolutionary Iran," in Eric Hooglund and Leif Stenberg (eds) *Navigating Contemporary Iran* (2010) London: Routledge.

7 The understood references to "pressure" and "going too far" in this conversation are to sexual relations, a subject which none of these young women would feel comfortable discussing openly with males. In these villages, it is still a very important social value for a girl to be a virgin when she gets married. Thus, when these young women talk about "Irani dates" the implication is that there are no sexual encounters.

8 For one short but insightful analysis of the *Basij-e khakharan*, see Fatemeh Sadeghi, "Foot Soldiers of the Islamic Republic's 'Culture of Modesty'," *Middle East Report*, 250 (spring 2009), pp. 50–55.

9 For more on the gender inequalities in the laws of Iran, see Chapter 1 by Louise Halper.

10 Ahmadinejad was Mayor of Tehran and came in first place in Tehran province, the country's most populous province. He also came in first place in Esfahan and Qom, where his well-organized supporters had campaigned effectively. The big leads in these populous areas more than compensated for his low votes in Fars and other provinces.

11 For an overview of U.S.–Iran cooperation in Afghanistan between September and December 2001, see Kenneth M. Pollack, *The Persian Puzzle: The Conflict between Iran and America* (New York: Random House, 2004), pp. 345–349.

12 For the text of George W. Bush's 2002 State of the Union Address in which he named Iran, Iraq, and North Korea as forming an "axis of evil" see: http://georgewbush-whitehouse.archives.gov/news/releases/2002/01/print/20020129-11.html   (accessed June 19, 2010).

9 Women's employment trends

Advance or retreat?

Roksana Bahramitash and Shala Kazemipour

There has been growing concern about women's poverty, and as a result there has been an increasing literature on women and development, much of it focused on the issue of women's employment/unemployment and poverty, but this is not the case with women in the Muslim world. Consequently, research and documentation of women's economic status in Muslim countries remains scarce. This is true despite the fact that a rich body of literature on women in Muslim countries exists. Part of the problem is related to the fact that there is a tendency to overlook women's economic role owing to the persistence of stereotypical assumptions even among academics to treat Muslim women as victims. As discussed in the introductory chapter, there has been a recent proliferation of literature by academics of post-colonial feminist theory that is critical of the mainstream literature on women in the Muslim world.[1] They are critical of focuses on the way Muslim women are being viewed as victims and the most oppressed "Other," and the effective creation of a dichotomy where Western women are the Self and Muslim women are the Other. The critiques challenge essentialist views of the impact of Islam upon women and argue that such essentialized views create barriers to understanding and analysis of women's reality in the Muslim world. In the context of Iran, ccommonly held assumptions about Iran are that in the aftermath of the Revolution and owing to Islamic ideology, female employment declined and the Shah's modernization plan was reversed. In this chapter as we shall see, the reality of women's employment indicates that in the past 50 years women's employment has continually increased. This process was interrupted in the aftermath of the Revolution in the decade following the Revolution, yet there are several factors other than Islamism at work. It is true that female employment remains relatively low in comparison with other regions of the world. Yet, at the same time, Iranian women's employment, like female employment in the rest of the Middle East and North Africa region (MENA), has increased at a much faster rate than any other region in the world.[2] Ironically, contrary to what is commonly believed, this high increase has been concurrent with rising support for Islamism.

A review of female employment in the post-revolutionary era may shed some light on the apparent contradiction between rising support for Islamism in MENA and the rapid increase in women's employment. Within Iranian studies literature many have argued that following the 1979 Revolution, women's employment declined.[3] While this is true of the decade immediately following the Revolution, an overall view of the changes in the past half century shows a steady increase in female employment. Others have argued that the process of Islamization has mobilized women of low income and traditionalist classes as volunteers in the decade following the Revolution.[4] This perhaps could explain some of the reasons for the decline in the 1980s.

Before proceeding to the analysis of this chapter, it is important to review some problems that exist when measuring female employment. Jennifer Olmsted in her analysis of Iranian women's employment has pointed out a problem in Iran similar to that in Egypt, and argues that "measuring female labor force participation is fraught with difficulties."[5] She quotes Anker and Anker who

> estimate that female employment levels in Egypt vary from 6.2 to 41.3, depending on the way work is defined. The World Bank (2004, p. 87) more recently discusses some of the problems with measuring female labor force participation, in Iran, Egypt, Jordan, Lebanon and Tunisia, suggesting that although scholars, statisticians and policy makers have become more aware that this is an issue in recent years, these problems are far from being resolved.[6]

Olmsted points out that much analysis of female employment has relied on census statistics, "which are the most conservative in terms of their estimates of women's employment and clearly underestimate women's participation in a number of ways."[7] However, with regard to pre-revolutionary Iran, Olmsted raises an interesting question about the possibility of a willingness on the part of the data-gathering process to demonstrate a higher participation for women as part of a political will to show that modernization and the incorporation of women into the economy has taken great strides.

Documentation of women's work in Iran has encountered yet another problem: their engagement in the informal sector. Official data do record some of the work done by women in the informal sector but fail to capture the entire informal sector, and this adds to the problem of undercounting. This is a major problem, particularly given that the state may be inefficient in gathering accurate data. This sector is already significant in the Iranian economy and increasingly as a source of employment for many. Generally however, this type of employment characteristically tends to be undercounted, particularly for women who become engaged in this sector in their home in a gender-segregated society.

Formal employment, overall trend: does Islam work against women?

As discussed in the previous section, female labor force participation has increased over the past two decades, according to the latest data gathered in the 2006 census.[8] Table 9.1 indicates that over the course of the past 50 years

(1956–2006), the female labor force has increased from 0.6 million to 3.6 million, a six-fold increase. The increase is even sharper in the urban areas, from 0.19 million in 1956 to 2.5 million in 2006, an increase of 13.5 times, compared with a 7.9-fold increase for men. This has led to an increase in women's share of the total labor force from just under 10 percent in 1956 to almost 16 percent in 2006. The fact that female employment has increased more than that of men is significant. However, the data also show that the rise in female labor was interrupted following the Revolution during the 1976–1986 period, when the urban labor force increased by only 1.5 times for women, which is very close to that of men, namely 6.0.

This trend clearly complicates simplistic assumptions about the overall impact of the Revolution and Islam. Especially when a panoramic view of the general economic performance of the country is taken into account, one sees that there was a decline in overall employment as a result of economic decline in the 1980s. Interestingly, a general overall decline of the economy had begun before the Revolution, as data from 1976 show, a trend that accelerated and continued into the 1980s and ended in the 1990s (after reaching a high in 1993).[9] A large part of that decline is related to Iran's dependence on oil revenues and the world oil market in particular; During the 1980s, the war and economic sanctions against Iran illustrate the economic reasons for the drop in employment in the decade following the post-revolutionary period. One result of an overall decline of the economy has been a decline in employment for both men and women.

As stated above, it is true that in the aftermath of the Revolution, many women were either forced or chose to leave their jobs because of imposed dress codes and/or their alleged or real affiliation to the deposed monarchy and/or proscribed counter-revolutionary organzations. Yet, when one looks more carefully into rural and urban dynamics, another interesting pattern appears. The data

Table 9.1 Share of women in the labor force, employment, and unemployment for population aged ten years and over (percent)

Census year	1956	1966	1976	1986	1996	2006
Labor force						
All Country	9.5	13.2	14.8	10.2	12.7	15.5
Urban	9.9	11.5	11.3	10.5	11.7	15.8
Rural	9.3	14.1	17.6	9.8	14.2	14.7
Employment						
All Country	9.7	13.3	13.8	8.9	12.1	13.6
Urban	10.3	11.8	11.2	8.8	11.3	13.9
Rural	9.4	14.1	16.0	8.9	13.4	12.8
Unemployment						
All Country	1.3	12.4	23.8	18.3	18.7	28.3
Urban	1.2	7.6	13.0	20.1	16.6	30.0
Rural	1.4	13.7	26.9	15.7	21.5	25.4

Source: Bahramitash and Esfahani (2011).

show that overall employment for women in the urban areas declined very marginally in the period following the Revolution, while the fall in female employment was primarily a rural phenomenon. As Table 9.1 shows, the share of female participation and employment rises from 9.5 and 9.7 percent respectively in the mid-1950s to 14.8 and 13.8 percent in 1976, but declines to 10.2 and 8.9 during the 1980s before rising to 15.5 and 13.6 in 2006. When one looks at urban–rural dynamics, one sees that much of the decline in the 1980s took place in the rural areas, which were simultaneously experiencing major migration to cities. Table 9.1 shows that labor force participation[10] and employment in urban areas rises from 9.9 in 1956 to 11.3 in 1976, then declines marginally to 10.5 in 1986, compared to figures in rural areas where the labor force is 9.3 in 1956, increasing much rapidly to 17.6 in 1976, but then there is a sharp decline in 1986 to 9.8. The employment figures are very similar to those of the labor force which indicate that much of the post-revolutionary decline of female labor was a rural phenomenon. These data provide a real challenge to the allegation that Islamism was the reason for the decline, because those living in rural areas tended to be religious, and the Islamic Revolution did not significantly impact upon their traditional attitudes about or practices of Islam. Thus, if Islamism does not provide a sufficient explanation for the decline of female employment in the 1980s, what other factors can explain this decline?

One possible factor may be that during the Shah's rule prior to 1979, there could have been a tendency to inflate the female employment figure in order to have a higher statistic to show that Iranian women were 'modern' and also that the 'modern' state's record and documentation of female employment was efficient. Other possible factors may be related to several economic changes. After the Revolution, economic factors also contributed to the decline of female employment, such as the decline in the carpet industry due to an economic embargo on Iran. Zahra Karimi, for example, argues that "after Islamic Revolution (1979), due to US sanctions against Iran, production and exports of Persian carpets declined significantly. For example, during 1978–1982 exports of carpets declined from 1.84 to 0.71 million square meters and carpet production decreased from 5 to 1.4 million square meters."[11] Karimi argues that due to the fact that much of female employment in the textile industry was in rural areas, the decline in the carpet industry affected female employment in the rural sector significantly. She documents that from "1976–86, the number of workers in Iran's textile industry decreased from about 1,010,000 to 830,000. Women in rural areas lost about 340,000 jobs; mainly carpet-weavers."[12]

In addition to this there was a massive effort on the part of the state for better education. The rise in education has been significant.[13] Table 9.2 shows how literacy rates increased, particularly among young females aged ten and above: 7.3 in 1956 to 96.1 in 2006. Considering the fact that illiteracy was high in the rural areas in the mid-1950s, some of the post-revolutionary decline in the rural sector employment for girls may be explained by the expansion of basic literacy even for those between the ages of 15 and 24. For these women, there has been an increase in literacy rate from 10 percent in 1956 to 96.1 percent in 2006. There

Table 9.2 Literacy rate

Census year	1956	1966	1976	1986	1996	2006
Literacy rate of population aged 10 years and over						
Female	7.3	16.5	30.5	47.6	71.7	79.5
Youth literacy rate aged 15–24						
Female	10.0	23.6	41.2	65.4	90.3	96.1
Total	19.0	37.6	54.1	75.1	92.9	96.6

Source: Bahramitash and Esfahani (2011).

has also been a major increase in primary and secondary education as well as tertiary education, which is discussed by Reza-Rashi in Chapter 4.

Having discussed achievements, it is important to point to one of the most important challenges for women in contemporary Iran: that of unemployment. The unemployment problem is a major dilemma for Iran. This is related to the fact that the Iranian population is very young: 70 percent of the population is below the age of 35. Moreover, the country is dependent upon oil and has embarked on many capital-intensive industries such as automobile production. The latter started during the time of the Shah and continued into the post-revolutionary period. As illustrated in Table 9.1, the total figure for unemployment is 28.3 percent; this is much higher among urban women, many of whom are educated. In fact, one of the most challenging dilemmas facing Iranian women is their lack of access to jobs matching their education and skills.

Where are the women? And what are they doing?

We have seen that female employment in the urban area in fact has experienced an increase with a fairly marginal decline during the 1980s. We also know that education has increased among women (see Chapter 4); therefore, there are many educated women in urban areas and in the labor force. Now that more women of higher education are in the labor force it is worth asking the question: where are they and what kinds of jobs they are doing?

The data show that from 1966 to 2006 the percentage of female employed in the executive, administrative, and managerial sectors has increased; much of the increase interestingly has occurred in the period from 1986 to 2006. Although the overall percentage remains low and women continue to suffer from the glass ceiling problem, nonetheless, some of the increase in urban employment has been in top positions. By far the largest increase has taken place in the professional and technical where nearly half employed women seem to be. This is to some extent related to the expansion of education which is segregated by gender (as it had been under the monarchy). The issue of gender segregation itself is interesting and is discussed separately in the following section, but here it is worth nothing that, owing to gender-segregated education and in some cases the

Table 9.3 Distribution of female employment by occupational categories (percent of total female employment in each area)

Census year	1966	1976	1986	1996	2006
Urban areas					
Executive, administrative, and managerial	0.1	0.3	0.3	3.9	4.5
Professional and technical	13.2	36.9	59.9	52.8	49.3
Administrative support, clerical, services, and sales	4.7	14.7	15.8	15.9	21.8
Farming, forestry, and fishing	2.3	2.2	2.4	1.7	1.2
Industrial production, transportation, and simple labor	60.7	30.6	13.5	21.7	19.3
Rural areas					
Executive, administrative, and managerial	0.0	0.01	0.02	0.4	0.6
Professional and technical	0.6	2.4	6.1	5.6	9.0
Administrative support, clerical, services, and sales	0.3	0.4	1.5	3.1	5.7
Farming, forestry, and fishing	31.7	28.8	54.3	30.7	35.8
Industrial production, transportation, and simple labor	65.4	66.5	34.8	57.0	45.1

Source: Bahramitash and Esfahani (2011).

healthcare system, new employment opportunities for women in post-revolutionary Iran have been created. These employment opportunities, however, have declined as public education declined owing to population decline and reduction in public spending in the 1990s.

Census data indicate that the percentage of women employed in administrative support, clerical, services, and sales has grown from 4.7 percent in 1956 to 21.8 percent in 2006. This in fact is very apparent in major cities such as Tehran, Isfahan, and Shiraz where increasingly women are entering the service sector. Some of this corresponds with a global trend toward women entering the service sector of the economy but sexual segregation also plays a role. Women are entering all female business clientele such as the sale of women's and children's clothing.

Another significant change which has occurred is in the pattern of employment category. The role of women as employers seems to have peaked from 1996 to 2006 in the urban economy. This as we shall see may be related to the expansion of the informal sector in the urban areas. Corresponding figures for the self-employed in both rural and urban areas have increased and this is indeed highly related to the informal sector where the type of employment often falls into the category of self employment. Here it is significant to note that numbers of unpaid family workers have dropped more dramatically in the rural areas and this may well be related to the decline of the carpet industry since the production is home-based cottage industry. The significance of the rising share of women as particularly employers and self-employed and the decline of unpaid family

Table 9.4 Distribution of female employment across private sector positions (percentages of total female employment in each area)

Census year	1956	1966	1976	1986	1996	2006
Share of private sector in female employment – urban areas	**86.3**	**78.9**	**50.0**	**20.4**	**31.2**	**48.8**
As employers	0.8	1.01	0.59	1.04	0.92	4.61
As self-employed	10.9	12.8	8.7	9.2	12.7	16.6
As private employees	72.5	59.5	29.8	7.8	13.1	25.3
As unpaid family workers	2.1	5.6	11.0	2.4	4.4	2.3
Share of private sector in female employment – rural areas	**98.5**	**98.6**	**96.2**	**87.1**	**86.5**	**85.2**
As employers	0.5	0.44	0.35	1.79	0.92	2.82
As self-employed	28.5	26.5	12.1	28.8	28.6	34.6
As private employees	44.1	41.3	24.6	12.8	15.6	15.9
As unpaid family workers	25.4	30.3	59.2	43.8	41.5	31.9

Source: Bahramitash and Esfahani (2011).

workers in rural and urban areas reflects some of the important changes which have occurred, particularly during the past decade. In the following section on the informal sector and findings from research conducted in Tehran, these data will be discussed in more detail.

Gender segregation and the informal sector

The literature on women's employment indicates that there is gender segregation in the workplace everywhere in the world and that includes the developing world.[14] This situation is true of women in Islamic countries. Generally, gender segregation works against women both in the formal and the informal sector since women tend to fill jobs which are at the margin of the labor market and are the lowest paid. This is true of Iran. However, in the context of Muslim countries the situation is a little more complex. In fact, it is not clear whether gender segregation hinders women's access to employment quite in the same way as in other countries. Gender segregation is a barrier to entry into some professions such as women working as judges, a case which happened in Iran. Yet, at the same time, it has opened other doors in a sexually segregated labor market and as an example it has created jobs particularly in education because of job opportunities. This was very apparent during the decade after the Revolution when, for instance, in the case of male high schools teachers were not allowed to be teachers and a desperate shortage of female math and physics teachers occurred, leading to rising demand for these subjects. This translated into encouraging girls to take up math and physics at higher education. This may explain why the percentage of women in fields such as engineering is relatively high in Iran. More generally the expansion of education led to a rise in demand for female teachers at primary and tertiary level. In the case of Iran's family planning, a new career opportunity was opened up to young women in rural areas as health workers (*behvarz*).[15] This is also true of other professions, particularly sports and recreational centers where the space is female only. Throughout the country public sports centers (as well as those that are privately owned) have been forced to hire women instructors. More recently, other jobs such as female taxi drivers have entered the market on a large scale.[16] These types of professions are reflected in Table 9.4 in the category of self-employed in the private sector.

My research in Iran suggests that gender segregation has created opportunities for women to engage in all-female production of goods and services.[17] In the informal sector, this has been confirmed by Fatemeh Moghadam's research.[18] Female-only goods and services such as women's underwear, women's and children's clothes, religious performances (*molidy* singing), to name a few are the types of goods and services from which men by and large are excluded and this is definitely the case in the informal economy. My fieldwork led me to the important observation that female spaces, such as hair salons, are simultaneously places where women engage in a host of commercial activities. During one of my pieces of fieldwork as a participant observer of a formal hair salon in a middle-income nighborhood, I was able to record different types of activities such as sales of different items from cosmetics, to underwear, to private personal training. When I asked for a rental apartment for myself as a single woman, another set of activities around real state and rental was revealed. The owner and other customers came up with an extensive list of rentals and offered to act as a mediator and guarantor for me. This opened my eyes to the existence of a shallow economy working through a female network, some of it for pay and in return for monetary reward. The issue of female networks will be discussed more in the context of low-income households later in this chapter and separately because, based on my fieldwork observation, neighborhood ties and community bounds are stronger and therefore the role of information gatekeeping was more pronounced.

Another point about gender segregation is that some women may prefer spaces which are all-female for reasons such as sexual harassment. In one of the interviews conducted, a female home gallery owner preferred to work from home because she could dress how she liked, not have to drive to work and have her students come home, and most importantly avoid sexual harassment. This is not to argue that gender segregation, whether based on the structure of the labor market or on religion, is ideal and/or desirable, of course, but only to point to the possible complexities involved.

Gender segregation and the informal sector are in some cases very closely tied together because many informal professions are home based where women create female-only spaces. In these cases women's work tends to fall into a domain which has the highest tendency to invisibility.[19] Often, women's work, particularly in home-based micro-enterprises, is hard to document and easy to overlook. This is an even larger challenge in the context of a sexually segregated society of Muslim countries. When women's work becomes invisible it seizes to exist, feeding stereotypes and Othering of Muslim women.

There has been a failure to document and see women's work in the informal sector of the economy as serious, particularly in the context of the current global trend toward formalization of the economy. In the case of Iran, the United Nations has estimated that the informal sector constitutes 65 percent of the country's GNP.[20] This is to some extent a general world pattern. Typically this sector of the economy is low paid and exploitive but increasingly it is becoming the only source of employment for many of the working poor. This is exacerbated by the decline of the role of the state and the public sector. For example, in a survey research on the informal sector in Tehran, which was carried out in five different neighbourhoods – very high income, high, medium, medium low and low income – sample interviews revealed a great deal of economic activity not captured by official statistics. It also found that the women interviewed had not reported their activities when national census data were gathered in 2006.[21] The research chose its sample from three different categories of women: formally employed women, informally employed women, and housewives. In our research we found that a positive relationship existed between those who came from a low-income background and their employment in the informal sector. The issue of over-representation of low-income women in our sample in the informal sector resonates with general findings in other countries. For this reason and to address the lack of documentation of low-income women in this sector, I decided to take the research further and to focus on women from low-income backgrounds. I started with a few focus groups in different low-income neighborhoods.

At this stage, four focus groups were held, each comprising four to six women from low-income households. A total of 18women were interviewed. I asked only a few questions of the women participating in the focus groups and allowed women to speak freely of their work and their access to credits and loans. The results were codified and combined with open-ended questions to interview an additional 12 women, taking the total number of women interviewed to 30.

The focus groups were organized based on the social ties of our network of friends and university students, as well as in collaboration with a local woman NGO. In one of the focus groups in a Molavi neighborhood (an old and poor neighborhood in the south of Tehran.), the neighborhood is dominated by migrants from Azerbaijan (a north-western province) who established themselves as a community in the neighborhood. This meant that their system of social networks, as a migrant community, expanded beyond the networks of women. They were proud of their heritage and by settling in close proximity to each other they continue to maintain their ties. Within this tight-knit community women are important gatekeepers and play a major role in the maintenance of social networks. The social network is vital to the community not just at a social level but at an economic level, where business in the informal sector relays on the network for credit and sale.

The literature on the informal sector indicates that owing to the low capital requirements of this sector of the economy, the community and community resources are important sources of credit which may be drawn from the family and the community. The informal finance raised and distributed through social networks and within the extended family and local community can be a source of start-up capital for a business as well as financial support necessary in times of economic problems. In the research with Shahla Kazemipur, we found that among our sample of more than 100 women where capital was required, nearly everyone raised their start-up capital through informal finance (there were only two cases where women used sources other than their family). Raising funds is part of a social network and social capital which women may draw upon within the informal sector.

This is not limited to Iran; both Diane Singerman and Homa Hoodfar have documented how the informal economy is tied to women's role in the community and how it is related to informal finance. Singerman discusses reciprocity and women's importance,[22] while Hoodfar documents how women's role in the community and the practice of reciprocity are linked to savings clubs in urban Cairo, where they play a major role in the informal sector. Women, particularly older women, are highly involved in community saving clubs.[23] These types of credits are tied to the family and to the community. This I found to apply to the case of Iran where women of low-income households in particular were involved in credit clubs, called *garzol hassaneh*.

However, the issue of female networks and the informal sector goes beyond simply women's economic status. Mansoureh (the name has been changed), a hairdresser in her late thirties, was one of the women from the focus groups. She had started her hairdressing business working as an apprentice but had slowly learned enough to run her own business and eventually turn her house into a hair salon as her parents grow old. By working hard, she had helped her brothers to buy their own home by taking out a mortgage on the house and, as well as working, she is caring for her elderly parents. She was single and had no plans to get married, yet in spite of her relatively young age she enjoyed a great deal of community respect. She was highly involved in community events and organized all women's tours and pilgrimages, and charity funds for those in need but more significantly she was a community trustee and her house acted as a shelter for battered women. Because of her good reputation and her highly respectable social standing, her house was used as a shelter whenever a woman was battered by her husband. Her house had been turned into a sanctuary and a place no man could prevent his wife from going to without being shunned by the community. This case is particularly striking and worth mentioning individually to illustrate the extent to which women can, through their role in the informal economy, rise to become community organizers and community leaders.

Some scholars argued that the informal economy and women's access to employment in this sector are a source of economic empowerment.[24] In fact, this may be relevant to our fieldwork finding as all-female businesses have a potential for women who are in need of access to cash for their businesses. This is complemented by a non-monetary flow of goods and services which can act as both social and economic capital. A recent World Bank working paper about rural Bangladesh points out that "access to transfer and credit, whether cash or in kind, is a major source of poverty alleviation in many developing countries."[25] The same paper documented that "The informal financial sector is also a key source of social protection … the informal sector … includes transactions [of such items] as gifts, loans from relatives, friends and neighbours."[26] The extent of such transactions is huge, and the paper points out that in the Philippines gifts and loans comprise 80 percent of what is received informally.

Before ending this chapter, I would like to mention in passing that the informal sector is different for different social classes. As argued before, women of middle- and high-income households have a tendency to prefer working in the informal sector for reasons such as being able to avoid taxes, male harassment, and not having to observe the dress code. In the case of the low-income informal sector, it is less about choice and more about necessity and in some of the jobs available to those on a low income terms of employment are less than desirable. This is particularly the case with domestic care givers and street vendors. In my research on street vendors in Tehran and Mashhad, the average income of those interviewed was five dollars a day (30 interviews were conducted).[27] In the case of daily care givers, my research remained at a preliminary observation and it seemed that this is a type of job which leaves women at the mercy of their employers. However, the interesting point was that those who found employment through their social network and who worked within their own community or close circles fare much better than those who had migrated from rural areas and had no social network.

Conclusion

This chapter began with the post-colonial feminist critique and drew from the introductory chapter on challenging the mainstream views of Muslim women as victims and then turned to the case of Iranian women's employment. Unlike the case of Afghanistan under the Taliban regime but similar to other countries in MENA, female employment in Iran has increased over the past three decades. There are two points to be made here. On the one hand, Islamic religious fundamentalism in cases such as Afghanistan under the Taliban did lead to the banning of women from all public domains, which may suggest that there are variations within the Islamist movement; on the other hand, even though overall female employment in MENA is rising fast, it remains comparatively low. The latter point is relevant to the case of Iran where female employment is low compared with other countries outside of the MENA region (it falls within the regional pattern). Therefore, even though there has been overall growth in the past few decades, the total employment figures are not particularly impressive.

Nonetheless, women have increased their participation despite a decline in the early post-revolutionary period. In fact, a close look at the decline in the 1980s revealed that the phenomena were related more to issues such as an overall decline of employment due to war and an economic embargo. Moreover, most of the jobs lost were rural and not necessarily urban (the decline in female employment in urban areas was relatively marginal). The rural dynamic of employment decline makes it hard to argue that Islamism was the reason for the decline in female employment because rural Iran had been more religious before the Revolution. The decline of rural employment was itself related to the decline of the carpet industry due to an economic embargo. In addition, expansion of education played an important role in the rural employment figures, as becomes apparent when looking at the literacy rate of girls above the age of ten as well as the high enrollment of girls in primary and secondary education. Moreover, the percentage of unwaged family workers has declined, suggesting that those in the cottage carpet industry were sent to school. Furthermore, data on unwaged family workers had been declining, further suggesting that the rural labor decline was related to education.

Yet, the issue of high female unemployment, particularly in the case of educated women, is a major problem. Thirty percent unemployment among urban women is perhaps one of the most serious challenges for Iranian women, many of whom are well educated and given the fact that more than half of university students are women. Thus, it is no surprise that the informal sector is significant, since employment in this sector of the economy is more accessible than in the formal sectors. This type of employment, however, remains invisible. It is very possible that a more careful examination of the informal sector would push up employment figures for women.

Part of this invisibility is related to the fact that there is sexual segregation and women's work, particularly in the informal sector, takes place in all-female space. As discussed in the chapter, gender segregation typically against women in the context of Iran has closed the doors to certain professions but ironically it has opened others. Women in the informal sector have managed to become active in all-female clientele businesses. In the case of low-income households, they are involved in different types of activities and such activities are tied to the community network and vital to survival strategies and the social safety net.

It seems that far from women becoming victims of Islam, contemporary women in Iran are in the labor force more than they ever have been in the past and are in professions that are increasingly atypical of traditional female employment. With regard to gender segregation, it appears that it has been turned on its head, particularly in the context of the informal sector where gender segregation has been used to enter professions from which men cannot be excluded. Contemporary Iran does not lend itself to a society plagued by backwardness and female oppression but one where women have resisted, negotiated, and succeeded in removing some of the barriers and who continue to challenge and press for more change.

Notes

1 See, e.g., Partha Chatterjee, P. (1986) *Nationalist Thought and The Colonial World: a Derivative Discourse* (London: Zed Books); Minh-Ha, T. (1989) *Women, Native, Other* (Indianapolis: Indiana University Press); Mernissi, F. (1985) *Beyond the Veil* (Bloomington: Indiana University Press); Yegenoglu, M. (1998) *Colonial Fantasies: Towards a Feminist Reading of Orientalism* (Cambridge: Cambridge University Press); Leila Ahmed (1992) *Women and Gender in Islam: Historical Roots of a Modern Debate* (New Haven, CT: Yale University Press); Abu-Lughod, L. (2001) "Orientalism and Middle East feminist studies," *Feminist Studies*, 27, 1, pp. 101–113; Moallem, M. (2005) *Between Warrior Brother and Veiled Sister* (Los Angeles: University of California Press); Mohanty, C. (2003) *Feminist without Borders: Decolonizing Theory, Practicing Solidarity* (Durham, NC: Duke University Press); and Olmsted, J. (2005) "Is paid work the (only) answer? Neoliberalism, Arab women's well-being and the social contract," *Journal of Middle East Women's Studies*, 1, 2 (spring): pp. 112–139.
2 See Shafik, N. (2001) "Closing the gender gap in the Middle East and North Africa," in Mier Cinar (ed.)*The Economics of Women and Work in the Middle East and North Africa* (London: Elsevier Science).
3 See, e.g., Moghadam, V. (1991) "The reproduction of gender inequality in Muslim societies: a case study of Iran in the 1980s," *World Development*, 19, 10, pp. 1335–1349; Moghadam, V. (1995) "Women's employment issues in contemporary Iran: problems and prospects in the 1990s," *Iranian Studies*, 28, 3–4, pp. 175–202; Moghissi, H. (1996) *Populism and Feminism in Iran: Women's Struggle in a Male-defined Revolutionary Movement* (New York: St. Martin's Press); Afshar, H. (1997) "Women and work in Iran," *Political Studies*, 45, 4, pp. 755–767; Alizadeh, P. and Harper, B. (2003) "The feminization of the labour force," in Ali Mohammadi (ed.) *Iran Encountering Globalization: Problems and Prospects* (New York: Routledge), pp. 180–196, 269–286; Behdad, S. and Farhad, T. (2006) *Class and Labor in Iran: Did the Revolution Matter?* (Syracuse, NY: Syracuse University Press).

4 For more examples see Paidar, P. (1995) *Women and the Political Process in Twenti-eth Century Iran* (Cambridge: Cambridge Middle East Studies); Poya, M. (1999) *Women, Work and Islamism* (London: Zed Books); Mehran, G. (2003) "The paradox of tradition and modernity in female education in the Islamic Republic of Iran," *Comparative Education Review*, 47, 3, pp. 269–286; Roksana Bharmaitash and Hadi Esfahani (eds) (2011) *Veiled Employment: The Political Economy of Female Employment in Iran* (Syracuse, NY: Syracuse University Press); and Goli Reza-Rashti (Chapter 4) and Jaleh Taheri (Chapter 6), this volume.

5 See Olmsted, J. (2005) "Is paid work the (only) answer? Neoliberalism, Arab women's well-being and the social contract," *Journal of Middle East Women's Studies*, 1, 2 (spring), pp. 112–139.

6 See Olmsted, J. (2011) "Gender and globalization; the Iranian experience," in Roksana Bahramitash and Hadi Esfahani (eds) *Veiled Employment: The Political Economy of Female Employment in Iran* (Syracuse, NY: Syracuse University Press).

7 Ibid.

8 Ibid.: Esfahani.

9 Ibid.

10 Female labour force participation refers to the number of women who are employed as well as those who are unemployed as a proportion of a specific age group (usually 16–65).

11 Karimi, Z. (2011) "The effects of international trade on gender inequality in Iran: the case of women carpet-weavers," in Bahramitash and Esfahani (eds) *Veiled Employment: The Political Economy of Female Employment in Iran* (Syracuse, NY: Syracuse University Press).

12 Ibid.

13 Bahramitash, R. (2006) "Female employment and globalization during Iran's reform era (1997–2005)," *Journal of Middle East Women Studies*, 3, 2 (spring), pp. 56–86.

14 See Joekes, S. (1987) *Women in the World Economy: United Nations International Research and Training Institute for the Advancement of Women* (New York: Oxford University Press); Anker, R. (1998) *Gender and Jobs: Sex Segregation of Occupations in the World* (Geneva: International Labour Office.); and Anker, R. (2001) "Theories of occupational segregation by sex: an overview," in Martha F. Loutfi (ed.) *Women, Gender and Work* (Geneva: International Labour Office), pp. 129–157.

15 Bahramitash, R. (2007) "Family planning, Islam and women's human rights in Iran," *International Development Studies Journal*, ISJ 4, 1 (summer), pp. 33–50.

16 *Time* magazine. Available online at www.time.com/time/world/article/0,8599,1847151,00.html (accessed May 26, 2010).

17 Bahramitash, R. and Kazemipour, S. (forthcoming) "Veiled economy: gender and the informal sector," in Bahramitash and Esfahani (eds) *Veiled Employment: The Political Economy of Female Employment in Iran* (Syracuse, NY: Syracuse University Press).

18 Moghadam, F. (forthcoming) "Iran's missing working women," in Roksana Bahramitash and Hadi Esfahani (eds) *Veiled Employment: The Political Economy of Female Employment in Iran* (Syracuse, NY: Syracuse University Press).

19 Ibid.

20 United Nations (2003) *United Nations Common Country Assessment for the Islamic Republic of Iran* (Tehran: UNCR), p. 40.

21 Bahramitash, R. and Kazemipour, S. (forthcoming) "Veiled economy: gender and the informal sector," in Bahramitash and Esfahani (eds) *Veiled Employment: The Political Economy of Female Employment in Iran* (Syracuse, NY: Syracuse University Press).

22 Singerman, D. (1997) *Avenues of Participation: Family, Politics and Networks in Urban Quarters of Cairo* (Egypt: The American University in Cairo Press).

23 Hoodfar, H. (1997) *Between Marriage and the Market: Intimate Politics and Survival in Cairo* (Berkeley: University of California Press); Chant, S. (1997) *Women Headed*

Households: Diversity and Dynamics in the Developing World (London: Macmillan), pp. 217–219.

24 See, e.g., Chant, S. (1991) *Women and Survival in Mexican Cities: Perspectives on Gender, Labour Markets, and Low-income Households* (New York: Manchester University Press).

25 McKernan, S-M., Pitt, M., and Moskowitz, D. (2005) "Use of the formal and informal financial sectors: does gender matter? Empirical evidence from rural Bangladesh." Available online at www.urban.org/uploadedpdf/411160_financial_sectors.pdf (accessed May 26, 2010), p. 1.

26 Ibid., p. 5.

27 See further Bahramitash, R. and Kazemipour, S. (2011) "Veiled economy: gender and the informal sector," in Bahramitash and Esfahani (eds) *Veiled Employment: The Political Economy of Female Employment in Iran* (Syracuse, NY: Syracuse University Press).

10 Extra legal/informal settlements

Does gender matter?

Roksana Bahramitash and Zohreh Fanni

This book has documented some of the opportunities and challenges women in Iran face in different spheres of their lives from culture and attitudes toward education to employment and law at both the macro and micro levels. In this chapter we wish to start a preliminary discussion on the issue of shelter. According to UN-Habitat, it is estimated that the world's slum population will double in the next 30 years and the problem is a global challenge facing our future world.[1] With increasing UN-approved economic sanctions on Iran and the global financial meltdown on the one hand and government mishandling of the economy on the other hand, the relevance of the housing problem for vulnerable populations has become highly important. Moreover, there is a growing literature that documents the vital role women play in community development and housing in general, and in informal settlements in particular.[2] Here our emphasis is on the major role that women play in poverty alleviation and sustainable urban planning, rather than on greater gender equality, although we recognize that gender inequality is a subject of great magnitude that affects the strategies women adopt to deal with poverty. In addition, while we recognize that a comprehensive analysis of the housing situation in the case of rising property values and rentals and their impact on those in the lower strata of society is essential, in this chapter we wish to focus on just one aspect of housing, that of the informal, or extra-legal settlements.

Rising urban population as the result of a declining agricultural sector and population growth in Iran has been documented in the work of academics.[3] The trend had started under the Shah during the 1960s and accelerated during the first two decades of the Islamic Republic (*c*.1980–2000).[4] A rising urban population, growing poverty, and the need for low-income housing led to the expansion of shanty towns adjacent to Iran's cities. Asef Bayat, for example, has written comprehensively on the topic and has elaborated on slum settlements and their relationship to the rise of urban popular movements.[5] In fact, growing poverty in the shanty towns of south and east Tehran was an embarrassment to the Shah's glorification of modernization that characterized his pre-revolutionary governments. The intention may have been to set up small satellite cities for different income groups as part of the Shah's third development plan, but these state-funded projects were inadequate to address the housing needs of the poor and did not prevent the growth of illegal settlements on government land, such as *Zurabad* [founded by force] next to Karaj. These illegal settlements, or to borrow from Hernando de Soto's terminology 'extra-legal settlements,'[6] did not disappear no matter how hard the government tried to discourage them, including the infamous bulldozing of illegal houses in east Tehran in the summer of 1977.

As Iran's poor and economically marginalized were mobilized for the Revolution, post-revolutionary Iran sought to address their problems by legalizing what before the Revolution were illegal settlements. Since the idea of the revolution was based on fighting disempowerment and many of those living in slums were mobilized for the Revolution, illegal/extra-legal settlements slowly came to be part of the habitat of the new, increasingly urbanized Iran. Here we need to make clear that these extra-legal settlements were (and are) not homogenous and vary according to their size and the quality of shelter they provide, nor are they static (they keep changing over time). Some of these extra-legal/informal settlements are comparable with low-income housing in inner cities (such as those of Tehran) while others are merely shanty towns, such as those outside of Zahedan (the capital of Sistan and Baluchestan, the least economically prosperous provinces in Iran). As the boundaries of mega-cities such as Tehran expand, extra-legal settlements become part of the mega-city, which means that municipalities and the Ministry of Urban Development and Planning have to be prepared to keep track of these settlements and the government, both at the national and local levels, has to provide services such as access to tap water and electricity as well as other basic services such as communications.

According to data from the Ministry of Housing and Urban Development (MHUD) in 2003, household income is highly related to home ownership. We do not have any time series data at this point, but it is highly probable that the problem of poverty is related to rising inflation and high unemployment, two conditions for which we do have data, and in this book there are numerous references to increases in unemployment (see, for example, Chapter 11 by Elhum Haghighat-Sordellini). Nor do we have data on extra-legal housing. However, the MHUD has divided households into five categories by income levels: very high (5), high (4), medium (3), low-medium (2) and low-income (1) and some 80 percent of those from the highest income own their homes.[7] The Ministry data also illustrate that substandard housing was very typical among those in the lowest household income levels: levels 1, 2, and 3 household incomes.

Table 10.1 shows the percentage of informal settlements in different cities. It shows that Zahedan, in the far southeastern part of the country near Iran's borders with southern Afghanistan and southwestern Pakistan, has one of the highest percentages of informal settlements: 26 percent of inhabited areas are part of informal/illegal settlements, and 36 percent of its population live in this type of housing. An even higher percentage of the population – 39 percent – live in extra-legal settlements in the Persian Gulf port of Bandar-e Abbas; however, the illegal housing units account for only 7.7 percent of all households in Bandar Abbas. Different provinces show different percentages both in terms of the area of urban settlement classified as extra-legal and the percentage of the population

Table 10.1 Number of illegal/extra-legal housing in different cities of Iran in 1980

City	Population	% areas of informal settlements	% population of informal settlements (compared with total of population)
Zahedan	650,000	26	36
Kermanshah	692,986	7.7	39
Bandar Abbas	457,000	30	30
Tabriz	1,191,042	6	20
Sanandaj	325,618	15.6	53.3
Mashhad	2,400,000	4	27
Ahwaz	1,100,000	5.9	27.2
Arak	381,682	27	9.3
Ardabil	391,455	14	29
Shiraz	1,053,025	4.4	9.8
Ilam	140,301	11.7	39
Hamadan	464,162	8.2	20

Source: Housing and Urbanism Ministry, Improvement and Renewing of Informal Settlements.

living in it. For example, the city of Sanndaj, the capital of Kurdestan province in the west and bordering northern Iraq, had the highest percentage of inhabitants living in extra-legal dwellings – 53.3 percent – even though such settlements comprised only 15.6 percent of the city's total area. Like Zahedan, Sanandaj is close to an international border where security and government control are very weak in the rural areas, especially at night; and both cities are populated predominantly by ethnic (Kurds in Sanandaj, Baluchis in Zahedan) and religious minorities (Sunni Muslims in both cities); ethnic and religious tensions exacerbate housing problems in both cities.

These statistics have been alarming for some government officials, as they show that the problem of extra-legal settlements can have consequences for national security as well as the goal of poverty alleviation. Iran's first post-revolutionary governments had to deal with the problem from the start. In the initial nine months following the Revolution, the drafters of the new constitution made it a state responsibility to address the issue of empowerment of the poor and the marginalized [*mostazafin*]. The 1979 constitution stipulated that illegal housing must become legalized (thereby making the state responsible for providing them with basic services). At the same time, several other measures were taken, such as the 1980 law requiring that vacant dwellings (if identified) had to be rented to those who were living in illegal settlement areas; absentee landlords could be penalized by having their properties rented or sold to people with no land or property ownership.[8] Nonetheless, after the revolution and throughout the 1980s, the government enacted a series of laws and regulations, under the *arazi mavat* [unutilized properties], *arazi shahri* [urban properties], and *zamin shahri* [urban real states], in efforts to stop a booming, urban real state market.[9] More importantly, in 1993 Parliament passed a law, *ghanon-e tahiyeh-e maskan*

baraye afrad-e kamdaramad [law providing dewellings for low-income indi-
viduals], that made it mandatory for the state to provide housing for the poor.
This law came into effect in 1997, with various ministries, such as the Ministry
of Economics, Energy, and Housing and Urban Development, together with
public foundations such as the Imam Khomeini Relief Committee and the
Housing Foundation, mandated to provide low-income housing for economically
marginalized groups.

Despite these legal, governmental, and non-governmental measures, the
dilemma of extra-legal settlements has not disappeared, and the situation may
have deteriorated since 2000. In fact, during the early 2000s, extra-legal housing
became part of the everyday reality for many cities. In 2002 the World Bank in
collaboration with the Office of Urban Development and Rehabilitation tackled
the issue. Bandar Abbas, Kermanshah, and Zahedan were some cities where the
World Bank carried out research on the problems of extra-legal settlements. One
year later, a joint declaration by an intera-ministerial committee was formed to
come up with a common definition of informal settlements in order to incorporate the matter into the fourth development plan of the post-revolutionary era.
For this reason, the Center for National Empowerment with Regard to Informal
Settlement (CNERIS) was formed. This new initiative brought together the Ministries of Urban Development, Interior, Health, Energy, Labor and Welfare,
Industry and Mining, National Security, Environment, and Justice as well as the
Center for Management and Planning. The CNERIS, an organization responsible
to each of the aforementioned ministries, was assigned the task of dealing with
the informal settlements and to prevent the formation of new ones.

Where women come into the picture? Two case studies

All of the aforementioned efforts had no focus on gender and this is a problem,
as we shall see in micro-level analyses of two case studies. A short drive in a
taxi in almost any mega-city, especially Tehran, no doubt will lead to the topic
of the economy. Invariably, concern over economic issues will focus on rising
prices, especially the cost of living, including housing. In fact, housing is perceived as one of the highest priorities of basic needs. Housing impacts upon
entire families, so the natural question might be: Why should we pay attention to
women specifically with respect to housing issues? This is, indeed, a valid question, and one about which we hope to start an important discussion: How do
extra-legal settlements affect women differently than men, and what role do
women play in the welfare of their communities in these low-income neighborhoods? To answer these questions, we drew upon a vast literature about gender
and informal settlements in the context of developing countries.[10] One of the
ways in which this literature highlights the importance of paying attention to the
issue of gender is the fact that women are more closely linked with local community and take pride in their immediate family and community, whereas men
tend to be less concerned with such matters as the condition of the neighborhood.[11] Moreover, women as part of their reproductive role spend more of their

time at home than do men, and therefore issues related to home and housing inevitably affect them disproportionately. More recently the issue of a rise in female-headed households makes it imperative to examine extra-legal housing from a gender perspective, and highlights why the lack of a gender perspective in urban planning is of great consequence.

To illustrate the above points, we bring together data from two different illegal settlements and examine them from a gender perspective. The first case is from Islamabad in Tehran province. The shanty town is located in the north-west of Tehran and on the margin of Evin Darakeh. In the beginning (the settlement was started in 1971), the inhabitants used tin as basic material to build shelters, or they set up tents in which as many as four to five households (who had migrated from rural areas) lived. The first migrants were from Amol, a city in northern Iran's Caspian coastal plain, who came to Tehran because they had received no or inadequate land under a partial land reform program and they were in search of better economic opportunities.[12] Since the area was part of a dried-up river bed, it was not owned by anyone. Due to the possibility of flooding, permanent housing projects were not perceived as lucrative, and therefore the landowning class has not sought to bring it under legal ownership.[13] Therefore the place had remained "unclaimed" by landowners. Yet, as the population grew and the shanty town expanded, people started to form a local council and lobbied the government to make their landownership legal.[14]

Although the majority of households are headed by men, there are female-headed households. The inhabitants in this shanty town tend to work in the informal sector as unskilled laborers or vendors (for instance, flower sellers). Men who have some capital and own a car are part of the informal transport system and work as unofficial taxi drivers, while those with no capital work as unskilled or semi-skilled construction workers. However, their income is barely enough to support a family, and in many cases women have to enter the labor market and take jobs as domestic workers, vendors, or end up as recipients of various welfare programs run by governmental and non-governmental charity organizations.

More than 90 percent of the population in Islamabad had six years or more of education and only 6 percent were uneducated in 2007.[15] Some households were able to send their children to university. Research on the informal sector in other countries shows that women's income tends to be spent on the welfare of the family and in this case women's work in shanty towns contributes to the greater welfare of their children.[16] Similar results for Iranian shanty towns were documented in a study by Roksana Bahramitash and Shala Kazemipour, in which many women expressed high aspirations to send their children to university.[17] More recently, eco-feminists have argued that in the context of global environmental deterioration, urban planning must pay attention to the role of women in ecological sustainability.[18] Eco-feminists argue that slum dwellers suffer from environmental hazards and that women tend to adopt more environmentally friendly methods of habitation than do men. However, due to problems associated with conducting interviews in slums, such as a general lack of trust in strangers and government surveillance of research-gathering data, it was difficult to document how women try to deal with environmental issues, although some of the interviews shed light on the principal concerns of women that are similar to women in slums as documented in gender and development literature. Specifically, many women were concerned with the well-being of their families and the education of their children, since they perceived the latter as a means of social mobility and getting out of the poverty trap.

For example, during an interview with Belghis (a pseudonym to protect the identity of the interviewee), a 32-year-old woman who lived in a dwelling which had been put up overnight with one room and a toilet, she said her family got electricity from the main street line into which they had illegally tapped. However, they have no running water and have to get water through their neighbors. She said they had migrated to Islamabad five years ago from a village close to Meshgin Shahr (in north-western Iran) as a result of a drought. She considered her conditions to be better than her previous life in rural Meshgin Shahr:

> We don't have a school here, but we believe soon there will be one. But there are two mosques. My six-year old daughter didn't go to school because we couldn't afford to pay her transport. But to me her education is the most important thing after her health. My husband isn't really concerned with what happens at home and this drives me crazy because they [the City] can throw us out any minute. I was the one who insisted we move and now it is all up to me to bring food.[19]

Another interviewee, Mino, 40 years old, said that since her husband has a van and is a driver, he can work as a mover, a gardener, or a cleaner of homes. However, like Belghis, she expressed uncertainty about the future:

> We aren't sure what will happen to us. My husband works all day but in the end the City may just decide to throw us out of our home. I am really concerned about my children's education. They are going to school and the university.[20]

Many of the women interviewed were extremely concerned about crime and drug addiction. During the research it was deemed prudent not to inquire about the sex trade, given the sensitivity of the topic, but Iran's slums are generally places where illegal activities persist, and they pose a major hazard to the local communities. Nevertheless, the issue of drug addiction is a major concern in Islamabad, as was mentioned in the interviews. Drug addiction is a nationwide problem, with illegal drugs being smuggled into Iran through the borders with Afghanistan. The number of drug addicts has been increasing since the mid-1990s, with the majority of addicts being men, particularly young, unemployed males. This means that women as wives and mothers not only have to support their own family but in some cases live with the insurmountable problem of economic drain due to male drug addiction.[21]

Drug addiction was certainly an even more serious problem in our second case example, the extra-legal shanty town of Shirabad, adjacent to Zahedan, in the province of Sistan and Baluchistan. As in Islamabad, the issue of male drug addiction was mentioned as a high priority for the community. However, while in Islamabad drug addiction was just one of many problems, in Shirabad the community was consumed by the plague of illicit drugs. The settlement was formed following an extended period of drought in south-eastern Iran lasting for over seven years.[22] The original "illegal" inhabitants were local farmers displaced by the drought, which made it impossible to grow crops or maintain livestock. The shanty town's population subsequently increased with an influx of refugees from Afghanistan. Since Zahedan is close to the area where the borders of Iran, Afghanistan, and Pakistan meet, the region has become a major center for drug traffickers and arms smugglers, both of whom tend to have more power than the security forces of the Iranian, Afghan, or Pakistani governments. Ironically, throughout the region as well as outside the region, shanty towns like Shirabad are disturbingly similar. Informal settlements of this type – that is, where crime is rampant and government security is virtually absent – have familiar characteristics, whether outside of Mexico City, Jakarta, or Cairo: The unfamiliar familiarity of the shanty town is startling and at the same time overwhelming.

Unlike in Islamabad, where the majority of households were headed by men, in Shirabad, the majority of households were de facto female-headed. This means that even when men were present, they did not provide for their family's economic needs. High drug addiction meant that much of the economic burden was shouldered by the women. Moreover, due to lack of employment opportunities, many men were inevitably forced into illegal activities, especially drug trafficking and arms smuggling. These "occupations" are highly dangerous at the local level, and men involved with them can end up either in jail or being killed in gun battles with security forces. The number of casualties among both traffickers and the police are not statistics that are released publicly, although those gun battles in which many government personnel are killed do attract extensive media coverage. What is certain is that this border region is a highly dangerous zone for both low-level traffickers and law-enforcement officials, some of whom end up losing their lives and leaving their families female-headed.

Shirabad was established on vacant land forcibly occupied overnight [*zurabad*] in imitation of Islamabad and other *zurabad*s in the Tehran area. Yet, in sharp contrast with Tehran province, the province of Sistan and Baluchestan is the most impoverished part of the country, and, according to official statistics (see Table 10.1), its only major city, Zahedan, 36 percent of its population live in extra-legal settlements. Furthermore, Zahedan, unlike Tehran, is economically depressed and has few legitimate employment opportunities, which is why so many men become involved in the illicit drug and arms trade. One consequence has been the waging of a low-intensity form of warfare between the settlers in Shirabad and the local government and law-enforcement officials. Close to Shirabad are other shanty towns which rely solely on the drug trade and are in direct conflict with law enforcement. In fact, there have been instances where local police would be called upon only to be surrounded and attacked by people who want to make sure that the police stay outside of their neighborhoods. This low-intensity warfare is not only a result of the drug trade but is intertwined with ethnic (rural Baluchis and Afghan refugees, many of whom are also Baluchis) and religious conflict (Shi'i government officials versus local Sunni Muslim settlers), all of which helps to fuel lethal tensions in the face of the collapse of the rural economy.[23]

Since there is little state presence in Shirabad, non-governmental organizations have embarked upon development projects. For example, a joint initiative based on the South Asian Poverty Alleviation Program was implemented in collaboration with various governmental and non-governmental organizations, including the Office of Management and Planning, the Family and Sustainable Development Fund (an NGO funded by the first lady of the time, the wife of President Khatami, with a budget allocated by the United Nations) in collaboration with the United Nations Development Program. The project was not designed specifically to address the issue of extra-legal settlement but rather as a program to alleviate poverty.

Being in close proximity to a high-intensity war zone area in Afghanistan and Pakistan, the idea was to start a micro-credit program which would boost the local economy (to reduce reliance on illegal drug trafficking and arms smuggling) and to mobilize the poor based on self-help, public mobilization, and a bottom-up model of development.[24] The project started as a community effort that involved both men and women and was concurrent with similar projects elsewhere in the province of Sistan and Baluchistan. However, it ended up becoming an all-women's project, as men seemed to have no interest in participating in a micro-credit program. By the time the project ended in 2005, it was an all-female micro-credit program for de facto and *de jure* female heads of households.[25]

Unlike the case of Islamabad, shelter was not an immediate concern in Shirabad. This may be related to the fact that economic survival (rather than legalizing ownership) in a situation where the rural economy had collapsed and the urban economy had little to offer made daily survival a higher priority that consumed the energy of women. Nevertheless, as in Islamabad, women were highly concerned about the fate of their children and their education. According to one mother, Fatemeh:

> I want birth certificates for my children so that they can attend public schools.[26] I joined to get credit to set up a store. It helped me start the store but I could afford a refrigerator and fresh fruits and vegetables don't last in this weather. I couldn't get more loans to buy a refrigerator and my store is barely making ends meet. I want my children to have an education and to get real job [in the formal sector].

More generally, the research in Shirabad resonates with that of Asef Bayat, as the evidence from this shanty town demonstrates that although extra-legal settlements are a site of oppression, they are also a site of resistance. In the case of Shirabad, for example, economic marginality had led to collective action against the municipality of Zahedan to force it to legalize the settlement. Toward the end of the project, women had been mobilized to lobby the City and to demand collectively for access to clean water and electricity. Although they were not able to force the local government to provide running water, electricity, and other services, they managed to prevent the local government from trying to destroy their housing and thus implicitly accept their settlement. In this sense the effort to legalize extra-legal housing was more successful in Shirabad due to the precarious condition of the region as a whole than that of Islamabad in Tehran province.

By the way of conclusion, it is vital to bear in mind that men and women have different experiences due to women's reproductive role and their domestic responsibilities as home-makers. Moreover, as we have illustrated, women are highly concerned with the welfare of their families and thereby are vital to any poverty alleviation program. In addition, women play a major role in environmentally friendly uses of resources, and therefore it is vital to examine their roles closely and separately from those of men. This is especially important from the perspective of urban policy-making. Lastly, keeping in mind that this book is about women pushing boundaries, we have seen how women in Zahedan's Shirabad settlement have mobilized to negotiate with the local government and the municipality. It is true that women use softer and less violent means of resistance; nonetheless, they are present where there is room for change, a fact that may escape the attention of those who see Muslim/Iranian women as weak and passive, or as victims.

Notes

1 See UN-Habitat (2003) *Slums of the World: The Fact of Urban Poverty in the New Millennium*. Available online at: www.unhabitat.org/pmss/listItemDetails. aspx?publication ID=1124 (accessed June 8, 2010); J. Beall and S. Fox (2007) "Urban poverty and development in the 21st century: towards an inclusive and sustainable world," *Oxfam Research Report*. Available online at: http://eprints.lse.ac.uk/2903/1/ urban_poverty_and_ development_in_the_21st_ century.pdf (accessed May 2010); Joint Ministerial Committee (2003) *National Plan for Empowerment and Rehabilitation of Informal Settlement* [*sanad-e meli tavan-e mandsazi va samandehi-ye sokonat-gahha-ye gir-e rasmi*], Tehran: Ministry of Housing and Urban Planning, Office of Development and Urban Improvement, Action Committee on Empowerment. Zohreh Fanni has worked on the topic of small cities and sustainable development in Iran; see her paper presented at the SEAGA conference in 2006. Available at: www.hsse. nie.edu.sg/staff/changch/seaga/seaga2006/proceedings/Full%20Papers/day2_fullpaper/ session14_zohreh.pdf (accessed June 2010).

2 See, e.g., S. Stall and R. Stoecker (1998) "Community organizing or organizing community? Gender and the crafts of empowerment in gender and society," *Gender and Social Movements, Special Issue Part I*, 12, 6, pp. 729–756; C. Moser (1995) "Women, gender and urban development policy: challenges for current and future research," *World Development*, 17, 2; idem (1989) "Gender planning in the third world: meeting practical and strategic gender needs," *World Development*, 17, 11,

pp. 1799–1825; J.H. Momsen (2004) *Gender and Development*, London: Routledge; N. Datta (2006) "Joint titling: a win-win policy? Gender and property rights in urban informal settlements in Chandigarh, India," *Feminist Economics*, 12, 1 and 2, pp. 271–298; A. Todes (1995) "Gender in metropolitan development strategies: the case of Durban," *Cities*, 12, 5, pp. 327–336; J. Leavitt (2003) "Where's the gender in community development?," *Journal of Women in Culture and Society*, 29, 1, pp. 208–231; and C. Doss, C. Grown and D. Deere (2008) "Gender and asset ownership: a guide to collecting individual level data," paper presented at the World Bank.

3 See S. Kazemipour and M. Mirzaie (2005) "Uneven growth of urbanization in Iran," paper presented at the IUSSP XXB International Population Conference, Tours, France, July 18–23, 2005. Available at: http://iussp2005.princeton.edu/download. aspx?submissionId=51663 (accessed May 2010).

4 E. Hooglund (1982) *Land and Revolution in Iran* (University of Texas Press), pp. 115–121.

5 See A. Bayat (1997) *Street Politics: Poor People's Movements in Iran* (New York: Columbia University Press).

6 De Soto's work has attracted a great deal of attention. He argues that the informal sector is crucial to the economy and has become legalized in order to bring prosperity to the economy; his ideas have become adopted by powerful organizations such as the World Bank. Peru seems to have benefited from legalizing the informal sector. In his work De Soto calls the informal sector the extra-legal economy. He has been criticized by those who argue that efforts to bring people from the margins of the mainstream economy into the mainstream does not bring about greater equality but merely gives opportunities to some while leaving others still economically disempowered and politically disenfranchised. See further H. De Soto (2002) *The Other Path, The Economic Answer to Terrorism* (New York: Basic Books).

7 Office of Management and National Planning (1983) *First Development Plan Legal Addendum* (Tehran).

8 To what extent properties of absentee owners were actually confiscated and sold remains a contested issue, but one that, to date, has not been researched.

9 Office of Management and National Planning, *First Development Plan.*

10 See, e.g., the citations in n. 2, supra.

11 See C. Moser (1989) "Gender planning in the third world: meeting practical and strategic gender needs," *World Development*, 11, 11, pp. 1799–1825; J. Beall (1996) "Participation in the city: where do women fit in?," *Gender and Development*, 4, 4, pp. 9–16.

12 On the inequities of the 1962 to 1971 land reform program as a catalyst for rural to urban migration in pre-revolutionary Iran, see Hooglund, op. cit.

13 The entire process of land entitlement can be highly complicated in Iran, especially with respect to land that historically was regarded as having no economic value, such as dried-up river beds prone to brief flash floods in spring. The government tries to rely on local community authority for creating or regulating ownership of such land, but whenever changing conditions endow once useless land with value, those with capital can drive up property prices and/or bribe local officials to prevent equal access and a just system of land distribution.

14 This is also related to the fact that property prices in Iran experienced the same global property boom typical of the 1990s and the early 2000s.

15 See Z. Fanni (2006) "Small cities and regional sustainable development in Iran," paper presented at the NIE-SEAGA conference, November 28–30.

16 See International Development Research Center, *Gender in a Macroeconomic Framework: A CGE Model Analysis.* Available online at www.idrc.ca/en/ev-69008-201-1-DO_TOPIC.html (accessed May 2010); IFAD, *Rural Women in Ifad's Projects: The Key to Poverty Alleviation.* Available online at www.ifad.org/pub/other/! brocsch. pdf (accessed May 2010); and R. Bahramitash (2005) *Liberation from Liberalization: Gender and Globalization in Southeast Asia* (London: Zed Books).

17 R. Bahramitash. and S. Kazemipour (2011) "Veiled economy: gender and the informal sector," in R. Bahramitash and H. Esfahani (eds) *Veiled Employment: Islamism and Political Economy of Women's Employment in Iran* (Syracuse, NY: Syracuse University Press).

18 See further M. Mies and V. Shiva (1993) *Ecofeminism* (London: Zed Books); and I. Diamond and G.F. Orenstein (eds) (1990) *Reweaving the World: The Emergence of Ecofeminism* (New York: Random House). Ecofeminists argue that there is a parallel between the oppression of women and that of nature. When their argument gets translated into public policy, it relates to the role of women in ecological sustainability. In the case of Iran, many women's groups have been formed to protect the environment; on environmental initiatives in Iran; see R. Foltz (2001) "Environmental initiatives in contemporary Iran," *Central Asian Survey*, 20, 2, pp. 155–165.

19 Fanni (2006) "Small cities and sustainable development."

20 Ibid.

21 Some of the social problems of addiction, including the impact on low-income families, is discussed in M Vosooghi (2005) "Treatment of addicts in a Tehran drug rehabilitation center," *Critique*, 14, 1 (spring), pp. 89–100.

22 Bahramitash gathered data about Shirabad during a research trip there in 2005.

23 Bahramitash filed research notes from n. 22 supra.

24 See further Bahramitash and Kazemipour, op. cit.

25 See Roksana Bahramitash, "Female-headed households in Iran: micro-credit versus charity," in Bahramitash and Esfahani (eds) *Veiled Employment.*

26 Parents in remote villages often did not bother to go to faraway government offices to obtain official birth certificates for their children; this only became a problem if the families subsequently migrated to cities. In Shirabad and elsewhere in Zahedan, parents lacking such documents had the extra burden of proving that they and their children were legal citizens of Iran and not refugees from Afghanistan.

11 Iran within a regional context

Socio-demographic transformations and effects on women's status

Elhum Haghighat-Sordellini

Contrary to what is often depicted in the Western mainstream media and a body of academic literature, Iranian society continues to experience economic development, modernization and urbanization, and has improved its employment and educational attainment of men and particularly women during the past three decades. Iranian society reflects a complex set of cultural, political, and demographic patterns, and understanding the process of change requires an in-depth analysis within its social context. Rather than accept the common myth that women's low social status in Iran and other Muslim Middle East and North African (MENA) countries is solely a consequence of Islam, I question and argue that women's status is a consequence of societal and demographic changes. In this chapter, I make a point of illustrating how socio-demographic changes contribute to social forces and continue to transform Iranian society. There is no doubt that women continue to struggle to gain equal social and legal rights, higher levels of political participation, as well as a higher level of gainful employment. At the same time, women are significant and vibrant agents of social change, and active participants in improving Iranian society and their own social status.

Path to social and economic change in Iran and the MENA region

Most countries in the MENA region gained independence from Western European imperialism and foreign rule shortly after World War II. The influence of European colonialism, however, was supplanted by the growing influence of the United States and the former Soviet Union. After the fall of communism, the United States emerged as the dominant foreign power in the MENA region, and through its reach into the oil industry it contributed to the political turmoil that had been smoldering since the 1940s. The MENA region had experienced rapid economic development during the 1950s, and the oil boom of the 1970s contributed to further economic, political, and demographic changes. The rapid rise in wealth from oil revenues created some rich governments that became the main political and economic powers in the region. Nevertheless, political turmoil, including several major wars, continued to afflict the region even as it experienced a population explosion and rapid economic development. Population growth and development stimulated significant demographic changes, including an influx of foreign labor, rural-to-urban migration, and rapid urbanization.

Much of the MENA region may be characterized as functioning with a predominantly patriarchal social structure.[1] Although patriarchal structures are resistant to social changes, the increasing modernization and urbanization of the region still managed to lead to important transformations in gender roles. Iran as one of the oil producers in the region has played a significant role in the political and economic changes in the MENA region and continues to make strides in the political landscape of the region.

Iran and MENA in a global context

During the 1950s and 1960s – the post-World War II era – when the Western world was flourishing economically, the modernization perspective provided the dominant theory for explaining the ways in which a society could achieve economic prosperity. Modernization was described as a process of transition: a society goes through one stage and enters another. The evolution begins with the society in the pre-industrial agricultural stage; it then moves into an industrialized, urbanized stage, and later on to the post-industrial stage.[2] Countries are defined as "modern" based on their degree of industrialization. Modernization is also a process that transforms (1) a society's intellectual and technological properties, and (2) helps the members of that society to take greater control of nature and their environment.[3]

During the transition, modernization theorists argue that new ways of life, which subsequently change a society's values and norms as well as its demographic characteristics, develop; the occupational structure of the society changes and educational opportunities for its citizens increase. Changes such as these can bring more opportunities and comfort to women's lives, especially when they are followed by reduced fertility and household responsibilities. Interestingly, women's participation in the labor force declines during the early transitional stages[4] and picks up momentum when the society enters the post-industrial service economy stage. As the formal labor market grows during the early stages and agricultural sector jobs decline, more women leave agricultural work. However, the absence of jobs for women in the early manufacturing economy leads to an overall decline in women's employment.[5] Later on, with job growth in the service and white-collar occupations, women's labor force participation increases again.[6] The transition from a pre-industrial agricultural economy to an early industrial urbanized economy, and later to a post-industrial economy, is explained by modernization theorists as having a U-shaped effect upon women's labor force participation. Thus, there is a *curvilinear* rather than a *linear* relationship between economic development and female employment.[7]

When women's employment declines during the transitional stage – from a pre-industrial agricultural to an industrial economy – changes are also taking

Table 11.1 Selected development and demographic indicators of MENA countries, compared with the world and other regions.

Country	Population mid-2007 (millions)	Rate of natural increase, 2007	Projected population change % 2007–2050	% urban, 2006	2006 GNI PPP per capita (US$)**	Life expectancy at birth (years), 2006 male female		% population living below US$2 per day	Energy use per capita 2002 (kg oil equivalent)
Algeria	34.1	1.7	47	49	6,900	71	74	15	985
Bahrain	0.8	1.8	56	100	18,770	73	75	–	9,837
Egypt	73.4	2.1	61	43	4,680	68	73	44	789
Iran	71.2	1.2	41	68	–	71	76	7	2,044
Iraq	29.0	2.5	114	67	–	55	59	–	1,199
Jordan	5.7	2.4	71	82	6,200	71	72	7	1,036
Kuwait	2.8	1.9	84	98	29,200	77	79	–	9,503
Lebanon	3.9	1.5	27	87	5,460	69	73	–	1,209
Libya	6.2	2.0	57	85	–	71	76	–	3,433
Morocco	31.7	1.5	43	55	5,000	68	72	14	363
Oman	2.7	2.2	42	71	14,570	73	75	–	4,265
Palestine*	4.0	2.9	120	72	–	71	74	–	–
Qatar	0.9	1.5	55	100	–	71	76	–	19,915
Saudi Arabia	27.6	2.7	80	81	16,620	73	77	–	5,775
Syria	19.9	2.5	75	50	3,920	71	75	–	1,063
Tunisia	10.2	1.1	29	65	8,490	72	76	7	846
Turkey	74.0	1.2	20	66	9,060	69	74	10	1,083
United Arab Emirates	4.4	1.5	90	74	23,990	77	81	–	9,609
Yemen	22.4	3.2	159	26	920	59	62	45	221
Region **									
World	6,625	1.2	40	49	9,940	66	70	53	1,669
More developed	1,221	0.1	3	75	29,680	73	80	–	4,878
North America	335	0.6	38	79	43,290	75	81	–	7,946
Europe	733	–0.1	–9	72	22,690	71	79	–	3,614

Region	(millions)				(per capita)			
Less developed	5,404	1.5	49	43	5,480	64	67	56	893
Less developed (excluding China)	4,086	1.8	61	42	4,760	62	65	59	869
Africa	944	2.4	107	37	2,550	52	54	66	692
Northern Africa	195	1.9	59	50	4,660	67	70	29	773
South America	381	1.5	38	80	8,790	69	76	76	
Western Asia	223	2.0	65	64	8,180	68	72	–	2,065
South Central Asia	1,662	1.7	56	30	3,620	63	64	75	598
United States	3,022	.6	38	79	44,260	75	80	–	7,943

Source: *World Population Data Sheet* (2005, 2007). Washington DC: Population Reference Bureau.

Notes

* Palestine includes the Arab population of the West Bank and Gaza Strip.

** Definition of region:

North America – U.S. and Canada.

Europe – Continent of Europe.

Africa – Continent of Africa.

North Africa – Algeria, Egypt, Libya Morocco, Sudan, Tunisia, Western Sahara.

South America – Argentina, Bolivia, Brazil, Chile, Columbia, Ecuador, French Guiana, Guyana, Paraguay, Peru, Suriname, Uruguay, Venezuela.

Western Asia – Armenia, Azerbaijan, Bahrain, Cyprus, Georgia, Iraq, Israel, Jordan, Kuwait, Lebanon, Oman, Palestinian Territory, Qatar, Saudi Arabia, Syria, Turkey, U.A.E., Yemen.

Table 11.2 Political leadership indicators and gender-related development indicators (GDI) in the MENA region compared with other regions

Country	Women as percent of Parliament 1995–2004	As percent ministerial and sub-ministerial officials 1998	GDI Rank, 2003** ***
Algeria	7	6	5	107
Bahrain	–	0	1	37
Egypt	2	2	5	120
Iran	4	3	1	106
Iraq	11	8	0	–
Jordan	1	6	1	90
Kuwait	0	0	5	46
Lebanon	2	2	0	83
Libya	–	–	5	61
Morocco	1	11	6	126
Oman	–	–	4	79
Palestine*	–	–	–	98
Qatar	–	–	0	44
Saudi Arabia	–	0	0	73
Syria	10	12	3	110
Tunisia	7	23	8	91
Turkey	2	4	13	96
United Arab Emirates	0	0	0	48
Yemen	1	0	0	148
Region				
World	12	16	11	–
More developed	14	20	14	–
North America	14	17	32	–
Europe	15	20	12	–
Less developed	11	14	9	–
Less developed (excluding China)	9	13	9	–

Africa	9	13	9	—
Northern Africa	4	9	—	—
South America	10	15	12	—
Western Asia	5	6	—	—
South Central Asia	6	9	4	—
United States	11	14	32	7

Sources: (1) *Women of Our World* (2002, 2005). Washington, DC: Population Reference Bureau;(2) United Nations Development Fund: http://hdr.undp.org/reports/global/2003/indicator/pdf/hdr03_table_22.pdf; (retrieved on August 30, 2007); (3) *2005 World Development Indicators*, Women in Development.

Notes
* Palestine includes the Arab population of West Bank and Gaza.
** The top ten countries with the highest GDI (Gender Development Indicator) rank are: Norway, Iceland, Sweden, Australia, U.S.A., Canada, Netherlands, Belgium, Denmark, and Finland.
*** A low number indicates a high GDI rank. For example, the U.S.'s GDI rank is 7 which means that the U.S. has a high GDI (women have more resources) compared with 148 for a country such as Yemen (low resources for women) or 126 for Morocco.
The top 10 countries with the highest GDI rank are: Norway, Iceland, Sweden, Australia, Netherlands, Belgium, U.S.A., Canada, Japan, and Switzerland.

place with respect to their households and family responsibilities. In pre-industrial societies women are able to combine housework and childcare with paid work.[8] Industrialization and urbanization divide the home and work spheres (work is done in an urban setting removed from the domestic residence). Because the domestic responsibilities remain primary to women, the physical separation of work and home lives limits their opportunities to participate in the market. Therefore, their rate of participation in the labor force declines.[9] In sum, the modernization process creates more favorable conditions for women to enter the labor force. Therefore, women's workforce participation increases with a higher degree of industrialization and urbanization.[10] Social and cultural changes, such as delaying marriage, declining fertility rates, and an increasing demand for a more educated labor force, all contribute to a larger supply of female workers. With the help of modern technology and smaller family size, women are freed from overburdening domestic responsibilities (i.e., early marriage, multiple pregnancies, and high rates of maternal death due to lack of access to healthcare resources, childcare responsibilities, and housework) and are therefore more available to be employed if job opportunities are available to them.

In this chapter, I place Iran in a global and regional context and compare Iran with the rest of the Muslim MENA countries; I reference 19 countries with a majority Muslim population that are traditionally included in the region designated as MENA. The countries included in North Africa are Algeria, Egypt, Libya, Morocco, and Tunisia; in the Persian Gulf/Arabian Peninsula: Bahrain, Kuwait, Oman, Qatar, Saudi Arabia, United Arab Emirates, and Yemen; and in the rest of the Middle East: Iran, Iraq, Jordan, Lebanon, Palestine (Gaza Strip and the West Bank), Syria, and Turkey. Table 11.1 represents selected development and demographic indicators of MENA countries, compared with the world and other regions. Egypt, Iran, and Turkey are the most populous MENA countries but only Iran and Turkey have the lowest rate of natural increase next to Tunisia. Yemen and Palestine show the highest rate of natural increase. Iranian society is highly urbanized with 68 percent of its population living in cities and urban areas. As Table 11.2 indicates, most of the MENA region is highly urbanized. Yemen is the least urbanized country in the region with only 26 percent of its population living in cities. The most urbanized countries in the region are Bahrain and Qatar with 100 percent of their population urban.

In terms of women's political leadership indicators and their access to societal resources in the MENA region, Iran shows an extremely low rate of women's participation in Parliament and women holding ministerial and sub-ministerial ranks. Among other types of measures commonly used are the systematic measures calculated by the United Nations Development Program (UNDP).[11] The only measure of gender status is the gender-related development index (GDI). UNDP describes it as a composite index measuring average achievement in the three basic dimensions captured in the human development index – a long and healthy life, knowledge, and a decent standard of living – adjusted to account for inequalities between men and women.[12] A low number indicates a high GDI rank. For example, the United States' GDI is 7, which translates to having a high GDI[13] compared with a GDI of 148 for Yemen or 126 for Morocco, indicating a low access to resources for women. Iran's GDI rank of 106 translates to a high level of gender inequality and lower access for women to societal resources.

The following sections take us through different demographic indicators while it positions Iran's socio-economic changes in context.

Fertility patterns and demographic changes in Iranian society

Iranian society has succeeded in lowering its fertility rate and improving both men's and women's educational attainment at an astonishing rate. The lowering of fertility has been achieved by political tactics before, during, and after the 1978 to 1979 Islamic Revolution and during the Islamic Republic period. Reduced fertility often is associated with the higher status of women and a greater access to societal resources. Access to family planning programs often helps reduce fertility, and can increase a woman's autonomy, which in turn encourages her participation in the paid employment sector.[14] The MENA region has made great improvements in terms of providing access to reproductive health services for women except in a few countries, notably Yemen. Most Muslim countries provide direct access to family planning services,[15] and most have succeeded in lowering their fertility rates during the past few decades. In fact, most MENA countries have a relatively high rate of contraceptive use (Table 11.3). In 2007, among MENA countries, Iran shows the lowest total fertility rate (TFR) (2.0) in the region next to Tunisia (2.1). Yemen clearly has the highest TFR in the region (6.2), next to Iraq (4.9) and Palestine (4.6). As Table 11.3 indicates, TFR declined for every MENA country from 2002 to 2007. Average TFR for MENA during 2002 was 4.0 and dropped to 3.2 in 2007 – an indication of a slow drop in the natural rate of increase in the region. Married Iranian women have the highest rate of use of any contraceptive methods compared to other MENA countries – an indication of family planning success in Iranian society. Abortion policies in the region vary from one country to another (Table 11.4). While most MENA countries prohibit abortion, countries such as Turkey have implemented liberal policies and the rest fall in the middle by placing some restrictions on abortion but not completely banning its practice. However, family planning programs are highly politicized and governments play a crucial role in banning or promoting them. For example, the institutionalization of an "ideology of female domesticity" or "housewifization" in Iran following the 1979 Revolution encouraged a pro-natalist ideology. Modern contraceptive methods were discouraged, abortion was banned, and contraceptive devices were removed from pharmacies and clinics.[16] Between 1976 and 1986 the population increased by 3.9 percent and the TFR was 5.6, which placed Iran among the fastest-growing countries in the region. In 1986 about 50 percent of the population was under the age of 15. By the end of the 1980s, the unfavorable effects of population increase were felt by the economy, health care services, the educational system, and the workforce. The government, influenced by religious leaders, reconsidered its earlier pro-natalist policies, which resulted in a drastic decline of fertility in Iran within a decade. Subsequently, Iran's fertility has reached its lowest rate among MENA countries and is comparable to that in many Western nations including the United States. In 2002, the United States' TFR was 2.1 compared with 2.0 for Iran. Its success with family planning was due to the crucial role of women as volunteers, many of whom ironically were mobilized by the clerics.[17]

The important role of the government in the promotion or discouragement of family planning programs has been influential in the success or failure of family planning programs in MENA countries. Although Islamic law does not prohibit the practice of family planning and does not encourage high fertility, the pro-natalist orientation of many Muslim majority countries is based not on direct injunctions but indirectly on the extant political conditions that are conducive to high fertility.[18] Countries such as Algeria and Iran, for example, saw fertility decline dramatically while experiencing the rise and domination of Islamic fundamentalism.[19] Scholars such as C.M. Obermeyer, in studying the impact of Islam on fertility behavior in Iran and Tunisia, concludes that the reproductive behavior in these countries is a function of the government's policy changes rather than the impact of the population's religious beliefs.[20] By addressing economic, social, and cultural barriers through the educational system and the media, governments can play an important role in facilitating the use of health and family planning services in Muslim countries. The governments of Egypt and Iran have played a crucial role in implementing successful family planning programs. The governments consciously use religion to manipulate the population depending on the needs of the economy. In Iran and Egypt, for example, religious leaders sent out messages or *fatwas* (religious rulings) in favor of modern contraception. Government healthcare facilities distribute contraceptive devices and therefore make them available to couples from all levels of economic and social classes.

The success of family planning programs supported by the Iranian government and the cooperation of the religious leaders is progressive in that the sole focus is not on a woman's responsibility for reducing fertility; they also place a great deal of importance on the man's role in reducing fertility. According to Janet Larsen,

> One of the strengths of Iran's promotion of family planning is the involvement of men. Iran is the only country in the world that requires both men and women to take a class on modern contraception before receiving a marriage license. And it is the only country in the region with a government-sanctioned condom factory. In the past four years, some 220,000 Iranian men have had a vasectomy. While vasectomies still account for only 3 percent of contraception, compared with female sterilization at 28 percent, men nonetheless are assuming more responsibility for family planning.[21]

At the opposite end of the spectrum, the Yemeni government has made no effort to control the country's high fertility rate (7.2), or to reduce the high child mortality rate and high maternal mortality; in fact, it deploys ideologies in the name of Islam to reinforce the practice of high fertility. Yemen has the least favorable demographic record (high fertility, high mortality, low women's status, low modernization, low women's employment, virtually no participation of women in politics) compared to other MENA countries. A high percentage of Yemeni women believe that Islam does not condone the use of contraception.[22] Therefore Yemeni women and men are reluctant to use birth control methods as it is considered "un-Islamic" to do so. Since Yemen has such a poor record of health-care, which leads to high mortality rates, a high rate of fertility is necessary to replace the population.[23]

Jennifer Olmsted,[24] in her study of the MENA countries, examines what she calls the "fertility puzzle." She tests variables such as income, government policies, women's labor force participation, and cultural factors, and finds that female education and age at marriage are among the most significant factors in determining fertility levels. Thus, Islam alone does not affect women's fertility patterns. Other studies link women's employment patterns to fertility rates. These studies show that when women have the opportunity to earn their own incomes, they tend to delay marriage and parenthood and hence bear fewer children in their lifetime.[25] Employment has an affect on fertility in both directions – women may choose not to work if they have children, and for women who are working, this may influence the number of children they choose to have. Social and cultural changes, such as a decline in fertility rates, an increase in age at marriage, and a demand for more educated men and women, all contribute to a larger supply of younger women who are freed, at least temporarily, from family responsibilities[26] and therefore more available to be employed. Singh, using cross-national data, evaluates the effect of women's contraceptive use and availability, and the use of health services by mothers at birth on fertility, mortality, women's education, and labor force participation in developing countries.[27] She finds that women's educational attainment (measured by school enrollments and/ or the number of school years completed) had a restraining effect on fertility and mortality rates. Needless to say, using contraceptives leads to a decline in fertility rates, and the availability of health services to mothers at birth leads to a lower rate of child mortality.

In general, similar to most of the developing world, the majority of Muslim societies face the dilemma of a high fertility rate (but declining) and, as a result, high population growth rates. The World Fertility Survey reports that fertility was the highest in the MENA region but currently the region holds the second highest rank in the world. The fertility rate has been declining in all regions over recent years, except in sub-Saharan Africa. Although the MENA region is experiencing one of the highest population growth rates in the world, it also has made dramatic improvements in reducing fertility in some of its countries such as Iran. The lingering effect of the previously higher rate of fertility is that countries still have a disproportionately large young population to educate, employ, and provide social services for. The economic instability in the region coupled with patriarchal tradition means that women are not the priority of the government and therefore are pushed aside. In sum, despite the declining fertility rates there

Table 11.3 Selected reproductive health indicators in the MENA region, 2000–2004

	Total fertility rate** 2002	Total fertility rate 2007	Married women 15–49, using any method of contraceptives (%)	Married women 15–49, using modern contraceptives (%)
Algeria	3.1	2.4	64	50
Bahrain	2.8	2.6	62	31
Egypt	3.5	3.1	56	54
Iran	2.6	2.0	74	56
Iraq	5.3	4.9	–	–
Jordan	3.6	3.5	56	39
Kuwait	4.2	2.6	52	39
Lebanon	2.5	2.3	63	40
Libya	3.9	3.0	45	26
Morocco	3.4	2.4	58	49
Oman	6.1	3.4	24	18
Palestine*	5.9	4.6	50	39
Qatar	3.9	2.8	43	32
Saudi Arabia	5.7	4.1	32	29
Syria	4.1	3.5	47	35
Tunisia	2.3	2.0	63	53
Turkey	2.5	2.2	64	38
UAE	3.5	2.7	28	24
Yemen	7.2	6.2	21	10
MENA	4.0	3.2	59	45

Sources: (1) Mensch, Barbara, Susheela Singh and John Casterline (2005) "Trends in the Timing of First Marriage among Men and Women in the Developing World." The Population Council, no. 202, p. 39; (2) Farzaneh Roudi-Fahimi (2003) *Women's Reproductive Health in the Middle East and North Africa*. Table 1, pp. 4–5. Washington DC: Population Reference Bureau; (3) 2002 *Women of Our World*. Washington, DC: Population Reference Bureau; (4) 2007 *World Population Data Sheet*, Washington, DC: Population Reference Bureau.

Notes
*Palestine includes the Arab population of West Bank and Gaza.
**Average number of children born to a woman in her life time.

Table 11.4 Selected reproductive health indicators and abortion policies in the MENA region, 2000

	Births attended by skilled personnel (both rural and urban) (%) (1)	Births conducted in health facilities (both rural and urban) (%)	Maternal deaths per 100,000 live births (2)	Abortion policy		
				Liberal (3)	Some restrictions (4)	Prohibited (5)
Algeria	78	76	140		X	
Bahrain	98	98	46		X	
Egypt	61	48	84			X
Iran	90	88	37			X
Iraq	54	–	290			X
Jordan	98	97	41		X	
Kuwait	98	98	5		X	
Lebanon	89	88	100			X
Libya	94	94	75			X
Morocco	40	37	230		X	
Oman	91	89	14			X
Palestine*	97	–	–	–	–	–
Qatar	98	98	10		X	
Saudi Arabia	91	91	23		X	
Syria	89	55	65			X
Tunisia	91	90	70	X		
Turkey	81	73	130	X		
UAE	99	99	3			
Yemen	22	16	350			X
MENA	70	64	130			X

Sources: (1) Farzaneh Roudi-Fahimi (2003) *Women's Reproductive Health in the Middle East and North Africa*, Table 1, pp. 4–5. Washington, DC: Population Reference Bureau; (2) *2002 Women of Our World*. Washington DC: Population Reference Bureau, pp. 46–59.

Notes

* Palestine includes the Arab population of West Bank and Gaza.
1 Percent of births attended by skilled personnel. Skilled personnel include doctors, nurses, and midwives. Data refer to the latest survey year through 2001.
2 Maternal deaths: The number of deaths to women per 100,000 live births that result from conditions related to pregnancy, delivery, and related complications. The estimates for most less developed countries are taken from 1995 consensus estimates of WHO, UNICEF, and UNFPA.
3 LIBERAL: Permitted on broad socioeconomic grounds or without restriction as to reason, with gestational limits. Certain other restrictions may apply, such as spousal and/or parental consent.
4 SOME RESTRICTIONS: Permitted on physical or mental health grounds – spousal and/or parental consent required in some countries.
5 PROHIBITED: Prohibited, or permitted only to save a woman's life.

has been *no comparable* increase in women's employment as would be projected by the modernization theory.

Education attainment

Approximately half of the countries in the MENA region have succeeded in significantly reducing illiteracy among their younger generations of women and men.[28] Those countries are Bahrain (1 percent), Iran (9 percent), Jordan (1 percent), Kuwait (7 percent), Lebanon (7 percent), Libya (7 percent), Oman (4 percent), Qatar (3 percent), and Turkey (6 percent). Iraq (71 percent), Yemen (54 percent), Morocco (42 percent), and Egypt (37 percent) still have a significant population of women in the 15 to 24 age bracket who are illiterate (Table 11.5). The illiteracy rate among women over age 15 is still high in several other countries in the MENA region where women are about twice as likely as men to be illiterate in that age group.[29] Thus, the gender gap in providing education is closing in the MENA region. Most children in the region are enrolled in primary school,[30] but not all countries have been able to provide equal access to secondary school enrollment. Only 62 percent of girls and 71 percent of boys were enrolled in secondary school (Table 11.6). Countries such as Libya and Bahrain have an impressive close to 100 percent rate for secondary school enrollment while Syria, Morocco, and Yemen show rates of 42, 36, and 27 percent for female enrollment in secondary school, respectively. However, in the two decades between 1980 and early to mid-2000, many countries experienced a dramatic jump in the enrollment of both male and female students in secondary school. For example, in 1985, 57 percent of age-appropriate girls in Libya were enrolled in secondary school compared with 108 percent in the year 2000. Oman and Tunisia provide other great examples; only 18 percent of girls in Oman and 32 percent in Tunisia were enrolled in secondary school in 1985. By the year 2000, 78 and 81 percent of girls were enrolled in Oman and Tunisia, respectively. Women's share of university enrollment is impressive in some of the GCC countries (Saudi Arabia, 56 percent; Oman, 58 percent; Bahrain, 60 percent; Kuwait, 68 percent; and Qatar, 73 percent) and low for Yemen and Iraq.[31]

A society's investment in education is generally assumed to pay off in the creation of more jobs (mainly in the non-agricultural sector) and better educated individuals in the workforce. For a society to receive returns on its investments on education, it needs to build a skilled and flexible labor force. Contrary to expectations, the MENA region's substantial investment in education has not been paying off as expected. There is little evidence that education has contributed to economic growth in the region.[32] The high rate of women's access to secondary and higher education in most of the MENA region is impressive, although much improvement is still needed. According to modernization theorists and based on the experience of many Western societies, more educated women are more empowered women. They claim that as educational access for women improves, it creates more favorable conditions for women to enter the labor force. Therefore, the number of women working increases with a higher degree of industrialization.[33] Social and cultural changes, such as marriage at a later age, declining fertility rates, and a demand for a more educated labor force, all contribute to a larger supply of female workers. The demand for a more educated labor force in modernizing societies is generally assumed to work in women's favor since modernization also increases women's access to better jobs.

And yet, as women's education level has increased in the MENA region, their labor force participation has not increased as expected. As of the year 2000, women's formal employment in the MENA region was as low as 27 percent, which is accompanied by a staggering unemployment rate – sometimes as high as 30 percent. Within the region, the GCC countries show the lowest rate of women's employment. In turn, as women in the region have become more educated, their labor force participation has not increased as expected. The low rate of women's employment[34] results from their lack of improved social status.[35] Despite women's high level of education, due to economic stagnation and regional political problems, the governments enforce traditional roles and values on women and run campaigns to legitimize discrimination against them. There is no doubt that the fact that these women have access to higher education contributes to the improvement of their status. On the other hand, if their status is not improved on a societal level, their higher education credentials will not help them to get far in the job market. Mirna Lattouf's observation as to why families support their daughters' higher educational attainment despite the questionable rate of economic return is about the relations of women to men; families support their daughters' higher education as a way to improve their daughters' chances of finding a suitable husband of a similar or higher social status, which in turn adds to the families' collective social status.[36]

Another similar study by Mitra Shavarini describes the experiences of women in present-day Iranian institutions of higher education and the challenges which female students face in their everyday life. Shavarini tries to answer two main questions in her ethnographic study: "1) what role does higher education play in the lives of Iranian women? and 2) what are the experiences of Iranian women at these institutions?"[37] Shavarini posits that women's ability to gain access to higher education at an increasing rate is explained in part by the "Islamic packaging" of higher education. She states that women's access to colleges "reveals that college has become the only viable institution through which young Iranian women can alter their public role and status."[38] She quotes one of her respondents:

> The only right women find that is granted to them and is encouraged is the
> right to an education.... In today's Iranian society, women are considered
> "second-class citizens." They have no rights; no place in society, is there a
> place for women's rights. Going to the university has become the only thing
> that we are allowed to do.[39]

Many of the women whom Shavarini interviewed had the full support of their families to obtain a higher education. However, the support and promotion of a college experience for women by their families was often mentioned as a way to improve their daughter's chances of finding a suitable husband of similar or higher social status. Many of these women were aware that they were facing societal discrimination when it came to finding jobs even with their higher education degrees. The discrimination is a consequence of living in an economically depressed country such as Iran, with a high inflation rate and a high rate of unemployment. Men are given priority in access to jobs and therefore highly qualified women with college degrees are unable to find suitable employment.

Discrimination against women is partially an expedient response to the faltering economy and has its roots in history and culture. For the most part, in a strongly patriarchal society men are the breadwinners, and many women are dependent on the male members of their family including father, brother, uncle, husband, and son. From a political standpoint, it makes sense to ensure that men are not facing competition from women for jobs, especially where there is a scarcity of work. The deep historical roots of the patriarchal social structure and support from religion for this system lead to discrimination against women in the labor force, which is further compounded by economic stagnation, political conflicts, and global events. The rate at which new jobs are created lags behind the growth in the number of young people entering the job market. The MENA region suffers from an unusually high rate of unemployment not only for women but for men as well. In 2006 the unemployment rate for men and women averaged 10 and 17 percent, respectively.[40] The unemployment rate is further complicated by age; the younger generation of men and women are experiencing even higher unemployment rates in the MENA region than the older age groups. For example, according to Roudi-Fahimi and Kent:

> While less than 15 percent of young men and women were unemployed worldwide, the ILO estimated that just over 20 percent of young men and just over 30 percent of young women in MENA were unemployed in 2005. The situation is particularly dire for members of MENA's youth bulge in some countries. More than 40 percent of Algeria's young men and women were unemployed in 2005, which may be why so many Algerians are emigrating [*sic*] to Europe and elsewhere in search of jobs. Between 21 percent and 31 percent of young men were unemployed in Tunisia, Jordan, Saudi Arabia, and several other MENA countries, along with between 29 percent and 50 percent of young women. Qatar, with a labor force dominated by foreign male workers, has relatively low unemployment for young men, but high unemployment for young women.[41]

To illustrate the severity of lower inclusion of and discrimination against women despite their high educational attainment, Shavarini (2006) describes the experience of a female engineering student in the highly competitive Tehran Polytechnic Institute. The female student expresses disappointment and a degree of anger with the discrimination she experiences each day and the lack of prospects for her future:

Table 11.5 Selected literacy indicators in the MENA region

Country	% illiterate (15 years or older), 2000		% illiterate (ages 15–24), 2000/2004		Literate women as % literate men (ages 15–24), 2000–2004
	Female	Male	Female	Male	
Algeria	43	24	16	7	91
Bahrain	17	9	1	2	101
Egypt	56	33	37	24	85
Iran	31	17	9	4	95
Iraq	77	45	71	41	49
Jordan	16	5	1	1	100
Kuwait	20	16	7	8	102
Lebanon	20	8	7	3	96
Libya	32	9	7	0.05	94
Morocco	64	38	42	24	79
Oman	38	20	4	0.5	98
Palestine*	16	6	–	–	–
Qatar	17	20	3	7	102
Saudi Arabia	33	17	10	5	96
Syria	40	12	21	5	96
Tunisia	39	19	11	3	93
Turkey	24	7	6	1	95
UAE	21	25	6	13	108
Yemen	75	33	54	17	60
Region					
MENA	42	22	23	11	–
Africa	48	30	31	19	–
Latin America/Caribbean	14	11	4	5	–
North America	–	–	–	–	–
More developed	–	–	–	–	–
Less developed	34	19	19	12	92
World	31	17	18	11	92

Sources: (1) *Women of Our World* (2005) Washington, DC: Population Reference Bureau; (2) *2005 World Population Data Sheet.* Washington: Population Reference Bureau; (3) United Nations Development Programme (UNDP) (2003) *Human Development Report 2003.* New York: UNDP; (4) Roudi-Fahimi and Valentine M. Moghadam (2003) *Empowering Women, Developing Society: Female Education in the Middle East and North Africa.* Washington, DC: Population Reference Bureau (November).

Note
*Palestine includes the Arab population of West Bank and Gaza.

Table 11.6 Selected education indicators in the MENA region

Country	% enrolled in primary school, 2000		% enrolled in secondary school 1985, 1993–1997, 2000/2003						Women as share of university enrollment (%), 2000	Public education as share of total government expenditure (%)
	Female	Male	Female	Male	Female	Male	Female	Male		
Algeria	107	116	44	59	62	65	74	69	—	16
Bahrain	103	103	97	98	98	91	99	91	60	12
Egypt	96	103	50	72	73	83	85	91	—	15
Iran	85	88	36	54	73	81	75	79	47	18
Iraq	91	111	39	68	32	51	29	47	34	—
Jordan	101	101	—	—	—	—	87	86	51	20
Kuwait	95	93	87	95	66	64	88	83	68	14
Lebanon	97	101	60	61	84	78	81	74	52	8
Libya	117	115	57	61	—	—	108	102	48	—
Morocco	88	101	28	42	34	44	36	45	44	25
Oman	71	74	18	35	79	80	78	79	58	16
Palestine*	109	107	—	—	—	—	—	—	47	—
Qatar	104	105	86	79	66	68	93	88	73	—
Saudi Arabia	—	—	31	48	57	65	65	73	56	23
Syria	105	113	48	68	40	45	42	47	—	14
Tunisia	115	120	32	46	63	66	81	78	48	20
Turkey	96	105	30	52	48	68	66	86	41	15
UAE	99	99	55	55	82	77	82	77	—	20
Yemen	61	96	—	—	14	53	27	65	21	22
Region										
MENA	91	100	43	54	50	60	62	71	—	—
World	—	—	23	33	55	63	62	67	—	—
Africa	—	—	—	—	32	38	36	41	—	—
Latin America/Caribbean	—	—	97	97	—	—	90	83	—	—
North America	—	—	94	93	98	99	93	95	—	—
More developed	—	—	31, 44	44	102	99	103	101	—	—
Less developed	—	—	—	—	47	57	55	61	—	—

Sources: (1) Roudi-Fahimi and Valentine M. Moghadam (2003) *Empowering Women, Developing Society: Female Education in the Middle East and North Africa.* Washington, DC: Population Reference Bureau; (2) *Women of Our World 2005.* Washington, DC: Population Reference Bureau; (3) *2005 World Population Data Sheet.* Washington DC: Population Reference Bureau; (4) United Nations Development Programme (UNDP) *Human Development Report 2003.*

Note
* Palestine includes the Arab population of West Bank and Gaza.

My battle starts the minute I walk out of my home each morning. As I am waiting to catch a ride, I endure honks and lurid comments by passing male motorists; during the ride I am made offers of *sigha* [temporary marriage]. At the university gate, I am stopped and told that my makeup and *hejab* are improper and in class my comments are dismissed or discredited by my male peers and male professors as "emotional female viewpoints." Do I think I will find a job after I graduate? What man in this society is going to take me, take us [women], seriously enough to hire us?[42]

There is no doubt that the fact that these women have access to higher education is a monumental improvement in their educational status. Nevertheless, if their status is not improved on a societal level, their higher education credentials will not help them to get far in the job market. As Shirin Ebadi, the Iranian human rights lawyer, activist, and the winner of the 2003 Nobel Peace Prize, concluded, "higher education is paradoxical: it both limits and expands women's possibilities in Iran."[43]

Employment/unemployment patterns

A vast body of feminist literature indicates that women's paid work is not only empowering and "status enhancing" but also beneficial to the collective well-being, and it is an important aspect of the production of goods and services in societies. Women's entry into the workforce is also argued to strengthen their position in the political system, to help them understand their rights, and to boost their political and collective action. However, another body of literature indicates that women's employment can also be disempowering and exploitative of women. Their labor is often exploited by their employers and oftentimes by their own family members, where they are used as unpaid and subjugated labor. From the global point of view, different tiers of women are exploited in the global economy even more so.

Therefore, as much as women's labor force participation has been assumed to contribute to their liberation and empowerment, in the MENA region, it is not obvious that employment is beneficial to women and their social status. If the society has not set up "social contracts" outside of the family and the kinship system, employment is not as attractive for women. There is little incentive for women to work outside of their homes if they are still held accountable for all the domestic responsibilities that traditionally have fallen to them. Societies arrange "social contracts" as guidelines to clarify an individual's and a society's responsibilities. They are set up as an exchange of goods and services. For example, in the Nordic countries the government takes responsibility for almost all social services including education, healthcare, childcare, and elder care. In societies with few or none of these services, as is the case in most Muslim countries, families and kinship systems meet these needs. In fact, in societies dominated by patriarchal family systems, women are expected to fulfill most of the familial responsibilities; whereas in non-familial regimes, that is to say, countries with social-democratic governments, the government would be expected to provide at least some of those services. Therefore, it is beneficial for governments to justify and perpetuate patriarchal family norms as is done in many of the MENA societies. In terms of women's position in the region, a "patriarchal gender contract"[44] or "sexual contract"[45] is argued to be the main factor determining participation or inhibition of women's involvement in the modern labor force. Women's status in society is the key determinant of their access to societal resources, which appears to be low in the MENA region. Societies might have set up certain arrangements through the patriarchal system to care for women and children, but once modernization is in place, compounded by economic and political failures, women have no guarantees of social and cultural support in these societies.

On the other hand, the unemployment rate in the region for both men and women is among the highest in the world, indicating a high demand for and a low supply of jobs. In the region, women's employment rate is much lower than men's while their unemployment rate is much higher than men's, indicating the multiple reasons for their lack of participation in the workforce. The unemployment rates for women are highest in Algeria, Egypt, Iran, Iraq, Jordan, and Syria. These countries also have a higher percentage of college-educated women among their younger population. Iran has the highest percentage of college-educated women among its younger population. The income disparity between men and women in the region is even more dramatic; the gap is much wider than in other regions. For example, Kuwaiti men earn three times more than women, Omani men four times more than women, Saudi men five times more than women (see tables 11.7 and 11.8).

As was discussed in the previous section, among the younger generation, the gap in educational attainment between women and men has narrowed tremendously in the MENA region. Furthermore, following the projections of modernization theory, many of the educated women are marrying later and having fewer children. In theory, higher education for women should lead to more employment opportunities. And yet Bahramitash,[46] in her study of contemporary Iranian women and the changes in their social status over the past decades, points to a lack of connection between education and employment. Iranian society has not been able to provide jobs for many of these women. The unemployment rate was as high as 20 percent for females and 12 percent for males in 2000 to 2004. It is all well and good to educate women, but if the underlying economy cannot support more workers, an advanced education does not necessarily offer an advantage. Furthermore, in recent decades, the poverty rate among women has increased dramatically due to higher inflation, higher male and female unemployment rates, and higher incidences of women not marrying, marrying later, or getting divorced, which leaves them without a male to support them financially. Rising poverty rates and high inflation force many educated and less educated women to seek employment. If women, both educated and non-educated, are competing for low wages and low-status jobs, then, Bahramitash argues, working "does not necessarily translate into economic empowerment for women."[47]

Table 11.7 Selected indicators of work, 2000–2004

Country	Estimated earned income (PPP US$) 2001		Income disparity between men and women** (%)
	Female	*Male*	
Algeria	2,784	9,329	30
Bahrain	7,578	22,305	34
Egypt	1,970	5,075	39
Iran	2,599	9,301	28
Iraq	–	–	–
Jordan	1,771	5,800	31
Kuwait	8,605	25,333	34
Lebanon	1,963	6,472	30
Libya	–	–	–
Morocco	2,057	5,139	40
Oman	3,919	17,960	22
Palestine*	–	–	–
Qatar	–	–	–
Saudi Arabia	4,222	21,141	20
Syria	1,423	5,109	27
Tunisia	3,377	9,359	36
Turkey	3,717	8,023	46
UAE	6,041	28,223	21
Yemen	365	1,201	30
High income countries			
Norway	23,317	36,043	65
Sweden	19,636	28,817	68
United States	26,389	45,540	58

Sources: (1) *2005 World Development Indicators, Women in Development*, Table 1.5 ; (2) *Human Development Report 2003*, Table 22, Gender-related development; (3) The World Bank Group, *GenderStats*, Database of Gender Statistics, available online at: http://devdata.worldbank.org/genderstats/genderRpt.asp?rpt=profile&cty=BHR,Bahrain&hm=home (retrieved on August 30, 2007).

Notes
*Palestine includes the Arab population of West Bank and Gaza.
** Income disparity is calculated as (female income/male income) * 100.

Simply, because statistically more women are working does not mean that they are seeing improvements in their wages or that overall they are a more economically empowered group. Rising employment for women in Iran and other countries in the region could be indicative of "economic exploitation rather than economic empowerment."[48]

Table 11.8 shows patterns of women's employment and unemployment from 1980 to 1990 and 2000 to 2004. The first column lists our select three countries, and the second column lists female labor force participation as a percentage of the total labor force. Only in Iran does one see that female labor force participation has increased between 1980 and 2004. The same data, grouped by region, show that overall in the MENA region female labor force participation has increased as is also witnessed in the United States. Female labor force participation for the

Table 11.8 Selected indicators of employment for men and women

Country	Female labor force participation (% of total labor force)			Unemployment			
				Total (% of total labor force)		Female (% of female labor force)	
	1980	1990	2000–2004	1990	2000–4	1990	2000–04
Algeria	20	23	30	19.8	29.8	15.9	29.7
Bahrain	11	17	19	–	–	–	–
Egypt	19	26	22	8.6	11	17.9	23.9
Iran	20	20	33	–	11.6	–	20.4
Iraq	16	17	19	–	28.1	–	16
Jordan	18	19	24	–	13.2	–	20.7
Kuwait	13	22	25	–	–	–	–
Lebanon	28	32	30	–	–	–	–
Libya	16	17	26	–	–	–	–
Morocco	21	24	25	15.8	10.8	–	–
Oman	15	11	16	–	–	–	–
Palestine*	–	–	–	–	–	–	–
Qatar	9	10	14	–	3.9	–	12.6
Saudi Arabia	8	11	15	–	5.2	–	11.5
Syria	23	26	30	–	11.7	–	24.1
Tunisia	19	21	27	15.3	14.3	–	–
Turkey	35	29	26	8.0	10.3	8.5	9.7
United Arab Emirates	5	10	13	–	2.3	–	2.6
Yemen	28	27	28	–	11.5	–	8.2
Region/economic category							
MENA	20	–	27	–	13.6	–	–
Lower middle income	41	–	42	3.9	5.9	–	–
High income	39	–	44	5.6	5.5	5.5	5.4
United States	41	44	46	5.6	6.4	6.8	6.6

Source: The World Bank Group, *GenderStats*, Database of Gender Statistics; available online at: http://devdata.worldbank.org/genderstats/genderRpt.asp?rpt=profile&cty=BHR,Bahrain&hm=home (retrieved on August 30, 2007).

Note
*Palestine includes the Arab population of West Bank and Gaza.

MENA region is as low as 27 percent. Despite the relative levels of rising employment for women, unemployment rates in the MENA region for both men and women are among the highest in the world, indicating a high demand and a low supply of jobs. In Iran women's employment rate is 33 percent – the highest in the region (still low compared to countries in other regions) – and the female unemployment rate is over 20 percent. While the unemployment rate in high-income countries is slightly lower for women than for men (6.8 percent for men and 6.6 for women in the United States), in the MENA region, women's employment rate is much lower than men's and their unemployment rate is much higher than men's. The highest recorded unemployment rates among these countries were in Algeria, Egypt, Iran, Iraq, Jordan, and Syria. These countries also have a higher percentage of college-educated women among their younger population,[49] once again countering the modernization theory's positive correlation between higher education and higher labor force participation. Table 11.8 also shows an income disparity between men and women among different regions and countries but more pronounced disparity in Iran, Turkey, and Yemen.

In examining the labor force dynamics in the MENA region, we encounter unique situations. Overall, women in the MENA region are not fully included in the labor force. They experience a low rate of employment and high rate of unemployment as a group, despite increasing education and reduced fertility rates. It should be mentioned that the process of modernization occurred gradually over three centuries in the Western world and allowed ample time for a gradual and unstoppable shift in social values and institutions. As modernization progressed, so did population sizes.[50] In Iran, modernization was spurred on by the global importance of oil and minerals. Its rapid expansion did not re-create the same environment that led to the development of the job market and industries as occurred in the Western modernization process. Thus, with the population bulge that ensued, a greater conflict between traditional social values and institutions was experienced.

Including women in the paid workforce will be advanced by a society if it is not facing economic and political failures and can support both men and women with jobs and social services. If the country is facing political turmoil and economic breakdown, women's employment is not a priority as we see in Iran. In those instances all sorts of cultural norms and ideological messages will be used to justify keeping women at home to attend to their families' care and well-being. Frequently, however, women of lower socio-economic status do not have the strong familial support and the societal system also is ill-equipped to protect them.

In sum, women enter the paid workforce when the country is politically stable and has a diversified and prosperous economy enabling it to provide jobs and competitive salaries for both men and women. When, instead, there is political instability or a lack of economic growth (or an economy based on a sole industry: oil) women's employment and improvements in their social status loses momentum and actually is discouraged. Cultural norms and ideological messages will be used to maintain the status quo (i.e., that a woman's duty is to her family). In many cases, in exchange for their services and care giving, women are taken care of through the patriarchal kinship system. Women with lower socio-economic status, however, might not have strong kinship support and cannot rely on their male family members in case of economic need. They are among the most disadvantaged groups in the region.

Conclusion

The way many MENA countries deal with women's issues, placing an emphasis on traditionalism in the name of Islam, has often been a political strategy for these nations to deflect attention from their economic failures, high inflation rates, lack of ability to provide employment for everyone, and lack of adequate social services.[51] The intent of this chapter has been to analyze Iran within the context of the MENA region and the multiple aspects that have affected women's status in Iran – factoring in economic, demographic, and political forces responsible for changes or the lack thereof. The view of the MENA as a region experiencing high population growth without a parallel growth in job creation may lead us to a pessimistic view of the future for Iran and other countries in the MENA region. This assumption, however, is not necessarily correct.

Studies of the modernization process have shown that women's status improves when they become essential to the financial system; when the forces of sustainable growth and a diversified economy are able to provide jobs at least equal to the demand. The data for educational attainment by women in MENA show the effects of modernization; as in recent decades, the percentage of women enrolled in higher education (university) has increased significantly. In some MENA countries, the majority of university students are female. According to Gary Becker,[52] this is indicative of a country's shift from underdeveloped to developed. The family dynamics change from having many children to provide labor for the family, to smaller families where the parents invest more in their children through education (quantity versus quality). In the latter case, in a developed society, there is a greater return when parents invest in a smaller number of children. Society also benefits from a more educated and smaller population.

Each MENA country has reached different levels of social reality pertaining to women's status. In the case of Iran's modernization and its affects on women's status, as compared with other MENA countries, one can see that Iran's fertility rate is the lowest in the group, at 2.0, with a low rate of maternal mortality.[53] Women play a small role in government with a 3 percent representation in Parliament (in 2004), which is consistent with the effects of converting the secular government to a religious one based on historically patriarchal traditions. In spite of the patriarchal system imposed by the government, female educational attainment from 1985 to 2003 increased more than it had during the programs of the previous secular political system. Female enrollment during this period rose from 36 to 75 percent with the university population being 47 percent female by 2000. Married women in Iran have the lowest rate of participation in the labor force compared to single and widowed women. Divorced women have the highest rate of participation in the labor force.[54]

The future of women's status is dependent on the next course of modernization. In spite of great wealth, MENA countries such as Iran that are dependent on a single industry (oil) actually suffered an incomplete modernization to the detriment of women. The political and economic status quo is maintained by reinforcing historically patriarchal ideologies. This status quo, however, has not necessarily led to political stability and prosperity. Improvement in the quality of life, and as a consequence improvement in women's status, will occur if the current trajectory of the modernization process is altered in accordance with lessons taken from the Western modernization process. This theme is reflected in the studies by Salehi-Isfahani.[55] His discussion is centered on the size and distribution of population in Iran (the "youth bulge"), and the effects this will have upon economic and social development in the next few decades. He points out how in Iran, the 1979 Revolution against the government was born among the disenfranchised youth.[56] Following the revolution, Iran's fertility rate increased dramatically, thus producing another, even larger, youth bulge. Hope, according to Salehi-Isfahani, lies in the government changing the country's base of economic growth from oil, to "human capital." The oil industry, based on a finite quantity of a natural resource, produced a financial windfall for the Iranian economy – not a sustainable economic model. This is also true for the other major oil-producing nations such as Kuwait, Saudi Arabia, and the United Arab Emirates. Wherever there is a tight relationship between per capita income and oil exports, further complicated by rapid population growth, social and political scientists will see the potential for civil unrest and instability. And it is clear that an oil export-based economy can have adverse affects on women's status.

The population boom seen across the MENA region in the 1970s and 1980s, followed by the rapid decline in fertility rates, can represent a danger to an oil-based economy or a valuable asset to an economy in expansion. Throughout the MENA region, a youth bulge followed by a decline in fertility means that over time, the ratio of adults to children changes to produce more teachers/nurturers to raise fewer children. This facilitates the transition of economic growth away from oil and more toward human capital. The timing of this transition is paramount. All the MENA countries with declining fertility rates need to make a rapid investment in their human capital and create a diversified economic base for sustainable growth before the current youth bulge reaches retirement.[57] At that point there will be a smaller cohort of working contributors to care for a larger elderly population. Investment in human capital today and diversification to a sustainable economy away from just an oil-based industry will provide tomorrow's generations with stability and prosperity.

Women's social status has been and continues to be conditioned by the economic and political realties of the region. When expedient, Islam and historical traditions of patriarchy have been engaged as frameworks and justifications for controlling the population. However, in Islamic countries where we see a more diversified economy, Islam has not been an altogether limiting influence. There-fore, we can predict a substantial improvement in the future of women's status in the MENA region if it is able to move away from reliance on oil exports and focus on an investment in human capital and a diversified economy with ample jobs. With the population growth under control, and women already achieving higher educational attainment, regional stability and prosperity lies in continued and intelligent modernization. Most importantly, women's status would improve by virtue of the natural economic forces that would ensue from stability and eco-nomic diversification.

Notes

1 Patriarchy is considered a system that enables men to dominate women and maintain power and control of resources. Women – especially younger ones – have minimal power and are dependent on men; see further M. Cain *et al.* (1979) "Class, Patriarchy, and Women's Work in Bangladesh," *Population and Development Review*, 5 (Sep-tember), pp. 405–438; and K.O. Mason (1986) "The Status of Women: Conceptual and Methodological Issues in Demographic Studies," *Social Forces*, 1(2), pp. 284–300. Deniz Kandiyoti defines classic patriarchy as a systematic unequal position of women in societies. She describes a patriarchal family as multigenerational and hierarchical, where younger women and children are placed in the lowest level of the hierarchy. The *paterfamilias,* as she calls it, is characterized by young women marry-ing men older than themselves (frequently significantly older). When the young bride enters the new household, she is placed at the lowest level of the hierarchy with the least amount of power. Upon bearing sons, she gains more status and eventually, by becoming a mother-in-law, she gains more power as an older female in the household. Marrying young girls is important because it legitimately extends the length of time that they can bear children. A young woman is also socialized more readily to an unequal role and inequitable entitlement to the family resources – even compared to her own children; see further D. Kandiyoti (1992) "Islam and Patriarchy: A Compara-tive Perspective," in N. Keddie and B. Baron (eds) *Women in Middle Eastern History: Shifting Boundaries in Sex and Gender* (New Haven, CT: Yale University Press), pp. 23–42; and Val Moghadam (ed.) (2004) *Gender and National Identity: Women and Politics in Muslim Society* (London: Zed Books for United Nations University World Institute for Development Economics Research (UNU/WIDER). What do women gain from their lower status with these inferior arrangements? In exchange for their low status and unequal access to resources, women are entitled to protection and maintenance. Kandiyoti (in *supra*) refers to this exchange as the "patriarchal bar-gains." According to A.G. Johnson, four dimensions characterize a patriarchal social structure: male domination – men predominantly hold the most prestigious and powerful roles and women hold the least powerful roles; patriarchal control – women are devalued and experience physical and psychological control, violence and fear of violence in their everyday lives because of the ideological need for men's control, supervision, and protection; male identified – most aspects of society that are highly valued and rewarded are associated with men and identified with male characteristics, while any other attributes less valued and rewarded are associated with women; and male centricity – public attention (e.g., the media, public spaces) is often granted to men, and women are placed in the background and on the margins. See further A.G. Johnson (1997) *The Gender Knot: Unraveling Our Patriarchal Legacy* (Philadelphia, PA: Temple University Press). Finally, M. Hughes *et al.* describe patriarchy as an institution where gender inequality is perpetuated by a set of complex processes referred to as sexism where patriarchy is rooted in cultural and legal systems that his-

torically gave fathers authority in family and clan matters, made wives and children dependent on husbands and fathers, and organized descent and inheritance through the male line; see M. Hughes *et al.* (1999) *Sociology, the Core,* 5th edn (Boston, MA: McGraw Hill), p. 250.

2 See further A. Inkles and D.H. Smith (1974) *Becoming Modern: Individual Change in Six Developing Countries* (Cambridge, MA: Harvard University Press); Wilbert E. Moore (1979) *World Modernization: The Limits of Convergence* (New York: Elsevier); and Talcot Parsons (1971) *The System of Modern Societies* (Englewood Cliffs, NJ: Prentice-Hall).

3 See further C.E. Black (1966) *The Dynamics of Modernization* (New York: Harper & Row); N. Black and A. Cottrell (1981) *Women and World Change* (Beverly Hills, CA: Sage); M.J. Levy (1966) *Modernization and the Structure of Societies: A Setting for International Affairs* (Princeton, NJ: Princeton University Press); and D.A. Rustow (1967) *A World of Nations: Problems of Political Modernization* (Washington, DC: The Brookings Institute).

4 From pre-industrial agriculture to an industrial manufacturing economy.

5 See further Richard Anker and Catherine Hein (1986) *Sex Inequalities in Urban Employment in the Third World* (London: Macmillan); Ester Boserup (1970) *Women's Role in Economic Development* (London: Allen & Unwin); Ann Oakley (1974) *Women's Work* (New York: Vintage Books); M.P. Ryan (1975) *Womanhood in America: From Colonial Times to the Present* (New York: New Viewpoints); and Louise Tilly and Joan Scott (1978) *Women, Work and Family* (London: Routledge).

6 Peter Evans and Michael Timberlake (1980) "Dependence, Inequality, and the Growth of the Tertiary," *American Sociological Review,* 45, pp. 531–552; Jeffrey Kentor (1981) "Structural Determinants of Peripheral Urbanization: The Effects of International Dependence," *American Sociological Review,* 46, pp. 201–211; and M. Semyonov (1980) "The Social Context of Women's Labor Force Participation: A Comparative Analysis," *American Journal of Sociology,* 86, pp. 534–550.

7 See Boserup, *Women's Role;* Elhum Haghighat-Sordellini (2002) "Culture, Development and Female Labor Force Participation: Disaggregating Different Sectors," *International Review of Sociology,* 12(3), pp. 343–362; idem. (2009) "Determinants of Female Labor Force Participation: A Focus on Muslim Countries," *International Review of Sociology,* 19(1), pp. 103–112; idem. (2010) *Women in the Middle East and North Africa: Continuity and Change* (New York: Palgrave-Macmillan); Valerie Oppenheimer (1970) "The Female Labor Force in the United States: Demographic and Economic Factors Governing its Growth and Changing Composition" (Berkeley, CA: Institute of International Studies); and Fred Pampel and Kazuko Tanaka (1986) "Economic Development and Female Labor Force Participation: A Reconsideration," *Social Forces,* 64(3) (March), pp. 33–60.

8 For example, petty trade, carpet and basket weaving, small-scale farming.

9 See, for example, Anker and Hein, *Sex Inequalities.*

10 John Durand (1975) *The Labor Force in Economic Development* (Princeton, NJ: Princeton University Press).

11 UNDP, *Human Development Indicators, 2003;* see Table 2 for these measures.

12 Ibid.

13 Women have access to more resources in the United States.

14 Considering the availability of job opportunities.

15 UN Report, *World Population Policies, 2003.*

16 Val Moghadam (1993) *Modernizing Women: Gender and Social Change in the Middle East* (Boulder, CO: Lynne Reiner).

17 Roksana Bahramitash (2007) "Family Planning, Islam and Women's Human Rights in Iran," *International Development Studies Journal,* 4(1) (summer), pp. 33–50.

18 R. Fagley (1965) "Doctrines and Attitudes of Major Religions with Regard to Fertility," paper presented at UN World Population Conference, Belgrade; Carla Makhlouf

Obermeyer (1992) "Islam, Women, and Politics: The Demography of Arab Countries," *Population and Development Review*, 18(1) (March), pp. 33–60; and idem. (1994) "Reproductive Choice in Islam: Gender and State in Iran and Tunisia," *Studies in Family Planning*, 25(1), pp. 41–51.

19 Phillipe Fargues (2003) "Women in Arab Countries: Challenging the Patriarchal System?," *Population et Societes*, 387 (February).

20 Obermeyer, "Reproductive Choice."

21 Janet Larsen (2001) "Iran's Birth Rate Plummeting at Record Pace: Success Provides a Model for other Developing Countries," *Earth Policy Institute*, p. 2; available at: http://www.earth-policy.org/Updates/Update4ss.htm (retrieved on August 30, 2007).

22 UNDP, *Human Development Indicators, 2003.*

23 Ibid.

24 Jennifer Olmsted (2003) "Reexamining the Fertility Puzzle in the Middle East and North Africa," in Eleanor Doumato and Marsha Pripstein-Posusney (eds) *Women and Globalization in the Arab Middle East: Gender, Economy and Society* (Boulder, CO: Lynne Reiner), pp. 73–92.

25 See further Karin Brewster and Roland Rindfuss (2000) "Fertility and Women's Employment in Industrialized Nations," *Annual Review of Sociology*, 26, pp. 271–296.

26 For example, early marriage, subsequent pregnancies, childcare responsibilities, and housework.

27 R.D. Singh (1994) "Fertility–Mortality Variations across LDCs: Women's Education, Labor Force Participation, and Contraceptive Use," *Kyklos*, 47(2), pp. 209–221.

28 Nine of the 18 countries within the MENA region report illiteracy rates of less than 10 percent for both boys and girls aged 15 to 24 years.

29 UNIFEM (2004); and Jennifer Olmsted (2005) "Is Paid Work the (Only) Answer? Neo-Liberalism, Arab Women's Well-being, and the Social Contract," *Journal of Middle East Women's Studies*, 1(2) (spring), pp. 112–139.

30 Ninety-one percent of girls and 100 percent of boys.

31 Twenty and 34 percent, respectively.

32 Mustapha Nabli (2002) "Conference on Higher Education in the Middle East and North Africa: Challenges and Opportunities for 21st Century" (Institute de Monde Arab and the World Bank).

33 Durand, *Labor Force.*

34 Despite their improved educational attainment and lower fertility.

35 Mirna Lattouf (2004) *Women, Education, and Socialization in Modern Lebanon* (New York: University Press of America); and Mitra Shavarini (2006) "Wearing the Veil to College: The Paradox of Higher Education in the Lives of Iranian Women," *International Journal of Middle East Studies*, 38, pp. 189–211.

36 Lattouf, *Women.*

37 Shavarini, "Wearing the Veil," p. 189.

38 Ibid., p. 193.

39 Ibid., p. 199.

40 See ILO, "Global Employment Trends for Women, 2007."

41 Farzaneh Roudi-Fahimi and Mary Kent (2007) "The Population Puzzle" (Washington, DC: Population Reference Bureau), p. 206.

42 Shavarini, "Wearing the Veil," p. 206.

43 Quoted in ibid., p. 190.

44 Moghadam (ed.) *Gender*; and Jackline Wahba (2003) "Women in MENA Labor Markets," *Newsletter of the Economic Research Forum for the Arab Countries, Iran & Turkey*, 10(1) (spring).

45 Carole Pateman (1988) *Sexual Contract* (Stanford, CA: Stanford University Press); and Olmsted, "Paid Work."

46 Bahramitash, "Family Planning."

47 Ibid., p. 104.
48 Ibid.
49 With the exception of Iraq.
50 Changed from a low population growth to high and then to almost no population growth.
51 Nadia Hijab (1988) *Womenpower: The Arab Debate on Women at Work* (Cambridge: Cambridge University Press); Moghadam, "Development and Patriarchy"; and Obermeyer, "Islam, Women, and Politics."
52 Gary Becker (1991) *Treatise on the Family* (Cambridge, MA: Harvard University Press).
53 Both are indicators of modernization.
54 Djavad Salehi-Isfahani (2000a) "Demographic Factors in Iran's Economic Development," *Social Research*, 67(2) (summer), pp. 599–620.
55 Ibid.
56 Ibid.; and D. Salehi-Isfahani (2000b) "Microeconomics of Growth in MENA – the Role of Households," Global Research Project, Global Development Networks.
57 Estimated around 2040.

Bibliography

Abu-Lughod, L. (1998) "Introduction: feminist longings and postcolonial conditions," in *Remaking Women: Feminism and Modernity in the Middle East*. Princeton, NJ: Princeton University Press, pp. 3–31.

Abu-Lughod, L. (2001) "Orientalism and Middle East feminist studies," *Feminist Studies*, 27, 1, pp. 101–113.

Abu-Lughod, L. (2002) "Do Muslim women really need saving? Anthropological reflections on cultural relativism and its others," *American Anthropologist*, 104, 3, pp. 783–790.

Acemoglu, D., Simon, J., and Robinson, J.A. (2001) "The colonial origins of comparative development: an empirical investigation," *American Economic Review*, 91, 5, pp. 1369–1401.

Adelkhah, F. (2004) *Being Modern in Iran*, trans. J. Derrick. New York: Columbia University Press.

Afary, J. (1996) *The Iranian Constitutional Revolution, 1906–1911*. New York: Columbia University Press.

Afshar, H. (1997) "Women and work in Iran," *Political Studies*, 45, 4, pp. 755–767.

Ahmed, L. (1992) *Women and Gender in Islam*. New Haven, CT: Yale University Press.

Alavi, N. (2005) *We are Iran*. Brooklyn, NY: Soft Skull Press.

Alizadeh, P. and Harper, B. (2003) "The feminisation of the labour force in Iran," in Mohammadi, A. (ed.) *Iran Encountering Globalization: Problems and Prospects*. London: Routledge.

Alloula, M. (1986) *The Colonial Harem*. Manchester: Manchester University Press.

Amawi, A. (1996) "Women and property rights in Islam," in Sabbagh, S. (ed.) *Arab Women: Between Defiance and Restraint*. New York: Olive Branch Press, pp. 151–158.

Amesden, A. (1985) "The state and Taiwan's economic development," in Evan, P., Rueschemeyer, D., and Skocpol, T. (eds) *Bringing the State Back*. Cambridge: Cambridge University Press.

Amin, S. (1989) *Eurocentrism*. New York: Monthly Review Press.

Amy, L. (1997) "Gender, development and urban social change: women's community action in global cities," *World Development*, 25, 8, pp. 1205–1223.

Andoni, L. (1995) "President's daughter rallies for women's sports in Iran," *Christian Science Monitor*, March 28, p. 7. Available at: http://web.ebscohost.com (accessed May 10, 2010).

Anker, R. (1999) *Gender and Jobs: Sex segregation of occupations in the world*. Geneva: International Labour Office.

Anker, R. (2001) "Theories of occupational segregation by sex: an overview," in Loutfi, M.F. (ed.) *Women, Gender and Work*. Geneva: International Labour Office.

Anker, R. and Hein, C. (eds) (1986) *Sex Inequalities in Urban Employment in the Third World*. London: Macmillan.

Ayotte, K.J. and Husain, M. (2005) "Securing Afghan women: neocolonialism, epistemic violence, and the rhetoric of the veil," *National Women's Studies Association Journal*, 17, 3, pp. 112–133.

Badran, M. (1995) *Feminists, Islam and Nation*. Princeton, NJ: Princeton University Press.

Bahramitash, R. (2003) "Islamic fundamentalism and women's economic role: the case of Iran," *International Journal of Politics, Culture and Society*, 16, 4, pp. 551–558.

Bahramitash, R. (2004a) "Myths and realities of the impact of political Islam on women: female employment in Iran and Indonesia," *Development in Practice*, 14, 5, pp. 508–520.

Bahramitash, R. (2004b) "Market fundamentalism versus religious fundamentalism: women's employment in Iran," *Critique*, 13, 1, pp. 33–46.

Bahramitash, R. (2005a) *Liberation from Liberalization: Gender and Globalization in Southeast Asia*. London: Zed Books.

Bahramitash, R. (2005b) "The war on terror, feminist orientalism and orientalist feminism: case studies of two North American bestsellers," *Critique*, 14, 2, pp. 221–235.

Bahramitash, R. (2007a) "Family planning, Islam and women's human rights in Iran," *International Development Studies Journal*, 4, 1, pp. 33–50.

Bahramitash, R. (2007b) "Female employment and globalization during Iran's reform era (1997–2005)," *Journal of Middle East Women Studies*, 3, 2, pp. 56–86.

Bahramitash, R. (2011) "Female-headed households in Iran: micro-credit versus charity," in Bahramitash, R. and Esfahani, H. (eds) *Veiled Employment: The Political Economy of Female Employment in Iran*. Syracuse, NY: Syracuse University Press.

Bahramitash, R. and Esfahani, H. (2009) "Nimble fingers no longer! Women's employment in Iran," in Gheissari, A. (ed.) *Contemporary Iran: Economy, Society, Politics*. Oxford: Oxford University Press.

Bahramitash, R. and Esfahani, H. (2011) "The transformation of female labour market," in Bahramitash, R. and Esfahani, H. (eds) *Veiled Employment: The Political Economy of Female Employment in Iran*. Syracuse, NY: Syracuse University Press.

Bahramitash, R. and Kazemipour, S. (2011) "Veiled economy: gender and the informal sector," in Bahramitash, R. and Esfahani, H. (eds) *Veiled Employment: The Political Economy of Female Employment in Iran*. Syracuse, NY: Syracuse University Press.

Balakrishnan, R. (ed.) (2002) *The Hidden Assembly Line: Gender Dynamics of Subcontracted Work in a Global Economy*. Bloomfield, CT: Kumarian Press.

Bamdadan, B. [Dustdar, A.] (1997) *Derakhsheshha-ye tireh* [Somber incandescences]. Paris: NP.

Bayat, A. (1997) *Street Politics: Poor People's Movements in Iran*. New York: Columbia University Press.

Beall, J. (1996) "Participation in the city: where do women fit in?," *Gender and Development*, 4, 4, pp. 9–16.

Beall, J. and Fox, S. (2007) "Urban poverty and development in the 21st century: towards an inclusive and sustainable world," *Oxfam Research Report*. Available online at: http://reprints.lse.ac.uk/2903/1/urban_poverty_and_development_in_the_21st_century. pdf (accessed May 2010).

Becker, G. (1991) *Treatise on the Family*. Cambridge, MA: Harvard University Press.

Beckford, J. (2003) *Social Theory and Religion*. Cambridge: Cambridge University Press.

Bellah, R.N. (1957) *Tokugawa Religion: The Values of Pre-industrial Japan*. Glencoe, IL: Free Press.

Benería, L. (1999) "Globalization, gender and the Davos man," *Feminist Economics*, 5, 3, pp. 61–83.

Benería, L. (2003) *Gender, development and globalization: economics as if all people mattered*. New York: Routledge.

Benería, L., Floro, M., Grown, C. and MacDonald, M. (2000) "Globalization and gender," *Feminist Economics*, 6, 3, pp. vii–xviii.

Bhagwati, J.N. and Desai. P. (1970) *India: Planning for Industrialization*. London: Oxford University Press.

Black, C.E. (1966) *The Dynamics of Modernization*. New York: Harper & Row.

Black, N. and Cottrell, A. (1981) *Women and World Change*. Beverly Hills, CA: Sage.

Bollag, B. (2000) "For Iranian women, conservative dress fosters liberal views on campus," *Chronicle of Higher Education*, 7 (August), p. 1. Available online at: http://web.ebscohost.com (accessed May 27, 2010).

Boroujerdi, A. (1995) "Women's position in Islam," paper presented to the First International Conference on The Role of Woman and Family in Human Development, Tehran, Iran, May 22–24. Available online at: http: www.salamiran.org/Women/News/The_Role_of_Woman_andFamily_in_Human_Development.html (accessed May 26, 2010).

Boroujerdi, M. (1996) *Iranian Intellectuals and the West: The Tormented Triumph of Nativism*. Syracuse, NY: Syracuse University Press.

Boserup, E. (1970) *Women's Role in Economic Development*. New York: St. Martin's Press.

Boserup, E. (1990) "Economic change and the role of women," in Tinker, I. (ed.) *Persistent Inequalities: Women and Development*. New York: Oxford University Press.

Bott, E. (1971) *Family and Social Network*, 2nd edn. London: Tavistock.

Brewster, K. and Rindfuss, R. (2000) "Fertility and women's employment in industrialized nations," *Annual Review of Sociology*, 26, pp. 271–296.

Bricker, M. (2008) "The Islamic Republic's women at the wheel," *Time* magazine. Available online at www.time.com/time/world/article/0,8599,1847151,00.html (accessed May 26, 2010).

Cagatay, N., Elson, D., and Grown, C. (eds) (1995a) "Introduction," in *Gender, Adjustment and Macroeconomics*. New York: Elsevier Science.

Cagatay, N., Elson, D., and Grown, C. (1995b) "Gender, adjustment and macroeconomics," *World Development*, special issue, 23, 11, pp. 1826–1827.

Cain, M., Khanom, S.R., and Nashar, S. (1979) "Class, patriarchy, and women's work in Bangladesh," *Population and Development Review*, 5 (September), pp. 405–438.

Chant, S. (1991) *Women and Survival in Mexican Cities: Perspectives on Gender, Labour Markets, and Low-income Households*. New York: Manchester University Press.

Charusheela, S. (2004) "Postcolonial thought, postmodernism, and economics: questions of ontology and ethics," in Zein-Elabdin, E. and Charusheela, S. (eds) *Post-colonialism Meets Economics*. New York: Routledge.

Chatterjee, P. (1986) *Nationalist Thought and the Colonial World: A Derivative Discourse*. London: Zed Books.

Corden, W.M. and Neary, P.J. (1982) "Booming sector and deindustrialization in a small open economy," *The Economic Journal*, 92 (December), pp. 825–848.

Creswell, J. (2007) *Educational Research: Planning, Conducting, and Evaluating Quantitative and Qualitative Research*, 3rd edn. Upper Saddle River, NJ: Prentice Hall.

Dabashi, H. (2006) "Native informers and the making of the American empire," *Al-*

Ahram Weekly. Available online at: http://weekly.ahram.org.eg/2006/797/special.htm (accessed December 2, 2008).

Dabbagh, M. (1996) "Zanan va naqsh-e anan dar majles" [Women and their role in the Majles], *Neda*, 17–18 (winter).

Datta, N. (2006), "Joint titling: A win-win policy? Gender and property rights in urban informal settlements in Chandigarh, India," *Feminist Economics*, 12, 1 and 2, pp. 271–298.

Deeb, L. (2007) *An Enchanted Modern: Gender and Public Piety in Shi'i Lebanon*. Princeton, NJ: Princeton University Press.

De Soto, H. (2002) *The Other Path: The Economic Answer to Terrorism*. New York: Basic Books.

Diamond, I. and Orenstein, G.F. (eds) (1990) *Reweaving the World: The Emergence of Ecofeminism*. New York: Random House.

Dignard, L. and Havet, J. (eds) (1995) *Women in Micro- and Small-scale Enterprise Development*. Boulder, CO: Westview Press.

Doss, C., Grown, C., and Deere, D. (2008) "Gender and asset ownership: a guide to collecting individual level data," paper presented at the World Bank, Washington.

Drakich, J. and Stewart, P. (2007) "40 years later, how are university women doing?," *Academic Matters*, February, pp. 6–9.

Durand, J.D. (1975) *The Labor Force in Economic Development*. Princeton, NJ: Princeton University Press.

Dustdar, A. (1359/1980) *Molahezat-e falsafi dar din, elm va fekr* [Philosophical considerations on religion, science and thought]. Tehran: NP.

Early, E.A. (1994) "Getting it together: Baladi Egyptian businesswomen," in Tucker, J. (ed.) *Arab Women: Old Boundaries, New Frontiers*. Bloomington: Indiana University Press.

Easterly, W. (2001) *The Elusive Quest for Growth: Economists' Adventures and Misadventures in the Tropic*. Cambridge, MA: MIT Press.

Easterly, W. (2006) *The White Man's Burden: Why the West's Efforts to Aid the Rest Have Done So Much Ill and So Little Good*. New York: Penguin Press.

Ebn-Eddin, F. (1992) "Lozoum-e eslah-e qavanin-e talaq, t'addud-e zojat va hezanat" [The necessity for the reform of laws concerning divorce, polygyny, and child custody], *Payam-e Hajar*, 28–29, September 10.

Elson, D. (1993) "Gender aware analysis and development economics," *Journal of International Development*, 5, 2, pp. 176–190.

Elson, D. (1995) "Gender awareness in modeling structural adjustment," in Cagatay, N., Elson, D., and Grown, C. (eds) *World Development*, 23, 11, pp. 1851–1868.

Escobar, A. (1995) *Encountering Development: The Making and Unmaking of the Third World*. Princeton, NJ: Princeton University Press.

Esfahani, H.S., Gary, M., and Lyn, S. (forthcoming) *Diversity in Economic Growth*. Northampton, MA: Edward Elgar.

Esfandiari, H. (2001) "The politics of the woman question in the Islamic Republic: 1979–1999," in Esposito, J. (ed.) *Iran at the Crossroads*. New York: Palgrave.

Esfandiari, H. (2005) "Iranian women, please stand up," *Global Newsstand: Foreign Policy*, November/December, pp. 84–85.

Evans, P. and Timberlake, M. (1980) "Dependence, inequality, and the growth of the tertiary," *American Sociological Review*, 45, pp. 531–552.

Fagley, R. (1965) "Doctrines and attitudes of major religions with regard to fertility," paper presented at the U.N. World Population Conference, Belgrade, quoted in Schieffelin, O. (ed.) (1967) *Muslim Attitudes Toward Family Planning*. New York: The Population Council.

Fanni, Z. (2006) "Small cities and regional sustainable development in Iran." Paper presented at NIE-SEAGA conference, November 28–30. Available online at: www.hsse. nie.edu.sg/staff/chanch/seaga2006/proceedings/full%20Papers/day2fullpapers/session-14zohreh.pdf (accessed June 2010).

Fargues, P. (2003) "Women in Arab countries: challenging the patriarchal system?," *Population et Societes*, 387 (February).

Feyerabend, P. (1987) *Farewell to Reason*. London: Verso.

Fischer, M.M.J. and Abedi, M. (1990) *Debating Muslims: Cultural Dialogues in Postmodernity and Tradition*. Madison: University of Wisconsin Press.

Foltz, R. (2001) "Environmental initiatives in contemporary Iran," *Central Asian Survey*, 20, 2, pp. 155–165.

Frank, A.G. (1967) *Capitalism and Underdevelopment in Latin America*. New York: Monthly Review Press.

Gallaway, J. and Bernasek, A. (eds) (2002) "Gender and informal sector employment in Indonesia," *Journal of Economic Issues*, 36, 2, pp. 313–321.

Gerhardt, M. (2002) "Sport and civil society in Iran," in Hooglund, E. (ed.) *Twenty Years of Islamic Revolution*. Syracuse, NY: Syracuse University Press.

German, L. (1996) "Do women want to stay at home?," *Socialist Review*, 198, pp. 17–19.

Gheissari, A. (1997) *Iranian Intellectuals in the Twentieth Century*. Austin: University of Texas Press.

Gheytanchi, E. (2000) "Appendix: Chronology of events regarding women in Iran since the Revolution of 1979," *Social Research Journal*, 67, 2, pp. 439–452.

Goldin, C. (1994) "The U-Shaped Female Labour Force Function in Economic Development and Economic History," Working Paper No. 4707. *National Bureau of Economic Research*. Available online at: www.nber.org/papers/w4707.pdf (accessed June 2008).

Gorgi, M. (1993) "Zan va zamamdari: negahi beh hokoumat-e malakeh-ye saba dar qoran" [Women and leadership: a look at the Queen of Sheba's reign in the Qur'an], *Farzaneh*, 1, pp. 9–29.

Gran, J. (1977) "Impact of the world market on Egyptian women," *MERIP Reports*, 58, pp. 3–7.

Haddad, Y.Y. and Smith, J. (2002) "Adjusting the tie that binds: challenges facing Muslim women in America," in Jawad, H. and Benn, T (eds) *Muslim Women in the United States and Beyond*. Boston, MA: Brill.

Haeri, S. (1989) *Law of Desire: Temporary Marriage in Shi'i Iran*. Syracuse, NY: Syracuse University Press.

Haghighat-Sordellini, E. (2002) "Culture, development and female labor force participation: disaggregating different sectors," *International Review of Sociology*, 12, 3, pp. 343–362.

Haghighat-Sordellini, E. (2009) "Determinants of female labor force participation: a focus on Muslim countries," *International Review of Sociology – Revue Internationale de Sociologie*, 19, 1, pp.103–125.

Haghighat-Sordellini, E. (2010) Women in the Middle East and North Africa: Continuity and Change. New York: Palgrave-Macmillan.

Hakim, C. (2000a) *Research Design: Successful Designs for Social and Economic Research*. London: Routledge.

Hakim, C. (2000b) *Work–Lifestyle Choices in the 21st Century: Preference Theory*. Oxford: Oxford University Press.

Hakim, C. (2003) "Competing family models: competing social policies," *Family Matters*, 64, pp. 52–61.

Halper, L. (2005) "Law and women's agency in post revolutionary Iran," *Harvard Journal of Law*, 28, 1, pp. 85–106.

Halper, L. (2007) "Law, authority and gender in post-revolutionary Iran," *SUNY Buffalo Law Review*, 54, 4, pp. 1137–1189.

Harrison, F. (2006) "Women graduates challenge Iran." BBC online, September 19. Available online at: www.bbc.com (accessed October 10, 2006).

Hasso, F.S. (2005) "Problems and promise in Middle East and North Africa gender research," *Feminist Studies*, 31, 3, pp. 653–679.

Heintz, J. and Pollin, R. (2003) "Informalization, economic growth and the challenge of creating viable labor standards in developing countries," Working Paper, University of Massachusetts Amherst.

Higgins, P. and Shoar-Ghaffari, P. (1994) "Women's education in the Islamic Republic of Iran," in Afkhami, M. and Friedl, E. (eds) *In the Eye of the Storm: Women in Post-Revolutionary Iran*. London and New York: I.B. Tauris.

Hijab, N. (1988) *Womanpower: The Arab Debate on Women at Work*. Cambridge: Cambridge University Press.

Hillenbrad, C. (2003) "Women in the Seljuq period," in Nashat, G. and Beck, L. (eds) *Women in Iran from the Rise of Islam to 1800*. Urbana: University of Illinois Press.

Hine, C. (2000) *Virtual Ethnography*. London: Sage.

Hoodfar, H. (1997) *Between Marriage and the Market: Intimate Politics and Survival in Cairo*. Berkeley: University of California Press.

Hoodfar, H. (1999a) "The Women's movement in Iran: women at the crossroads of secularization and Islamization," *Women Living under Muslim Laws, The Women's Movement Series*, 1.

Hoodfar, H. (1999b) "Volunteer health workers in Iran as social activists," *Women Living Under Muslim Laws*, 10, pp. 112–123.

Hooglund, E. (1982) *Land and Revolution in Iran, 1960–1980*. Austin: University of Texas Press.

Hooglund, E. (1997) "Letter from an Iranian Village," *Journal of Palestine Studies*, 27, 1 (autumn), pp. 76–84.

Hooglund, E. (2009) "Thirty years of Islamic revolution in rural Iran," *Middle East Report*, 250 (spring), pp. 34–39.

Hooglund, E. (ed.) (2002) *Twenty Years of Islamic Revolution: Political and Social Transition in Iran since 1979*. Syracuse, NY: Syracuse University Press.

Hooglund, E. & Stenberg, L. (eds) (2011) *Navigating Contemporary Iran: Challenging Economic, Social, and Political Perceptions*. London: Routledge.

Hooglund, M. (1980) "The village women of Aliabad and the Iranian Revolution," *Iranian Political Economy and History*, 4, 27, pp.47–57.

Hoqouq-e Zanan (2001), nos 19–20, March.

Hughes, M., Kroehler, C., and Zanden, J.V. (1999) *Sociology, The Core*, 5th edn. Boston, MA: McGraw Hill.

Hunt, J. and Kasynathan, N. (2002) "Reflections on microfinance and women's empowerment," *Development Bulletin*, 57, pp. 71–75.

IFAD (2008) *Rural women in Ifad's projects: the key to poverty alleviation*. Available online at: www.ifad.org/pub/other/!brocsch.pdf (accessed May 2010).

Inkeles, A. (1964) *What is Sociology? An Introduction to the Discipline and Profession*. Englewood Cliffs, NJ: Prentice Hall.

Inkles, A. and Smith, D.H. (1974) *Becoming Modern: Individual Change in Six Developing Countries*. Cambridge, MA: Harvard University Press.

International Development Research Center (2007) *Gender in a macroeconomic framework: a CGE model analysis*. Available online at: www.idrc.ca/en/ev-69008-201-1-DO_TOPIC.html (accessed May 2010).

International Labor Office (2007). *Global Employment Trends for Women*.

Joekes, S. (1987) *Women in the World Economy: United Nations International Research and Training Institute for the Advancement of Women*. New York: Oxford University Press.

Johnson, A.G. (1997) *The Gender Knot: Unraveling Our Patriarchal Legacy*. Philadelphia, PA: Temple University Press.

Joint Ministerial Committee (2003) *Sanad-e meli tavan-e mandsazi va samandeha-ye sokonatgahha-ye gir-e rasmi* [National plan for empowerment and rehabilitation of informal settlements]. Tehran: Ministry of Housing and Urban Planning, Office of Development and Urban Improvement, Action Committee on Empowerment.

Jones, S. (1995) "Understanding community in the information age," in Jones, S.G. (ed.) *CyberSociety: Computer-mediated Communication and Community*. Thousand Oaks, CA: Sage.

Jones, S. (1997) "The internet and its social landscape," in Jones, S.G. (ed.) *Virtual Culture: Identity and Communication in Cybersociety*. London: Sage.

Kabeer, N. (1994) *Reversed Realities: Gender Hierarchies in Development Thought*. London: Verso.

Kabeer, N. (2001) *The Power to Choose: Bangladeshi Garment Workers in London and Dhaka*. London: Verso.

Kabeer, N. and Simmen, M. (2003) "Globalization, gender and poverty: Bangladeshi women workers in export and local markets," *Journal of International Development*, 16, 1, pp. 92–109.

Kadkhodayi, A.A. (2009) "Iran does not rule out female presidency." Available online at: www.radiofarda.com/content/o2_women_iran_election/1606943.html (accessed February 27, 2010).

Kandiyoti, D. (1992) "Islam and patriarchy: a comparative perspective," in Keddie, N. and Baron, B. (eds) *Women in Middle Eastern History: Shifting Boundaries in Sex and Gender*. New Haven, CT: Yale University Press, pp. 23–42.

Karimi, Z. (2011) "The effects of international trade on gender inequality in Iran: the case of women carpet-weavers," in Bahramitash, R. and Esfahani, H. (eds) *Veiled Employment: The Political Economy of Female Employment in Iran*. Syracuse, NY: Syracuse University Press.

Kazemipour, S. and Mirzaie, M. (2005) "Uneven growth of urbanization in Iran," Paper presented at the IUSSP XXB International Population Conference, Tours, France, July 18–23. Available online at: http://iussp2005.princeton.edu/download.aspx?submissionId=51663 (accessed May 2010).

Keddie, N. (1991) "Introduction: Deciphering Middle Eastern women's history," in Keddie, N. and Baron, B. (eds) *Women in Middle Eastern History*. New Haven, CT: Yale University Press.

Keddie, N. (2000) "Women in Iran since 1979," *Social Research*, special issue: *Iran: Since the Revolution*, 67, 2, pp. 405–438.

Keddie, N. (2007) "Iranian women's status and struggles since 1979," *Journal of International Affairs*, 60, 2, pp. 17–34.

Kentor, J. (1981) "Structural determinants of peripheral urbanization: the effects of international dependence," *American Sociological Review*, 46, pp. 201–211.

Kermali, S. (2008) "An 'oasis' inside Iran's holy city," *Al-Jazeera English*. Available online at: http://english.aljazeera.net/focus/iran/2008/2008/09/2008922143119456556. html (accessed September 20, 2008).

Khamenehi, A. (1995) *Cheshmeh-ye Nur* [Selecton of Khamenehi's Guidelines], vol. 9. Tehran: NP.

Khomeini, R. (1989) *Sahifeh-e Nour* [Selection of Ayatollah Khomeini's Questions and Opinions], vol. 9. Tehran: NP.

Khosrokhavar, F. (1993) *L'utopie Sacrifiée, Sociologie de la Revolution Iranienne*. Paris: Presses de la FNSP.

Khosrokhavar, F. (2004) "The new Iranian intellectuals in Iran," *Social Compass*, 51, 2, pp. 191–202.

Khosrokhavar, F. and Nikpey, A. (2009) *Avoir Vingt ans au pays des Ayatollahs* [Being 20 in the country of the ayatolahs]. Paris: Robert-Laffont.

Kian, A. (1997) "Women and politics in post-Islamist Iran: the gender conscious drive to change," *British Journal of Middle Eastern Studies*, 24, 1, pp. 75–96.

Kian, A. (1999) "Political and social transformations in post-Islamist Iran," *Middle East Report*, 212, pp. 12–16.

Kian, A. (2002a) "Women and the making of civil society," in Hooglund, E. (ed.) *Twenty Years of Islamic Revolution: Political and Social Transition in Iran since 1979*. Syracuse, NY: Syracuse University Press.

Kian, A. (2002b) *Les femmes iraniennes entre islam, état et famille* [Iranian women between Islam, state, and family]. Paris: Maisonneuve et Larose.

Kian, A. (2008) "From motherhood to equal rights advocate: the weakening of patriarchal order," in Katouzian, H. and Shahidi, H. (eds) *Iran in the 21st Century: Politics, Economics and Conflict*. London: Routledge.

Kian, A. (2010) "Le féminisme islamique en Iran: nouvelle forme d'assujettissement ou émergence de sujets agissants?" [Islamic feminism in Iran: new form of subjugation or emergence of active subjects?], *Critique Internationale*, 46, pp. 45–66.

Ladier-Fouladi, M. (2009) *Iran, un monde de paradoxes* [Iran, a world of paradoxes]. Paris: L'Atlante Publishers.

Lal, D. (1983) *The Poverty of "Development Economics."* London: Institute of Economic Affairs.

Larsen, J. (2001) "Iran's birth rate plummeting at record pace: success provides a model for other developing countries," Earth Policy Institute. Available online at: www.earth-policy.org/Updates/Update4ss.htm (accessed August 30, 2007).

Lattouf, M. (2004) *Women, Education, and Socialization in Modern Lebanon*. New York: University Press of America.

Leavitt, J. (2003) "Where's the gender in community development?," *Journal of Women in Culture and Society*, 29, 1, pp. 208–231.

Levy, M.J. (1966) *Modernization and the Structure of Societies: A Setting for International Affairs*. Princeton, NJ: Princeton University Press.

Lewis, A. (1955) *The Theory of Economic Growth*. London: Allen & Unwin.

Little, I.M.D. (1982) *Economic Development: Theory, Policy and International Relations*. New York: Basic Books.

Little, I.M.D. (1988) "The experience and causes of rapid labour-intensive development in Korea, Taiwan Province, Hong Kong, and Singapore and the possibilities of emulation in export-led industrialization," in Lee, E. (ed.) *Export-led Industrialization and Development*. Singapore: Koon Wah.

Loutfi, M.F. (2001) *Women, Gender and Work*. Geneva: International Labour Office.

Manz, B.F. (2003) "Women in Timurid dynastic politics," in Nashat, G. and Beck, L. (eds) *Women in Iran from the Rise of Islam to 1800*. Urbana: University of Illinois Press.

Martin, V. (2000) *Creating an Islamic State: Khomeini and the Making of a New Iran*. London: I.B. Tauris.

Mason, K.O. (1986) "The status of women: conceptual and methodological issues in demographic studies," *Social Forces*, 1, 2, pp. 284–300.

McClelland, D.C. (1964) "Business drive and national achievement," in Etzioni, A. and Etzioni, E. (eds) *Social Change: Sources, Patterns, and Consequences*. New York: Basic Books.

McKernan, S.-M., Pitt, M., and Moskowitz, D. (2005) "Use of the formal and informal financial sectors: does gender matter? Empirical evidence from rural Bangladesh." Available online at: www.urban.org/uploadedpdf/411160_financial_sectors.pdf (accessed May 26, 2010).

Mcleod, A.E. (1991) *Accommodating Protest: Working Women, the New Veiling and Change in Cairo*. New York: Columbia University Press.

Mehran, G. (1999) "Lifelong learning: new opportunities for women in a Muslim country (Iran)," *Comparative Education*, 35, 2, pp. 201–215.

Mehran, G. (2003) "The paradox of tradition and modernity in female education in the Islamic Republic of Iran," *Comparative Education Review*, 47, 3, pp. 269–286.

Meriwether, M.E. (1994) "Women and economic change in nineteenth-century Syria: the case of Aleppo," in Tucker, J. (ed.) *Arab Women: Old Boundaries, New Frontiers*. Bloomington: Indiana University Press.

Mernissi. F. (1985) *Beyond the Veil*. Bloomington: Indiana University Press.

Mernissi, F. (1991) *The Veil and the Male Elite: A Feminist Interpretation of Women's Rights in Islam*, trans. M. Lakeland. New York: Addison-Wesley.

Mies, R.M. and Shiva, V. (1993) *Ecofeminism*. London: Zed Books.

Milani, F. (2008) "On women's captivity in the Islamic world," *Middle East Report*, 38, 246, pp. 40–46.

Miller, D. and Slater, D. (2000) *The Internet: An Ethnographic Approach*. Oxford: Berg.

Minh-Ha, T. (1989) *Women, Native Other*. Indianapolis: Indiana University Press.

Mir-Hosseini, Z. (1993) *Marriage on Trial: A Study of Islamic Family Law: Iran and Morocco Compared*. New York: St. Martin's Press.

Mir-Hosseini, Z. (1996) "Women and politics in post-Khomeini Iran: divorce, veiling and emerging feminist voices," in Afshar, H. (ed.) *Women and Politics in the Third World*. London: Routledge.

Mir-Hosseini, Z. (1999) *Islam and Gender: The Religious Debate in Contemporary Iran*. London: I.B. Tauris.

Mir-Hosseini, Z. (2002a) "The conservative–reformist conflict over women's rights in Iran." *International Journal of Politics, Culture, and Society*, 16, 1, pp. 37–53.

Mir-Hosseini, Z. (2002b) "Religious modernists and the 'woman question,'" in Hooglund, E. (ed.) *Twenty Years of Islamic Revolution*. Syracuse: NY: Syracuse University Press.

Moallem, M. (2005) *Between Warrior Brother and Veiled Sister*. Los Angeles: University of California Press.

Moaveni, A. (2005) *Lipstick Jihad: A Memoir of Growing up Iranian in America and American in Iran*. New York: Public Affairs.

Moghadam, F. (1985) "An evaluation of the productive performance of agribusinesses: an Iranian case study," *Economic Development and Cultural Change*, 33, 4, pp. 755–776.

Moghadam, F. (2000) "The political economy of female employment in post-revolutionary Iran," in Slymovics, S. and Joseph, S. (eds) *Women and Power in the Islamic Middle East*. Philadelphia: University of Pennsylvania Press.

Moghadam, F. (2002) "Iran's new home economics: an exploratory attempt to conceptualize women's work in the Islamic Republic," in Cinar, E.M. (ed.) *The Economics of Women and Work in the Middle East and North Africa*. New York: Elsevier Science.

Moghadam, F. (2011) "Iran's missing working women," in Bahramitash, R. and Esfahani, H. (eds) *Veiled Employment: The Political Economy of Female Employment in Iran*. Syracuse, NY: Syracuse University Press.

Moghadam, V. (1988) "Women, work, and ideology in the Islamic Republic of Iran," *International Journal of Middle East Studies*, 20, 2, pp. 221–243.

Moghadam, V. (1991) "The reproduction of gender inequality in the Islamic Republic: a case study of Iran in the 1980s," *World Development*, 19, 10, pp. 1335–1350.

Moghadam, V. (1995) "Women's employment issues in contemporary Iran: problems and prospects in the 1990s," *Iranian Studies*, 28, 3–4, pp. 175–202.

Moghadam, V. (2002a) "Women, work, and economic restructuring: a regional overview," in Cinar, E.M. (ed.) *The Economics of Women and Work in the Middle East and North Africa*. New York: Elsevier Science.

Moghadam, V. (2002b) "The two faces of Iran: women's activism, the reform movement, and the Islamic Republic," in Reed, B. (ed.) *Nothing Sacred: Women Respond to Religious Fundamentalism and Terror*. New York: Thunder Mouth Press/Nation Books.

Moghissi, H. (1996) *Populism and Feminism in Iran: Women's Struggle in a Male-defined Revolutionary Movement*. New York: St. Martin's Press.

Mohammadi, A. (2003) *Iran Encountering Globalization: Problems and Prospect*. New York: Routledge.

Mohammadi, M. (2003) "Iran's way of constitutionalism after 1996: interpretations of Iran's constitution by the judiciary and the reformers." Paper presented at 2003 Annual Meeting of the Law and Society Association, Pittsburgh, Pennsylvania, June 5.

Mohanty, C.T. (2003a) *Feminist Without Borders: Decolonizing Theory, Practicing Solidarity*. Durham, NC: Duke University Press.

Mohanty, C.T. (2003b) "Under western eyes: feminist scholarship and colonial discourses," in Lewis, R. and Mills, S. (eds) *Feminist Postcolonial Theory*. New York: Routledge.

Moinifar, H. (2006) "Women in politics: whispers of power in Iran." Unpublished paper, Center for Women's Studies, University of Tehran.

Mojab, S. (2001) "The politics of theorizing 'Islamic feminism': implications for international feminist movements," *Feminist Review*, 69, pp. 124–146.

Mojtahed Shabestari, M. (2000) *Naqdi bar qara'at-e rasmi az din. bohranha, chaleshha, rah-e halha* [A critique of the official reading of religion: crises, challenges, and solutions]. Tehran: Tarh-e Now.

Momsen, J.H. (2004) *Gender and Development*. London: Routledge.

Moore, W.E. (1979) *World Modernization: The Limits of Convergence*. New York: Elsevier.

Moruzzi, N. (2001) "Women in Iran: notes on film and from the field," *Feminist Studies*, 27, 1, pp. 89–100.

Moser, C. (1989a) "The impact of recession and adjustment at the micro level: low income women and their households in Guayaquil, Ecuador," in *The Invisible Adjustment: Poor Women and the Economic Crisis*. New York: UNICEF.

Moser, C. (1989b) "Gender planning in the third world: meeting practical and strategic gender needs," *World Development*, 17, 1, pp. 1799–1825.

Moser, C. (1993) *Gender Planning and Development: Theory, Practice and Training.* New York: Routledge.

Moser, C. (1995) "Women, gender and urban development policy: challenges for current and future research," *World Development*, 23, 2.

Motee, N. (2000) *Population Council: Scientific and Cultural Exchange Program between Iranian and International Researchers*, app. 4. Available online at: www.iranngos.org/reports/SciCulExch/Women011ProfilesGovAgenResWo.htm (accessed November 9, 2004).

Mottaghi, M. [2004] "L'émergence du nouvel intellectuel religieux en Iran post-révolutionnaire." Unpublished doctoral dissertation, École des Hautes Études en Sciences Sociales, Paris.

Nabli, M. (2002) "Conference on Higher Education in the Middle East and North Africa: Challenges and Opportunities for the 21st Century." Institute de Monde Arabe, May 23. World Bank Group, Middle East and North Africa; available online at: http://lnweb18.worldbank.org/mna/mena.nsf/Attachments/Education-Nabli/$File/HigherEducation-Nabli.pdf (accessed July 27, 2006).

Najmabadi, A. (1991) "Women's autobiography in contemporary Iran." Harvard Middle Eastern monographs, Cambridge, MA: Harvard University Press.

Najmabadi, A. (1998a) "Feminism in an Islamic Republic: years of hardship, years of growth," in Haddad, Y. and Esposito, J. (eds) *Islam, Gender, and Social Change*. New York: Oxford University Press.

Najmabadi, A. (1998b) "Crafting an educated housewife in Iran," in Abu-Lughod, L. (ed.) *Remaking Women: Feminism and Modernity in the Middle East*. Princeton, NJ: Princeton University Press.

Najmabadi, A. (2005) *Women with Mustaches and Men without Beards: Gender and Sexual Anxieties of Iranian Modernity*. Berkeley: University of California Press.

Nomani, F. and Behdad, S. (2006) *Class and Labor in Iran: Did the Revolution Matter?* Syracuse, NY: Syracuse University Press.

North, D.C. (1990) *Institutions, Institutional Change, and Economic Performance*. Cambridge: Cambridge University Press.

Nozaki, Y., Aranha, R., Fix-Dominguez, R., and Nakajima, Y. (2009) "Gender gap and women's participation in higher education: views from Japan, Mongolia, and India," in Wiseman, A.W. and Baker, D.P. (eds) *International Perspectives on Education and Society*, vol. 10, *Gender, Equality, and Education from International and Comparative Perspectives*. Bingley, UK: Emerald Group Publishing.

Oakley, A. (1974) *Women's Work*. New York: Vintage Books.

Obermeyer, C.M. (1992) "Islam, women, and politics: the demography of Arab countries," *Population and Development Review*, 18, 1 (March), pp. 33–60.

Obermeyer, C.M. (1994) "Reproductive choice in Islam: gender and state in Iran and Tunisia," *Studies in Family Planning*, 25, 1, pp. 41–51.

Office of Management and National Planning (1983) *First Development Plan Legal Addendum*. Tehran: OMNP.

Olmsted, J. (2004) "Orientalism and economic methods: (re)reading feminist economic discussions of Islam," in Zein-Elabdine, E. and Charusheela, S. (eds) *Postcolonialism Meets Economics*. London: Routledge.

Olmsted, J. (2005) "Is paid work the (only) answer? Neoliberalism, Arab women's well-being and the social contract," *Journal of Middle East Women's Studies*, 1, 2, pp. 112–139.

Olmsted, J. (2007) "Globalization denied: gender and poverty in Iraq and Palestine," in

Cabezas, A., Reese, E., and Waller, M. (eds) *The Wages of Empire: Neoliberal Policies, Armed Repression, and Women's Poverty*. Boulder, CO: Paradigm.

Olmsted, J. (2011) "Gender and globalization; the Iranian experience," in Bahramitash, R. and Esfahani, H. (eds) *Veiled Employment: The Political Economy of Female Employment in Iran*. Syracuse, NY: Syracuse University Press.

Oppenheimer, V.K. (1970) "The female labor force in the United States: demographic and economic factors governing its growth and changing composition," Population Monograph Series No. 5. Berkeley: Institute of International Studies of the University of California.

Paidar, P. (1995) *Women and the Political Process in Twentieth Century Iran*. Cambridge: Cambridge University Press.

Paidar, P. (2001) "Gender of democracy: the encounter between feminism and reformism in contemporary Iran," in *Democracy, Governance, and Human Rights*, Paper 6, United Nations Research Institute for Social Development.

Palmer, I. (1991) *Gender and Population in the Adjustment of African Economies: Planning for Change*. Geneva: International Labor Organization.

Palmer, I. (1992) "Gender, equity and economic efficiency in adjustment models," in Afshar, H. and Dennis, C. (eds) *Women and Adjustment Policies in the Third-World*. London: Macmillan.

Pampel, F.C. and Tanaka, K. (1986) "Economic development and female labor force participation: a reconsideration," *Social Forces*, 64, 3 (March), pp. 599–619.

Parson, T. (1971) *The System of Modern Societies*. Englewood Cliffs, NJ: Prentice-Hall.

Pateman, C. (1988) *Sexual Contract*. Stanford, CA: Stanford University Press.

Patton, M. (2002) *Qualitative Research and Evaluation Methods*. California: Sage.

Pollack, K.M. (2004) *The Persian Puzzle: The Conflict between Iran and America*. New York: Random House.

Pooya, A. and Razavi, M. (2005) "Women's participation and employment in Iran: a critical examination," *Critique*, 14, 1, pp. 57–73.

Powell, A. (2003) "Iranian primary care produces big results," *Harvard Gazette*. Available online at: www.hno.harvard.edu/gazette/2003/01.23/07-iran.html (accessed January 21, 2003).

Poya, M. (1999) *Women, Work and Islamism*. London: Zed Books.

Ramazani, N. (1993) "Women in Iran: the revolutionary ebb and flow," *The Middle East Journal*, 47, 3, pp. 409–428.

Renia, L. (1996) *Gendering Orientalism: Race, Femininity and Representation*. London: Routledge.

Renia, L. and Mills, S. (eds) (2003) *Feminist Postcolonial Theory: A Reader*. Edinburgh: Edinburgh University Press.

Reskin, B. and Padavic, I. (1994) *Women and Men at Work*. Thousand Oaks, CA: Pine Forge Press, Sage.

Richards, P. and Roberts, B. (2004) "Social capital and economic development: toward a theoretical synthesis and policy framework," *Theory and Society*, 27, 2, pp. 151–208.

Rodrik, D. (2008) "The new development economics: we shall experiment, but how shall we learn?" HKS Working Paper no. RWP08–055. Harvard University.

Roldan, M. (1988) "Renegotiating the marital contract: intra-household patterns of money allocation and women's subordination among domestic outworkers in Mexico City," in Dwyer, D. and Bruce, J. (eds) *A House Divided: Women and Income in the Third World*. Stanford, CA: Stanford University Press.

Rosenstein-Rodan, P.N. (1943) "Problems of industrialisation of Eastern and South-Eastern Europe," *The Economic Journal*, 53, 210, pp. 202–211.

Ross, M. (2008) "Oil, Islam, and women," *American Political Science Review*, 102, 1 (February), pp.107–123.

Rostami-Povey, E. (2001) "Feminist contestations of institutional domains in Iran," *Feminist Review*, 69, pp. 44–72.

Rostow, W. (1956) "The take-off into self-sustained growth," *The Economic Journal*, 66, 26, pp. 25–48.

Roudi-Fahimi, A. (2002) "Iran's family planning program: responding to a nation's needs," Washington: Population Reference Bureau. Available online at: www.prb.org/pdf/IransFamPlanProg_Eng.pdf (accessed 2002).

Rustow, D.A. (1967) *A World of Nations: Problems of Political Modernization*. Washington, DC: The Brookings Institute.

Ryan, M.P. (1975) *Womanhood in America: From Colonial Times to the Present*. New York: New Viewpoints.

Sadeghi, F. (2009) "Foot soldiers of the Islamic Republic's 'Culture of Modesty,'" *Middle East Report*, 250 (spring), pp. 50–55.

Sadeghi, F. (forthcoming) "Double agency: women and power in the post-revolutionary Iran," in Eric Hooglund and Leif Stenberg (eds) *Contestation in Iran*.

Said, E. (1979) *Orientalism*. New York: Vintage Books.

Salehi-Isfahani, D. (2000a) "Demographic factors in Iran's economic development," *Social Research*, 67, 2 (summer), pp. 599–620.

Salehi-Isfahani, D. (2000b) "Microeconomics of growth in MENA – the role of households," Global Research Project. Global Development Networks.

Sedghi, H. (2007) *Women and Politics in Iran: Veiling, Unveiling, and Reveiling*. Cambridge, MA: Harvard University Press.

Semyonov, M. (1980) "The social context of women's labor force participation: a comparative analysis," *American Journal of Sociology*, 86, pp. 534–550.

Sen, G. (1987) *Development, Crises, and Alternative Vision: Third World Women's Perspectives*. New York: Monthly Review Press.

Shadi, J. (2001) "Officials concerned about controversy over women's employment and housewifery," *Zanan*. Available online at: www.netiran.com/?fn=artd (accessed 2001).

Shafik, N. (2001) "Closing the gender gap in the Middle East and North Africa," in Cinar, E.M. (ed.) *The Economics of Women's Work in the Middle East and North Africa*. London: Elsevier Science.

Shavarini, M. (2006) "Wearing the veil to college: the paradox of higher education in the lives of Iranian women," *International Journal of Middle East Studies*, 38, pp. 189–211.

Shaw, J. and Arezoo, B. (ed./trans.) (2001) *The Position of Women from the Viewpoint of Imam Khomeini*. Tehran: The Institute of the Compilation and Publication of Imam Khomeini's Works.

Shayegan, D. (1997) *Cultural Schizophrenia: Islamic Societies Confronting the West*. Syracuse, NY: Syracuse University Press.

Silver, D. (2000) "Looking backwards, looking forward: cyberculture studies 1990–2000," in Gauntlett, D. (ed.) *WebStudies: Rewiring Media Studies for the Digital Age*. Oxford: Oxford University Press.

Singerman, D. (1997) *Avenues of Participation: Family, Politics and Networks in Urban Quarters of Cairo*. Cairo, Egypt: The American University in Cairo Press.

Singh, R.D. (1994) "Fertility–mortality variations across LDCs: women's education, labor force participation, and contraceptive use," *Kyklos*, 47, 2, pp. 209–221.

Skocpol, T. (1985) "Bringing the state back in: strategies of analysis in current research," in Evan, P., Rueschmeyer, D., and Skocpol, T. (eds) *Bringing the State Back*. Cambridge, MA: Harvard University Press.

Sreberny-Mohammadi, A. and Mohammadi, A. (1994) *Small Media, big Revolution*. Minneapolis: University of Minnesota Press.

Stall, S. and Stoecker, R. (1998) "Community organizing or organizing community? Gender and the crafts of empowerment in gender and society," *Gender and Social Movements*, special issue, part I, 12, 6, pp. 729–756.

Standing, G. (1989) "Gender equity and globalization: macroeconomic policy for developing countries," *World Development*, 17, 7, pp. 1077–1095.

Szuppe, M. (2003) "Status, knowledge, and politics: women in sixteenth century Safavid Iran," in Nashat, G. and Beck, L. (eds) *Women in Iran from the Rise of Islam to 1800*. Urbana: University of Illinois Press.

Tabatabai, J. (1994) *Zaval-e andisheh-ye siasi dar Iran* [Decline of political thought in Iran). Tehran: NP.

Tazmini, G. (2009) *Khatami's Iran*. London: I.B. Tauris.

Tinker, I. (1997) "The making of the field: advocate, practitioners and scholars," in Lynn, D., Nisonoff, L., and Wiegersma, V. (eds) *Women, Gender and Development Reader*. London: Zed Books.

Todes, A. (1995) "Gender in metropolitan development strategies: the case of Durban," *Cities*, 12, 5, pp. 327–336.

Tohidi, N. (2003) "Islamic feminism: perils and promises," in *Middle Eastern Women on the Move*. Washington: Woodrow Wilson International Center for Scholars, pp. 135–146.

Tohidi, N. (2007) "Muslim feminism and Islamic reformation," in Ruether, R. (ed.) *Feminist Theologies: Legacy and Prospect*. Minneapolis: Fortress Press.

Tucker, J.E. (ed.) (1994) "Introduction," in *Arab Women: Old Boundaries, New Frontiers*. Bloomington: Indiana University Press.

UNDP (2004) Human Development Indicators, 2003. Available online at: http://hdr.undp.org/reports/global/2003/indicator/indic_207_1_1.html.

United Nations (2001) *Human Development Report: Iran, Islamic Republic*. Available online at: www.undp.org/hdr2001/indicator/cty_f_IRN.html (accessed 2001).

United Nations (2003a) *United Nations Common Country Assessment for the Islamic Republic of Iran*. Tehran: UNDP.

United Nations (2003b) *Slums of the world: the fact of urban poverty in the new millennium*. Available online at: www.unhabitat.org/pmss/listItemDetails.aspx?publication ID=1124; (accessed June 8, 2010).

United Nations (2006) "Towards the rise of women in the Arab world," in *The Arab Human Development Report*. New York: Regional Bureau for Arab States.

Vosooghi, M. (2005) "Treatment of addicts in a Tehran drug rehabiltation center," *Critique*, 14, 1 (spring), pp. 89–100.

Wade, R. (1992) *Governing the Market: Economic Theory and the Role of Government in East Asian Industrialization*. Princeton, NJ: Princeton University Press.

Wahba, J. (2003) "Women in MENA labor markets," *Newsletter of the Economic Research Forum for the Arab Countries, Iran and Turkey*, 10, 1 (spring).

Wallerstein, E. (1974) *The Modern World System: Capitalist Agriculture and the Origins of the European World Economy in the Sixteenth Century*. New York: Academic Press.

Wayne, E. and Inglehart, R. (2000) "Modernization, cultural change and the persistence of traditional values," *American Sociological Review*, 65, 1, pp. 19–51.

Weber, M. (2001) *The Protestant Ethic and the Spirit of Capitalism*, trans. Parsons, T. London: Routledge.

Whatley, S. (2003) "Iranian women film directors: a clever activism," *Off our Backs: The Feminist Newsjournal*, 33, 3, pp. 30–34.

Williamson, O.E. (1985) *The Economic Institutions of Capitalism: Firms, Markets, Relational Contracting*. New York: The Free Press.

World Bank GenderStats: *Capabilities and Human Capital—Iran, Islamic Republic*. Available online at: http://genderstats.worldbank.org/genderstats/genderRpt. asp?rpt=capability& cty=IRN,Iran,%20Islamic%20Rep.&hm=home2 (accessed 2007).

World Bank *Opportunity – Iran, Islamic Republic*. Available online at: http://genderstats. worldbank.org/genderstats/genderRpt.asp?rpt=opportunity&cty=IRN,Iran,%20 Islamic%20Rep.&hm=home2 (accessed 2007).

Yadigar, A.M. (1992a) "Qezavat-e Zan" [Women's judgment], *Zanan*, May 1, p. 5.

Yadigar, A.M. (1992b) "Ijtehad va marja'iyyat-e zanan" [Interpretation and women's religious authority]. *Zanan*, October 8.

Yeganeh, N. (1993) "Nationalism and national identities," *Feminist Review*, 44 (summer), pp. 3–18.

Yegenoglu, M. (1998) *Colonial Fantasies: Towards a Feminist Reading of Orientalism*. Cambridge: Cambridge University Press.

Zan-e Ruz (1993) "Determination of wages for work done," December 18.

Zein-Elabdine, E. and Charusheela, S. (eds) (2004) *Postcolonialism Meets Economics*. London: Routledge.

Index